MW00624665

"He skillfully provides the theoretical i
and ample resources for students explc
first time. There is such depth here, however, that graduate students
will find the chapters equally challenging and useful for extended research. The reference list of articles and books alone is a lasting treasure
for missiology students. Moreau spans a spectrum of approaches and
issues where the gospel intersects with cultures. This work is a spring-
board for various teaching styles and methods of presentation. The
well-planned layout of outlines, summaries, study questions, and key
word lists make travel through the material extremely manageable.
One shouldn't study contextualization without access to Moreau's
work."

—Paul W. Shea,
Associate Professor of Missions,
Houghton College

"In this new work, Moreau, a seasoned practitioner and an accomplished author and teacher, does the church and the academy a great
service. Having poured over and synthesized the vast contextualization literature of the past generation, Moreau offers a way forward—
a map—for evangelical intercultural workers to navigate the often
uncertain terrain of contextualization. In many ways, Moreau has
modeled this task well by addressing profound ideas that are made
accessible to the reader through an inviting and engaging style. This
timely book ought to be read in the curriculum of Christian colleges,
seminaries, and mission training centers."

—Edward Smither,
Professor of Intercultural Studies,
Columbia International University

"Scott Moreau provides us with a very thoughtful treatment of one
of the most important and controversial issues of the day—contextualization. Setting this issue in the context of history, current reality,
and future possibilities provides readers with a helpful framework to
deal with this topic. As evangelicals who are committed to the gospel
transformation of individuals, families, communities, and nations,
we must personally and corporately wrestle with the issues raised by

Moreau. I believe *Contextualization in World Missions* will help provide greater clarity, understanding, and hopefully unity as we serve our risen Lord in seeking to make disciples of all nations."

—Geoff Tunnicliffe,
CEO/Secretary General,
World Evangelical Alliance

"Jesus ate local food and spoke the local dialect. He honored his context. But contextualization is not bulletproof. There are many dangers. What term do we use for God? What rituals do we participate in? Is air conditioning contextual? Is the majority language contextual, or only the minority? If the second generation is influenced by global media, are their values as contextual as the first generation's? How much does it matter anyway? Aren't there other priorities that are more important than contextualization? For many years on the field and in the literature, Scott Moreau has explored this. Here is the fruit of his labor—nuanced, comparative, and inspiring."

—Miriam Adeney,
Associate Professor of World Christian Studies,
Seattle Pacific University

"Scott Moreau has produced an excellent compendium of the contemporary approaches to and philosophies that underlie the important subject of missionary contextualization. This is certainly the most comprehensive compilation available today and is thus an excellent resource for practitioners, students, and teachers alike. Scott's categorization of these approaches is well-conceived and his diagrams, charts, and appendices are all immensely helpful. Additionally, the author's evaluative comments regarding each of the approaches are refreshing to read and digest, particularly in this day of excessive neutrality."

—Larry Poston,
Professor of Religion,
Nyack College

"This is an exceptional overview of thirty years of dialog and debate among evangelicals on contextualization. It is a balanced and compelling review of the theological tensions that characterize this debate, reflecting on the diversity of theological perspectives, of method-ologies, and of praxis with reference to evangelism, discipling, and church planting among the major world religions. There is an excellent bibliography of sources for any student or scholar interested in the literature on evangelical contextualization. I welcome this work! It is an excellent contribution to evangelical scholarship on contextualization."

—Sherwood Lingenfelter,
Professor of Anthropology,
Fuller Theological Seminary

"Scott Moreau is doing a great service to all of us who got lost in the vast jungle of approaches to contextualization in world missions. His helicopter view provides us with a tremendously useful mapping of the landscape that will help us advance even further into what is eventually the cultures, minds, and hearts of peoples—the locale where the gospel is to be rooted."

—Birger Nygaard,
Danish Church Mission,
Denmark

"No one has read as widely or has a better grasp of the breadth of evangelical approaches to contextualization than Scott Moreau. His teaching, reading, and personal relationships have given him an unparalleled encyclopedic awareness of evangelical thinking and proposals for the theory and practice of contextualization for the past forty years. His book provides an accurate, comprehensive panorama of the landscape of evangelical contextualization. For missiological novices, it will open the door to two generations of voluminous writings. Among seasoned veterans, it will spark reflective, more evenhanded evaluation of what their brothers and sisters are saying. Moreau has a keen, analytical mind that is able to sort out hundreds of examples and present them in easy-to-comprehend categories. He is particularly strong in clarifying distinctions in evangelical approaches to contextualization that have become muddled over the years. The charts are outstanding; they simplify a vast amount of data, synthesizing and clearly explaining his analysis. Equally strong are the examples he has selected, which both illustrate his seven models of contextualization and demonstrate the creativity and variety of evangelical approaches. Moreau's 'map' is highly recommended as an accurate and comprehensive guide for anyone taking a serious trip into the land of evangelical approaches to contextualization."

—Steve Strauss,
Professor of World Missions and Intercultural Studies,
Dallas Theological Seminary

"The study and praxis of contextualization is often a theological and missiological mine field. This work provides an incredibly helpful map that guides the reader to a better understanding of the complexities of contextualization and provides a summary of evangelical approaches."

—Timothy R. Sisk,
Professor of World Missions,
Moody Bible Institute

"With *Contextualization in World Missions*, A. Scott Moreau has provided readers not only with a detailed map, but also with a reliable compass to navigate this vast and often daunting terrain of contextualization. Even experienced travelers in the world of evangelical contextualization will find Moreau the ultimate go-to guide."

—Craig Ott,
Professor of Mission and Intercultural Studies,
Trinity Evangelical Divinity School

"Moreau provides a travel guide through the evangelical landscape of contextualization. *Contextualization in World Missions* is an in-depth comparative survey of the theory and practice of communicating Christ across cultures. It is a timely text for serious students and practitioners in a day when ill-informed, superficial attacks and defenses of contextualization abound. Moreau provides a clean break, a fresh look at the ministry, art, and science of effectively communicating the gospel to, in, and through another culture. Moreau's research and scholarship are extensive and impeccable; yet the work is surprisingly readable and engaging. He defines keywords, provides questions for reflection and dialogue, and includes readings for further study. This book lays a solid foundation for the journey through the world of contextualization. Follow this guide and you are less likely to get lost and more likely to find your ultimate destination on your missions journey."

—Mike Barnett,
Dean, College of Intercultural Studies,
Columbia International University

"A contemporary, nuanced account of evangelical contextualization models fills a great need not only for missiologists and missionaries, but also among theologians and biblical scholars. Scott Moreau is a trustworthy guide, and his research will raise awareness of authentically global theology while further informing current hermeneutical discussions."

—Daniel J. Treier,
Professor of Theology,
Wheaton College

"Scott Moreau has done a masterful job of dealing with the vast amount of literature on contextualization. He has surveyed an incredible number of articles and books and in a masterful way helpfully presented and evaluated content and perspective to produce his study. The next time I teach a course on contextualization, this will be my text."

—Charles H. Kraft,
Professor Emeritus of Anthropology,
Fuller Seminary School of Intercultural Studies

Contextualization
in
World Missions

Mapping and Assessing
Evangelical Models

A. Scott Moreau

There are presentation slides in PowerPoint format available for this book on the Kregel website: www.kregeldigitaleditions.com.

Contextualization in World Missions: Mapping and Assessing Evangelical Models

© 2012 by A. Scott Moreau

Published by Kregel Publications, a division of Kregel, Inc., 2450 Oak Industrial Dr. NE, Grand Rapids, MI 49505-6020.

This book is available in digital format at www.kregel.com.

Unless otherwise noted, all Bible quotes are from the NIV. THE HOLY BIBLE, NEW INTERNATIONAL VERSION®, NIV® Copyright © 1973, 1978, 1984, 2011 by Biblica, Inc.™ All rights reserved worldwide.

Library of Congress Cataloging-in-Publication Data
Moreau, A. Scott, 1955-
   Contextualization in world missions : mapping and assessing evangelical models / A. Scott Moreau.
      p. cm.
   1. Christianity and culture. 2. Missions. 3. Evangelistic work. I. Title.
   BR115.C8M667 2012
   266.001—dc23

2011039899

ISBN 978-0-8254-3389-4

Printed in the United States of America
17 18 19 20 21 / 5 4 3 2

*Dedicated to my
friend and mentor Dr. John Gration.
John hired me to teach at Wheaton,
encouraged me to grow and develop in
my service to Christ and constantly
challenged my thinking.*

*I am deeply grateful for the
life of this servant of Christ
who went to his eternal reward
January 29, 2012.*

Contents

PREFACE

This book came into existence almost accidentally. Invited to participate in a World Evangelical Alliance consultation on contextualization, I was excited to hear what others had to say on the subject and to develop my own presentation. The organizers designed the consultation so that every participant would present a paper for the others to discuss. They distributed a list of topics for participants to consider. One grabbed my attention.

Organizers wanted one of the participants to develop a supplement to Stephen Bevans's excellent map that outlines the models of contextualization (1985; 1992; 2002). No one had volunteered, so I (perhaps not as wisely as I thought) jumped at the opportunity.

Bevans's map reduced almost all of the evangelical approaches to one or two models (the translation and countercultural models). A challenge for evangelicals is to develop a new map focused on evangelical models. My intention was not to compete with Bevans's map but to create a sub-map that would focus on evangelical models of contextualization. Creating this focused map requires a closer look at a smaller part of the terrain—like having a map of Nairobi as an insert to a map of Kenya.

As I prepared over the next few months, it dawned on me that this supplemental map of evangelical models of contextualization would require more than just a chapter in a book; it would take a whole book. I presented my approach at the consultation and received significant and helpful critique. Working through the revisions helped me finalize some thinking (Moreau 2010). It also opened doors to thoughts I had not considered. Eventually I put together a book proposal that Kregel generously accepted, which is what you now have in your hands (or on your screen).

While in graduate school, I spent hours in libraries browsing card catalogs and bookshelves and reading journal indices to find resources. A trip to the reference section, another trip to browse the right subject areas, and trips to the journal collections to browse by hand through all of the journals were all necessary parts of the research hunt.

Today, the immediate access to resources has changed the game completely. Google Scholar makes snippets of multiple millions of books available for almost instant searching. If the dreams of Google's owners come true, you and I will be able to search every book ever printed and buy those we want. Also, by virtue of the access granted to faculty at institutions like Wheaton College, I can search electronically every issue of major journals that are storehouses of evangelical contextualization ideas, proposals, and attempts. The complete issues of journals such as *Evangelical Missions Quarterly*, *International Journal of Frontier Missiology*, *Mission Frontiers*, *Swedish Missiological Themes*, *Missiology*, *International Bulletin of Missionary Research*, *Mission Studies*, *Journal of Asian Mission*, and *International Review of Mission* are all available. In less than an hour I can secure more electronic versions of articles from these journals (and many more) than I can read in a year.

That said, to explore the contours of what others are writing, I examined more than five thousand reference items, including articles, chapters, and monographs. I limited my reading to those most directly related to the purposes of this project, and you will see them in the reference list at the end of the book.

Although the resulting literature review is not exhaustive, it is comprehensive enough to give an accurate ethnography of contextualization as written by the spectrum of English-speaking evangelicals around the world. In the days of our global church, however, this is still only a small slice of what evangelical Christians from every nation of the world are doing to reach others for Christ. I hope, however, that it will give a clear picture of the incredible energy, creativity, and passion of that slice. This is an exciting vision!

ACKNOWLEDGEMENTS

Although I am the author of this book, such works are never the results of the efforts of one individual. As a part of Wheaton College, I have received continual support and help for research and reflection. The institution provides a fantastic evangelism and mission collection as well as access to incredible databases that I have enjoyed exploring. Wheaton College administrators encourage faculty to think carefully and clearly about our disciplines in light of the faith we share, and for 150 years have pushed us to do it all for Christ and his kingdom.

My colleagues in the intercultural studies department have been a constant encouragement and joy for me; their friendships and collegial partnership means more to me than I can adequately express. Additionally, I need to acknowledge my debt for thinking to four special students—Shane Dixon, Shane Gauthier, Mary Hawthorne, and Caleb Smith—who put up with me bringing thoughts and ideas to class and brainstormed with me on the mapping process. Special thanks for critical proofing work at various stages of the manuscript go to two additional students: Rachele Bargerstock and Todd Saur.

However, one person deserves special mention. John Gration was the department chair when I joined Wheaton, and he taught the contextualization course until he retired. I inherited his slot, and he provided abundant resources and thinking. It is on his shoulders that I stand. Even before I came to Wheaton, I used his fascinating article "From Willowbank to Wheaton" (1983) as a guide in my thinking and teaching of contextualization while on faculty at the Nairobi International School of Theology. Thanks to his clear thinking and ability to empower others for contextual thinking, I found solid grounding for my own development. Of course, wherever I have strayed from his foundations is my own responsibility.

INTRODUCTION

Perhaps one of the best ways to introduce contextualization is to tell a story. At the core of Simon's question are vital issues of the relationship between gospel and culture, and especially the gospel and this particular element of Simon's culture. As you read the story, consider how you might react to what he asks.

SIMON'S QUESTION

Ben churned inside over the implication of what Simon had asked. Given the circumstances, what could he say that would encourage Simon to walk faithfully in Christ despite the issues he would face once his conversion become known to his family?

Simon Mazikenda, a Swazi from Hlatikulu (a small town in southwest Swaziland) prayed to receive Christ one day at a bus stop when Ben, a teacher in Simon's school, presented the gospel to him. In Swazi culture, it is impolite to say no to anyone in a position of authority. Knowing this, Ben decided to involve Simon in a Bible study as a follow-up to discern if the decision had been genuine. Simon readily agreed and attended faithfully for the next several weeks. With exams coming, Simon faced the prospect of completing his studies and then returning home. An average student, Simon had little chance of qualifying for university studies (only one in thirty are accepted).

As Ben met Simon for the last time, he asked the question that had been troubling him since that day at the bus stop. "When I go home, I know that my father will ask me to sacrifice to the ancestors. What should I do?"

Having lived in Swaziland for two years, Ben knew some of the issues involved—at least in his head. The authority of elders in Swazi society, and especially parental authority, was not to be taken lightly. Should Simon openly rebel, he would face serious consequences, the least of which would be the beating he was sure to receive if he would not carry on the family traditions. The fear of family rejection in this strongly collective society ran deep—Simon's identity was tied to being a good family member.

Realizing that his answer could shape the rest of Simon's life, Ben initially asked for time and arranged for one extra meeting to answer the question. He spent that week talking to the Swazi Christians he knew, asking their advice. Unfortunately, he received mixed messages. Some insisted that all ancestral practices must be stopped no matter what the cost. Idolatry was one of the worst kinds of sin, and Swazi Christians had to put the traditions of fearing the ancestors behind them if people were to progress in Christ. Others, citing 2 Kings 5, maintained that a semblance of traditionalism was not wrong, as long as Simon maintained loyalty to God in his heart. They were quick to note that the ancestral traditions were not worship, as some missionaries called it, but simply a cultural way of showing respect for one's roots. Why risk the possible conversion of Simon's whole family over a non-essential issue? Ben weighed the arguments of both sides and gave himself over to prayer.

These and countless similar examples happen every day in cross-cultural work around the world. The question Simon asked is deeply connected to the central concerns all Christians face: how do we practice our faith in ways that honor God (and his Word) while at the same time respect our cultural values and traditions?

How Important Is Contextualization?

Revelation 7:9–10 bears eloquent testimony to the reality that our worship in heaven will not be monocultural:

> After this I looked and there before me was a great multitude that no one could count, from every nation, tribe, people and language, standing before the throne and in front of the Lamb. They were wearing white robes and were holding palm branches in their hands. And they cried out in a loud voice: "Salvation belongs to our God, who sits on the throne, and to the Lamb."

Without contextualization, people will not connect to Christ in a way that moves their hearts. Faith will feel foreign, and people will lose what they have grown up cherishing. Churches will never feel rooted in their own culture, and people will not see the true winsomeness of the gospel. They will never understand the fullest intent of the incarnation. As Byang Kato noted at the 1974 Lausanne Congress on World Evangelization, "Since the Gospel message is inspired but the mode of its expression is not, contextualization of the modes of expression is not only right but necessary" (1975, 1217).

Contextualization is at the "mixing point" of gospel and culture. It is not surprising then that the literature on contextualization has exploded over the past two decades. The sheer volume of writing, thinking, and experimenting with and about contextualization demonstrates its importance in mission. With thousands of ethnolinguistic groups, many with dialects and subcultural segments, the need to enable the Christian faith to be at home in each is a testimony to the need for contextualization.

What Do I Mean by "Evangelical"?

Because I focus on evangelical approaches, I need to define what I mean by evangelical. The term *evangelical* has a rich and varied history around the globe, and no single definition will satisfy everyone. For my approach I draw from two respected British sources. The first is British church historian David Bebbington, whose fourfold characterization of evangelicals (1989) is widely accepted. Bebbington characterizes evangelicals as those who emphasize *conversion* (the belief that lives need to be changed; Zoba adds that they have a personal relationship with Christ; 2005, 4–5), *activism* (the expression of the gospel in effort, especially evangelism and missionary work), *biblicism* (giving special importance to the Bible), and *crucicentrism* (Christ's atoning sacrifice on the cross is central).

To add depth to these characteristics, it is important to recognize the common theological frame that characterizes evangelicals. The best articulation I have found also comes from former British rector and theologian John Stott. He identifies three key theological constraints that are of importance to all evangelicals (2003, 25–30): 1) the gospel comes from God and not human ingenuity; 2) the gospel is Christological, biblical, historical, theological, apostolic, and personal;

and 3) the gospel is effective because God himself revealed it. Together these (overlapping) criteria offer a broad-based and yet appropriately constrained set of markers for determining contextual models and practices that can be identified as distinctively evangelical. They do so without imposing an artificial uniformity on the practitioners or ensuring agreement among them, as we shall see later in the book.

It will help readers to know that I am an evangelical. I typically use "I" or "we" rather than "they" throughout the book. I am not so naïve to think that I speak on behalf of all evangelicals or that all evangelicals agree with what I say. Rather, I indicate that I am one of the evangelicals whose ideas, values, orientations, and models of contextualization I discuss.

Purpose

"Contextualization" entered the missional lexicon in 1972, which means that we can confine our map to examples from 1972 and forward. Even in that brief time, evangelicals have used hundreds of fascinating approaches.

Metaphorically speaking, the contextual "world" is much larger than the evangelical "continent." Most of the maps produced so far attend to the world rather than our particular continent. In fact, very few have tried to chart or map our continent, and even fewer to categorize the types of terrain on it. It is as much a mistake to think of Africa as nothing but savannah as it is to think of all evangelical contextual approaches as the same "terrain."

Continuing this metaphor, I offer a "travel guide" of the evangelical continent rather than a global map. We know some of the parts of our continent very well and are quite comfortable with them. We know other parts less well, and they may seem strange but not threatening. However, we also need to explore some of the more challenging, even dangerous, corners of our continent, and the ways evangelicals warn fellow evangelicals to stay away from them.

In this book, I offer criteria by which evangelicals label sections of our continent (whether appropriate, good, and healthy or dangerous, syncretistic, and heretical). I offer short excursions to some carefully chosen landmarks in each type of terrain so that when you travel to them you will be better equipped to evaluate them.

To do this, I am more *descriptive* than *prescriptive* in my approach. This descriptive (or *phenomenological*) approach temporarily suspends judgment. We cannot ultimately avoid wise judgment. However, the astuteness we need to judge wisely comes only from an accurate understanding of what we judge (e.g., Hiebert, Shaw and Tiénou 1999, 31–44). This is particularly important when we want to appraise terrain in a new continent that we previously have not seen and thus are likely to misunderstand. In the nineteenth century, Europeans derided travelers who came home telling of a mountain in Africa that remained snow-capped in the summer heat. Those who judged the stories as patently false could not comprehend the possibility of a Kilimanjaro—there was no space for it in their assumptions. Unless we want history to judge us as similarly quick-tongued fools, we need to take the time and energy needed to *understand* before we *pronounce*.

Finally, a discerning reader will see that only occasionally do I draw on theologians and biblical scholars. They have much to say about our landscape, but I have chosen to develop this map from the ever-growing range of perspectives offered by missiologists. While this constraint limits the sophistication in some areas, it also frames the discussion in light of the perspectives of those who most deeply engage in and explore the landmass of evangelical contextualization.

Structure of the Book

In addition to developing my own map, I use *mapping* as a primary metaphor throughout the book. There is great flexibility and utility in this metaphor. Mapping is an *activity* involving exploring territories, drawing boundaries, identifying terrain, comparing size, climate, topography, environment, and so on. Mapping is also a *means* to gain a clear picture by using such tools as labels, markers, inserts, compass points, and scale. Further, in the process of mapping we apply *a chosen set of rules*. All of this results in the map, which is a *product*. We may choose, for example, scale that attends to a specific locale such as a neighborhood or a scale that includes the entire world. Along with our scale, we may determine to use an absolute direction (a "theological north") and to emphasize certain factors in the terrain while not indicating others. Each metaphorical element of maps and mapping—means, product, activity, rules—helps us better visualize and understand the things that concern us.

Maps are always mental constructs. No matter how complex, maps are always less complex than our real world. In creating maps, we filter out some things and emphasize others—depending on the choices we make. Every map reduces clutter but simultaneously reduces richness; it simplifies at the risk of reductionism. We do well to keep this in mind.

In the first section, using the map metaphor, I summarize how scholars map the entire world of Christian contextualization. These maps include the evangelical continent as one of the several such continents Christians of all types use.

To map the "evangelical contextualization continent," we must understand the values and rules that constrain what evangelicals consider necessary for inclusion on that continent. Thus, in the first section I zoom in on these values and rules. Evangelicals use them to guide, constrain, and ultimately evaluate contextual methods, processes, and products. I describe the assumptions evangelical cross-cultural practitioners and missiologists consider fundamental for contextualization as a whole (chapters 2 and 3) and the criteria we use to discern good from bad contextualization (chapter 4). Building on these, I explain significant concepts that shape and constrain evangelical contextual methods (chapter 5), and describe several of the tools we use to analyze, develop, and apply contextualization (chapter 6).

In the second section, I turn to the actual mapping project and briefly explain the important territories of that continent (chapter 7). Then I present guided tours through each major territory of the continent (chapters 8 through 13). In each tour, I introduce the territory, describe characteristics of that territory, and offer examples from the Bible and our contemporary world. I then note examples in the territory and conclude with a brief list of potential benefits and areas of concern. I conclude this section and the book with a brief speculation on the immediate future for evangelical contextualization, depicting contextual issues I anticipate evangelicals will face as we work toward incarnating Christian faith in every community in the world.

Whenever we map an intellectual landscape, we choose from multiple viable methods. In determining my method, I explored several ways evangelicals have mapped our contextual continent. The map I use does not depend on them, but for those who want to follow my examinations and understand why I did not use them, I include them in four appendices. Appendices A to C present three maps, and Appendix D has a composite derived from them. As I experimented with options for my map, I also developed a "visual map" of evangelical semantic domain for contextualization, explained in Appendix E. Finally, to supplement discussion in the text, I list in their respective categories the entire dataset of 249 examples used to construct the map I use in Appendix F.

Foundations for Evangelical Contextualization

Models and Maps of

Contextualization

CHAPTER OVERVIEW

In this chapter, I focus on helping the reader see how evangelical approaches fit within the larger set of approaches used by Christians of all theological persuasions. That scholars try to map the various attempts is not surprising. However, the number of proposals on how best to contextualize faith is staggering. Listing each individually does not help, so scholars who map them cluster examples with similar characteristics into categories. They refer to these categories as "models," so I start the chapter by explaining how I use the term *model*.

Not all readers will be familiar with the term *contextualization*, so I provide a synopsis of the history of the term with a concluding definition. In the synopsis, I focus on the American setting and the significant historical tensions between the more liberal (conciliar or mainline) segments of the church and the more conservative (evangelical) segments. These tensions weave into evangelical reactions to the term, in large part because it was coined in the conciliar circles. It is almost impossible to understand the ongoing debates and developments among evangelicals (fleshed out in the following chapters) without knowing the reality of these tensions.

Since the coining of *contextualization* as a missiological term in 1972, missiologists have developed several "maps" of the ever-growing number and variety of contextual models. I take the rest of the chapter to explain two of them. The first, developed by Catholic missiologist Stephen Bevans, is the map most commonly used today by missiologists. The second is that of Robert Schreiter, also a Catholic missiologist and a colleague of Bevans at Catholic Theological Union. The two maps converge in some ways but not in others. Understanding these two maps is important because 1) they (especially Bevans) are so widely used and 2) evangelicals who have developed their own maps draw heavily on them. Knowing the categories developed in these two maps gives us a necessary foundation for understanding the evangelical maps discussed in chapter 6.

CHAPTER OUTLINE

1. Models
2. What Is Contextualization?
3. Maps of Contextualization
   a. Stephen Bevans's Map
      i. Translation Models
      ii. Anthropological Models
      iii. Praxis Models
      iv. Synthetic Models
      v. Transcendental Models
      vi. Countercultural Models
   b. Robert Schreiter's Map
      i. Translation Models
      ii. Adaptation Models
      iii. Contextual Models

Imagine that I give you an assignment to write a description of each of twenty-five landmasses on the Earth to help someone from another planet learn about our planet. I also insist that every description be the same length. When you start working, you become frustrated because you have no more words to describe the Eurasian landmass than that of Iceland. You might try to indicate their relative importance by what you say in each description. However, you may wonder if readers will think that the two landmasses are of equal importance.

In some respects, this parallels the situation of the existing contextual maps. Rather than using "landmass" to describe the various approaches, missiologists use the term *model*. Both are metaphors, and before looking at the maps it is important to understand what we mean by "models."

Models

The idea of a model ranges from the physical (a small-scale replica, such as a model airplane) to the metaphoric (an ideal toward which we aspire, such as a model citizen) to the theoretical (an explanation of some object or idea, such as a model of the atom) (see Barbour 1974). Missiologists use the term in the third sense when discussing "categories" of contextualization. I clarify this early in the discussion because it is not the way Charles Kraft—a prominent evangelical missiologist—uses the term. In his landmark book *Christianity in Culture*, he uses *model* to refer to specific methods or propositions rather than larger categories (see 1979d, 31-33; 2005d, 25-26). This clarification will help readers familiar with his text understand how I use the term.

> A model is a case that is useful in simplifying a complex reality, and although such a simplification does not fully capture that reality, it does yield true knowledge of it.
>
> Stephen Bevans (2002, 31)

In describing contextualization *models*, missiologists may refer to a particular *type of* contextualization, *approach to* contextualization, or *orientation toward* contextualization. We usually identify at least one example or proposal of each model that we think best characterizes it. This example is a prototype or exemplar of the model. We cluster other approaches as additional examples of this model because they share common attributes with the exemplar.

We may include as common attributes of a model such things as the example's underlying assumptions, guiding orientation, methods, or goals. We can choose which of the many differing sets of attributes to use. However, some enable us to develop a better map than others. Depending on our purposes, we may develop several ways to group the same models, resulting in more than one map. To keep flexibility, we need models that are simplified and representative rather than highly detailed and specific. Indeed, too much specificity will result in each example being its own model, which is not helpful in our task!

A great example of what I mean is Richard Niebuhr's map of five categories (models) of the ways Christ and culture relate: 1) Christ *above* culture; 2) Christ *of* culture; 3) Christ *the transformer of* culture; 4) Christ and culture *in paradox;* and 5) Christ *against* culture (1951; see also Carson 2008). Niebuhr's map illustrates the sense that missiologists intend when we map contextualization.

In sum, I use *model* to indicate a category of contextual examples grouped together based on a particular set of criteria. A model is a conceptual category rather than a particular example. Central to the task of distinguishing one model from another is the need to identify carefully and choose the criteria we use. Once we choose the criteria, we can arrange contextual practices and the theories by those criteria (together called a rubric) into categories (models). I spend the majority of the book on the process of identifying and choosing the criteria (and developing rubrics) that yield a helpful map of the continent of evangelical contextualization.

What Is Contextualization?

To understand contextualization—especially the ever-expanding American evangelical models of contextual mission practice—we must see the term in light of elements in the history of twentieth-century American mission that evangelicals consider important for our identity.

Intellectuals of the nineteenth century increasingly challenged a variety of traditional Christian beliefs and practices, especially evangelism. One of the first major flashpoints for these challenges to missions within the U.S. Protestant church was the "Fundamentalist-Modernist" controversy (1910 on). As evangelicals saw it, the modernists increasingly promoted social engagement *as* evangelism (i.e., the "social gospel") together with other deviations from traditional Christian beliefs. New perspectives (e.g., internationalism as the kingdom of God) and pronouncements in ecumenical mission circles (e.g., the Hocking Report) in the 1920s and 1930s drove evangelicals increasingly away from modernist orientations and organizations. However, modernists gained increasing power in the mainline churches, private universities (e.g., Princeton), and the growing ecumenical movement.

From the 1930s through the 1960s, even though evangelicals grew rapidly in numbers and founded a host of new evangelical organizations (e.g., schools, mission agencies, denominations), evangelicals still experienced marginalization in mainline and ecumenical circles. In this context, evangelicals increasingly focused their rhetoric on evangelism and away from social engagement promoted by ecumenical organizations.

When the International Missionary Council (IMC) merged into the World Council of Churches (WCC) in 1961, the IMC became the Division on World Missions and Evangelism (DWME) and in 1973 the Commission on World Mission and Evangelism (CWME). Fearing that mission would be lost in the larger organization, a number of evangelicals left the IMC, depriving it of energy and passionate commitment to mission (Pierson 2003, 76).

During this phase the DWME focused on ideas such as evangelism as presence (versus proclamation), interreligious dialogue, moratorium, and seeing mission as centered on what God is doing in the world rather than what the church is doing (popularized through the term *missio Dei*). "Discern the signs of the times" and "Let the world set the agenda" embodied this shift in mission from evangelism toward the struggle for justice. Renowned South African missiologist David Bosch noted:

Whereas evangelicals seek to apply Scripture deductively—in other words, make Scripture their point of departure from which they draw the line(s) to the present situation—ecumenicals follow the inductive method; the situation in which they find themselves becomes the hermeneutical key. Their thesis is: we determine God's will *from* a specific situation rather than *in* it. The nature and purpose of the Christian mission therefore has to be reformulated from time to time so as to keep pace with events. In the words of the Uppsala Assembly: "The world provides the agenda." (Bosch 1980, 38)

By the end of the 1960s, ecumenists dropped the final "s" in missions and debated whether non-Christian religious adherents were actually "anonymous Christians" (see Yates 1994, 175–76). All of these debates and shifts in the ecumenical world, together with three mainline Protestant institutions ending formal missions training programs by 1973 (see Horner 1987, 121), were perceived by evangelicals as clear evidence that mission was eroding within ecumenical circles. Most evangelicals of the day would not have predicted that they themselves would wrestle with all of these ideas and come to accept several of them in the coming decades.

In the middle of this ferment Shoki Coe adapted the term *contextualization* and those in ecumenical circles widely promulgated it. Reflecting the rhetoric of the time, Coe noted that he intended

> . . . to convey all that is implied in the familiar term indigenization, yet seek to press beyond for a more dynamic concept which is open to change and which is also future-oriented. *Contextuality* (emphasis mine) . . . is that critical assessment of what makes the context really significant in the light of the *Missio Dei*. It is the missiological discernment of the signs of the times, seeing where God is at work and calling us to participate in it. (Coe 1976, 21–22)

The very fact that contextualization was coined in ecumenical circles left many evangelicals immediately suspicious (see discussion in Fleming 1980 and the historical overview in Kraft 2005d), even though Byang Kato used the term positively in his Lausanne address only two years after it was coined (Kato 1975, 1217–18). It is astonishing that by the end of that decade (see, e.g., Buswell 1978 and Kinsler 1978) the term would find a home in ecumenical *and* evangelical discussion and thinking, though with very different understandings. In 1984, David Hesselgrave pointed out that the controversy was not yet resolved: "Still in its infancy, that word has already been defined and redefined, used and abused, amplified and vilified, coronated and crucified" (1984, 693).

Given the history and differences in orientation, it is not surprising that evangelicals and ecumenicals would use the same word in significantly different ways (May 2005, 349). Nigerian Josphat Yego wrote, "It simply means the never-changing word of God in ever-changing modes of relevance. It is making the gospel concepts or ideals relevant in a given situation" (Yego 1980, 154). Echoing some of Coe's rhetoric, Filipino Rodrigo Tano nonetheless framed contextualization in light of biblical truth:

> The contextualization of the Gospel and Christian theology then calls for a discerning of the times, involvement in one's particular situation, and participation in the ongoing mission of the church wherever it is situated. It brings the text (Bible) into a dynamic interaction with the context (life-situation). From this interaction, a life-situation or contextual theology emerges. As a *theologia in via* (pilgrim theology), contextual theology is neither final nor complete. (Tano 1981, 10)

From an evangelical perspective, then, contextualization captures the tension of Christians having biblical revelation that is universally true and applicable while living in a world of societies that are widely diverse in their religious identities. "Simply stated, contextualization means that the message (or the resulting church) is defined by Scripture but shaped by culture" (May 2005, 350).

Tensions arise in trying to bring together three differing perspectives. First is the perspective of biblical revelation (mediated to us through numerous authors from a variety of cultural perspectives). The second set of perspectives are of those who adhere to biblical teachings (most of whom are from societies that differ significantly from the cultures of the biblical authors), which includes their history and church traditions. These we call the "agents" of contextualization.

The third is the set perspectives of the recipients (or receptors) of contextualized efforts. Complicating this is that everything happens in a world in which recipients' societies are often in a state of flux.

Evangelicals teach that we have a universal and applicable true revelation that we are commanded to share with those who have not yet heard of it. Of course, we do not see contextualization as only a "missions" term. "It is of crucial significance for *all* Christians—even those who never cross a cultural boundary—for every one of us lives in a cultural setting and has to incarnate the Word of God and the Christian faith appropriately into that setting" (Moreau 2005, 321).

In short, contextualization can be described as "the process whereby Christians adapt the forms, content, and praxis of the Christian faith so as to communicate it to the minds and hearts of people with other cultural backgrounds. The goal is to make the Christian faith *as a whole*—not only the message but also the means of living out of our faith in the local setting—understandable" (Moreau 2005, 323; building on Hesselgrave 1984, 694).

> Contextualization may be one of the most important issues in mission today. Unlike the "Death of God" movement in theology, contextualization is no mere missiological fad that will fade when another "hot topic" catches our attention.
>
> Darrell L. Whiteman (1997, 2)

Maps of Contextualization

In recent decades, several missiologists have developed maps showing all the ways Christians contextualize, applying their own criteria to identify the various continents (models) of their maps. For example, Hesselgrave differentiated models by the way proponents anchor them to the biblical text (Hesselgrave and Rommen 1989). Robert Schreiter distinguished models by the way each relates to the context in which theologizing is done (1985). Understanding these "global" maps is a necessary first step to understand the evangelical contextual continent.

A major difficulty in comparing and contrasting the maps is that missiologists have different purposes and use different principles to arrange the models into categories. Some focus on *descriptively* arranging the approaches into separate categories. They describe each model together with its strengths and weakness (e.g., Bevans 2002; Gilliland 2005; Van Engen 2005a). Others *prescriptively* developed criteria to separate appropriate models from inappropriate ones (e.g., Hesselgrave 1979; Nicholls 1979b; see chapter 4). The criteria for separating models include such things as orientation toward Scripture (Nicholls 1979b; Cortez 2005a), prioritization of Scripture or culture (Moreau 2005), theological method (Bevans 2002), and how each relates to the local cultural context (Schreiter 1985). While most contextual cartographers intend their maps to cover the entire world, some limit their maps to particular continents (Cortez 2005a, Gilliland 2005, and Van Engen 2005a; see Appendices A, B, and C).

In this chapter, I zoom in on two descriptive global maps developed by Roman Catholic scholars. Stephen Bevans (1989, 1992, 2002) and Robert Schreiter (1985) created maps of the entire world of contextual models, giving us their criteria for each model before delineating its strengths and limitations. In Table 1.2, I rearrange the models so that those across the same row are roughly equivalent to each other (shaded boxes indicate a lack of a discernable match). Bevans describes six separate models, and Schreiter groups his six distinguishable models into three categories.

Stephen Bevans's Map

Stephen Bevans developed the global map missiologists most commonly use today. He first published it as an article in 1985, expanded it in book form in 1992, and revised and expanded it even further in 2002. In his 2002 version, Bevans delineated six models that span the contextual globe: the 1) translation, 2) anthropological, 3) praxis, 4) synthetic, 5) transcendental, and 6) countercultural models. Bevans initiated the transcendental and countercultural models, therefore, there are no equivalent models for comparison. Bevans constructed his map in light of four clusters of issues that adhere to contextual theology: 1) theological method, 2) basic theological orientation, 3) criteria for orthodoxy, and 4) cultural identity (in relation to popular religiosity) and change (2002, 16).

Translation Models

The *translation* model (also called the accommodation or adaptation model; 2002, 44) is the most commonly used model of all (2002, 37). Krikor Haleblian (1983, 104–6) first coined the label to differentiate Charles Kraft's approach (1979b) from Robert Schreiter's (1985). Haleblian indicates that Kraft's model "involves the reinterpretation of a given phenomenon, whether the Bible, church structure, ritual, or symbol in a new context where the meaning and impact of the elicited response are equivalent to those felt by the first Christian community" (Haleblian 1983, 104). Haleblian applied "translation" to Kraft's approach because Kraft derived it from the linguistic translation methodology known as dynamic equivalence (discussed in chapter 6) with the intention that this would enable better communication (see Gilliland 1989b, 314).

TABLE 1.2: DESCRIPTIVE MAPS OF ALL CONTEXTUALIZATION MODELS	
Bevans	**Schreiter**
Classified by theological method	*Classified by how each relates to the cultural context*
Model (Alternate names)	**Model (Subtype)**
Translation (Accommodation, Adaptation)	Translation
Anthropological (Indigenization, Inculturation Ethnographic)	Contextual (Identity or Ethnographic approaches)
	Adaptation (Enculturative)
Praxis (Libration, Situational)	Contextual (Liberative)
Synthetic (Dialogical, Analogical)	Adaptation (Philosophical)
Transcendental (Subjective)	
Countercultural (Prophetic, Encounter)	

Bevans contends that evangelicals and conservative Catholics prefer the translation model because they posit an unchanging message of the gospel and require the faithful "translation" of this supracultural message (which they see as propositional in nature; Bevans 2002, 41) in new cultural settings. According to Bevans, practitioners see the message as a type of kernel. They work to separate this kernel from the husk of the whole Bible (and church tradition in the case of Catholics) so that the agent of contextualization can transplant the kernel in the new setting (40–41). Bevans characterized the translation model as examining the values and thought forms in the new cultural setting to discover how to embed the supracultural kernel into that setting rather than examining the local values to see if truth is already present (37).

Anthropological Models

The *anthropological* model (alternately called the indigenization model or ethnographic model, 61) is on the opposite end of the spectrum from the translation model. The initiation point for contextualization is not an unchanging message but ever-changing settings (32). The primary concern of proponents of the anthropological model is "the establishment of preservation of cultural identity by a person of Christian faith" (54). They value coming not to judge, tame, or conquer societies for Christ, but to learn from them. For example, they hope to learn how to understand their own faith better and how to be better Christians.

Christians using this approach (Bevans includes Schreiter in this category, e.g., 2002, 55 n.5, 59 n.26, and 60 n.28) recognize that all knowledge is culturally embedded. Therefore, they argue, we must see that God has already been at work in cultures making himself known (54–55). In contrast to the translation model, they examine the local setting for what it has to offer as a result of God's revelatory work within it, and not to learn how to embed an external message.

Praxis Models

In contrast to the other two models, the *praxis* (or liberation or situational, 78) model is framed in terms of a social change in a local setting (70). Practitioners do not just focus on words or ideas but insist that action for social change on behalf of the oppressed is part of the theological process. Following Marx, Bevans notes that they insist that "we know best . . . when our reason is coupled with and challenged by action" (72). Those who use this approach see theology not just in the framework of culture but also in the framework of history and acts of historical significance for the kingdom of God, following in the tradition of the Old Testament prophets such as Isaiah and Amos (70–71). The goal is not as much right thinking (*orthodoxy*) as it is right praxis (*orthopraxy*) (72), which is often (but not always) framed in terms of liberation theology.

Synthetic Models

The *synthetic* (or dialectical) model is a middle-of-the-road model in which advocates try to take the best from the three previous models and synthesize a both/and approach: "It takes pains to keep the integrity of the traditional message while acknowledging the importance of taking all the aspects of context seriously" (89). It is thus synthetic in the sense of being a synthesis rather than in the sense of being artificial (89). Synthetic contextualizers thus pull from a rich variety of sources (past and present; own culture and other cultures) to develop in dialectical fashion something that transcends the sources while retaining their strengths. With no set formula or recipe to follow, using this model to construct contextual theologies is more the work of an artist than a mechanic or scientist. They can blend the various ingredients in a multitude of ways to produce appropriate contextual theologies.

Transcendental Models

The *transcendental* (or subjective) model builds on the concept of the philosophical transcendental method initially developed by Kant in the 1800s and expanded by various thinkers, such as Bernard Lonergan (1972) since its initial development (Bevans 2002, 103). Generally speaking, the focus is more on the self who is reflecting than on the content or action of the reflection. Proponents contend that this is universally possible because of the universals that make up what it means to be human. Central to this model is the idea that we cannot know what is outside of ourselves unless we know the inside of ourselves. Knowing the inside of ourselves is the starting point for contextual theological development. The need for authenticity in knowing ourselves is critical for this process. It is also important to realize that no person is isolated or devoid of context, so understanding self-in-context—and learning to see God's revelation of himself in the midst of that context—is critical. Ultimately, according to proponents,

> to the extent that a person of faith obeys the transcendental precepts—"Be attentive, Be intelligent, Be reasonable, Be responsible"— in trying to articulate and deepen his or her faith, he or she is doing genuine theology. And to the extent that a person does this as an authentic human subject—conditioned by history, geography, culture and so forth—he or she is doing genuine contextual theology. (Bevans 2002, 106–7)

Countercultural Models

Bevans added the *countercultural* model (or prophetic encounter or epistemological model; Van Engen 2005b, 196–97) in his 2002 revision in response to continued reflection after the publication of his 1992 version. Practitioners of the countercultural model take context with utmost seriousness. At the same time, however, they are deeply suspicious of culture. While they do not see culture as inherently evil, they recognize that it is tainted and not trustworthy. As a result, their goal is to "truly *encounter* and *engage* the context through respectful yet critical analysis and authentic gospel proclamation in word and deed" (Bevans 2002, 119). Many of the proponents are from the West and look at their own cultures rather than other cultures. They recognize that contextualization is not only done "over there" but right here. Bevans lists as practitioners Lesslie Newbigin (1986), Lamin Sanneh (1989), and David Bosch (1991, 1995). He also includes the Gospel and Our Culture Network, though leaders such as George Hunsberger disagree with this placement (Bevans 2002, xvi).

Robert Schreiter's Map

The global contextual map of Robert J. Schreiter has three major continents with six "sub-continental" regions (1985, 6–16). He classifies the continents (models) by how each relates to the cultural context. In his map, each model exemplifies 1) a relationship between cultural context and theology, and 2) something about the relation between theology and the community in which it takes place.

Translation Models

The *translation* models of Schreiter and Bevans are the same. The core idea is that the context is a vessel into which we insert faith, and proponents focus on the transmission of faith. They do so in a two-step process. The first step is to free the Christian faith (kernel) from previous cultural traditions (husk). The second step is to translate the data of revelation (kernel) into a new setting. Every time agents go into a new setting they must repeat this process, so they repeatedly husk the kernel"

Adaptation Models

Schreiter's second classification is *adaptation* models, and he identifies three versions. In the first version, expatriates—either independently or together with local leaders—construct an explicit philosophical system for the society that in some way parallels a Western theological or philosophical system. They use this construct as the basis for developing a Christian theology for the local context. The second version is an extension of the first. In it, indigenous leaders themselves construct the system based on their training and/or exposure to Western models. These two versions have the same goal; the primary difference is in *who* controls the development of the philosophical/theological system. Therefore we can group them together as one form of adaptation model called *philosophical adaptation*, which parallels Bevans's synthetic model [see 2002, 93 n.17 and 94 n.22].

Schreiter's frames his third version of the adaptation approach as "planting the seed of faith and allowing it to interact with the native soil, leading to a new flourishing of Christianity, faithful both to the local culture and to the apostolic faith" (11). This can take place only where there has been no prior exposure to the Christian faith, so is increasingly rare as an option. Based on Schreiter's discussion, we can call this version *enculturative adaptation*. Schreiter cites Vincent Donovan's *Christianity Rediscovered* (1968) as an example of this type of adaptation, though Bevans cites the Donovan as an example of his anthropological model. That they both cite the same approach as examples for different models reminds us how difficult it can be to categorize the contextual methods that exist.

Contextual Models

Schreiter calls his third major category *contextual*. The name clearly indicates his preference for this model, which he also calls local theologizing. In contrast to the other two models, agents of contextual approaches attend first to the context. They try to address more directly than translation or adaptation models "the interaction between received apostolic faith and traditions of culture" (1985, 12). Processes built on the contextual approach have two steps. First, they begin with the needs of a people in a concrete place, starting with the questions of the people themselves. Once they elicit the people's questions, as a second step agents of contextual models move to the traditions of faith. They initiate dialogue with Christian tradition whereby that tradition can express questions genuinely posed by the local circumstances, rather than only those questions that Christian tradition has treated in the past.

All three types of models deal with important questions, but Schreiter indicates that the contextual approach is the most important and enduring. As a result, he builds his own approach as a composite the two types of contextual models he identifies. Both focus on context, but on different aspects of the context. The first, the *ethnographic* contextual model, focuses on identity theologies. It begins with the concrete situation of constant and rapid cultural change of the people and focuses on their need for cultural identity. Agents of ethnographic contextualization intend to build up or affirm an identity among the marginalized or denigrated. It has strong parallels to Bevans's anthropological model.

The *liberation* contextual model, by contrast, begins with the concrete situation of constant and rapid change which is oppressing and dehumanizing the people and focuses on the need for *social change* to repair the ills of society. It is equivalent to Bevans's praxis model. Agents of the liberation model are keenly concerned with justice and liberating people from oppression and degradation. Schreiter recognizes the various liberation theologies together as a—if not *the*—major force among the contemporary contextual models of theology.

Conclusion

We now have a framework for understanding the global map of contextualization. However, evangelicals, based on shared convictions about things crucial to the foundations of Christian faith, do not intend to move to contextual continents they consider irrelevant or even harmful to our faith. While Bevans and Schreiter accurately catalogue the majority of evangelical models under the descriptors "translation" and "countercultural," these two descriptors alone do not adequately convey the myriad of approaches used by evangelicals any more than the terms "China" and "India" adequately convey the richness and variety of all of the countries found on the Eurasian landmass.

Let's return to the imaginary assignment I gave in the introduction to the chapter. I asked you to portray each of the world's landmasses in equal length descriptions. As we saw in this chapter, Bevans (2002, 37) and Schreiter (1985, 6) agree that the translation model is the most popular and widely used of all models (see also Gilliland 2005, 512). It is, in effect, the largest landmass on the global map. However—as with your assignment—their global maps offer no greater detail on the innumerable variations of the translation model than they offer on any of the other five models.

It should be clear that Bevans's and Schreiter's maps leave readers with impression that the *translation* landmass and the *transcendental* landmass (for example) are equally significant on the contextualization globe. However, there are numerous examples of the translation model in every corner of the globe today in hundreds of variations. The average American Christian experiences, or knows of, translation model examples (e.g., Willow Creek, Saddleback, Mars Hill) without even knowing that these are translation models. In effect, the translation model is the metaphoric equivalent of the Eurasian landmass. By way of contrast, we find the *transcendent* model almost exclusively in Western academic settings with at most a handful of variations. The same average American Christian will likely *never* encounter an example of the transcendent model—let alone know that it exists. It is the metaphoric equivalent of the Iceland landmass.

Bevans's and Schreiter's global maps helpfully describe each land-mass in our contextual world. However, they do not provide the perspective we need on the relative significance of each landmass in relation to the others.

From here, I turn to the evangelical landmass. As a first step in gaining a better perspective on it, over the next two chapters I out-line key assumptions or presuppositions about contextualization that evangelicals cherish. These undergird the rules used by evangelicals to devise, implement, and evaluate contextualization—and how we understand contextualization.

KEYWORDS FOR REVIEW

Anthropological model: approach that sees all knowledge as culturally embedded; goal is see how God is *already at work in* every
culture and preserve cultural identity in Christian faith

Contextualization: the process whereby Christians adapt the whole
of the Christian faith (forms, content, and praxis) in diverse
cultural settings

Countercultural model: approach that truly *encounters* and *engages*
broken contexts through respectful yet critical analysis and
authentic gospel proclamation in word and deed

Enculturative Adaptation model: approach that plants the seed of
faith and allows it to interact with the native soil, leading to a
faith congruent with the local culture and the apostolic faith

Ethnographic Contextual model: two-step approach: 1) understand
the needs of the people in the setting as they express them; 2)
initiate dialogue of those questions with Christian tradition

Liberation contextual models: same as Praxis model

Map of contextualization: a mental schema of models that encompass
the ways Christians attempt to contextualize their faith

Model: a category, prototype, or idealization of contextualization
based on a particular set of criteria

Philosophical Adaptation model: approach in which practitioners
(whether expatriate or indigenous) construct an explicit philosophical system as the basis for developing a local Christian
theology

Praxis model: approach oriented to enact social change on behalf of
the oppressed or marginalized in a local setting

Synthetic model: approach that draws the best from the translation, anthropological, and praxis models to synthesize
contextualization

Transcendental model: approach built on human universals: we must
authentically know self in order to know "self-in-context" and
see God's revelation of himself in the midst of that context

Translation model: approach of faithfully translating a supracultural
unchanging message of the gospel in new cultural settings

QUESTIONS FOR REFLECTION

1. Why is contextualization important for all Christians?

2. In what ways does the incarnation of Christ correspond to contextualization? In what ways does it not correspond to contextualization?

3. As you consider churches in your area, what models would you say fit the style of ministry for each?

4. More than one million American Christians go on short-term mission trips every year. What would you want them to know about contextualization before they go?

5. Which model of contextualization most appeals to you? Why?

FOR FURTHER STUDY

Bevans, Stephen B. 2002. *Models of Contextual Theology: Revised and Expanded Edition*. Maryknoll: Orbis.

Coe, Shoki. 1972. "Contextualizing Theology." In *Mission Trends No. 3: Asian, African, and Latin American Contributions to a Radical, Theological Realignment in the Church*, ed. Gerald H. Anderson and Thomas F. Stransky, C.S.P., 19–24. Grand Rapids: Eerdmans.

Moreau, A. Scott. 2005. "Contextualization: From an Adapted Message to an Adapted Life." In *The Changing Face of World Missions*, ed. Michael Pocock, Gailyn Van Rheenen, and Douglas McConnell, 321–48. Grand Rapids: Baker.

Schreiter, Robert J. 1985. *Constructing Local Theologies*. London: SCM Press.

Whiteman, Darrell L. 1997. "Contextualization: The Theory, the Gap, the Challenge." *International Bulletin of Missionary Research* 21 (January): 2–7.

Presuppositional Concerns in Contextualization 1: Revelation

CHAPTER OVERVIEW

Due to attacks leveled against the Christian faith over the past 150 years, evangelicals are concerned with the presuppositions Christians have about their faith. This is true in contextualization, and in this chapter we focus on presuppositions related to the concept of revelation, especially how it applies to our understanding of the Bible and contextualization.

First, evangelicals presuppose that God actually revealed himself to the biblical authors in such a way that what they freely wrote was exactly what he wanted them to write. The result was an infallible Bible that reveals God to all humanity. The God who created human beings chose to reveal himself to them with a message that transcends human culture.

It is not surprising, then, that evangelicals consistently affirm that any expression of Christian faith must be congruent with biblical teachings. We consistently judge contextualization efforts that we perceive to be flawed in this regard as inadequate or inappropriate. We also challenge fellow evangelicals who, in our perception, jettison biblical congruence.

Given the belief that biblical authors freely wrote as God superintended, it is not surprising that evangelicals place greater weight on some portions of Scripture than others. In contextualization, this comes out in two considerations: 1) is there a "kernel" that can be separated from a "husk" of the Bible? and 2) how do we distinguish normative (supracultural) commands from relative (culturally-restricted) commands? I explore this issue, noting that the entire Bible cannot somehow be separated and must be held together.

In the last section, I tackle the concept of general revelation. All evangelicals agree that God reveals himself outside of the Bible. However, we do not all agree on the scope of general revelation or the extent to which we can use it in our contextual efforts. This is especially important, and part of the ongoing debates among evangelicals, in determining 1) *whether* we can use the teaching of non-Christian religions as bridges for the gospel and, if so, 2) the *extent* to which we can use them.

CHAPTER OUTLINE

1. The Importance of Presuppositions
2. The Bible
   a. A Revealed Bible
   b. Biblical Congruence
   c. The "Eternal Word" in "Changing Worlds"
3. General Revelation

AHMED'S DREAM

Jun lived in a Muslim setting. He learned the local language and developed friendships among the people he interacted with while attending to the necessities of life. Shopkeepers, waiters, and tradesmen—all politely curious when he first arrived—became used to seeing him. He often sat with them, sipping tea and chatting, during the long afternoon break common in the country.

One day Ahmed, a friend of one of the shopkeepers Jun knew, stopped by Jun's apartment. As was customary, Jun prepared tea, and he and Ahmed settled in to enjoy each other's company. They engaged in the small talk Jun had come to appreciate; it made him feel connected to the people. After awhile, the two simply sat together in comfortable silence. Jun noticed Ahmed staring at his cup and sensed he was wrestling with something. Jun waited quietly, occasionally sipping his tea. Finally Ahmed glanced up at Jun with a puzzled look on his face.

"Can I ask you something?" he asked.

Jun continued sipping his tea and nodded for Ahmed to continue.

Ahmed swallowed, and then spoke in a rush. "A week ago, I had a strange dream. Something big was chasing me; I was so scared that I was shaking even as I ran. I felt like it would never stop—and whatever it was kept getting closer and closer. Suddenly I tripped and fell on the ground, and my arms were like lead—I knew I couldn't get back up. I felt that if whatever was chasing me caught me, I would not survive."

Ahmed stopped—as if reliving the fear and panic of the dream. Taking a deep breath, he continued. "Just as it reached out, a man appeared between it and me. He told the creature to stop and leave. He said I belonged to him. Suddenly the thing screamed and just disappeared! The man looked at me—somehow I felt he knew me from the inside out. Then he disappeared just as suddenly as the thing had.

"I woke up shaking and could not get back to sleep the rest of the night. For the past week I've been afraid to go to sleep. I don't know what to do! I asked some of my friends, and they just laughed. They told me I'd been watching too many horror movies—but I don't even own a TV."

"I remembered hearing from my friend that you are a Christian. Somehow, I had the feeling that you were someone who could help me understand the dream and what it means."

After an awkward silence, Ahmed whispered the last line: "I don't know who else to ask."

What would you tell Ahmed?

Although this story is fictitious, it is the type of story recounted by cross-cultural workers in many parts of the world. Scott Breslin and Mike Jones, living in the Middle East, heard such dreams and the worried questions so often that they wrote *Understanding Dreams from God* (2004) to help Muslims make sense of their experiences.

Ahmed's dream—and others like it—raises important questions for contextualization. Westerners wonder if such dreams are real; the many Ahmeds of the world, however, have no doubt. Was it Jesus who appeared in Ahmed's dream to protect him? Do such experiences warrant the development of new methods of contextualization? Vinay Samuel and Chris Sugden note:

> It is the mission field on every inhabited continent of the world where the issues of Christian obedience are being hammered out as the church seeks to witness to the gospel in varied social, economic and political contexts. This is how it should be. This is what the daily reading of the Bible by people in different contexts should be producing. (1984, 163)

Since the inception of the church, Christians have been engaged in a wide variety of contextualization approaches. They commonly come not from theoretical developments but from the living questions and challenges of life in places where the gospel is taking root. How should we handle questions such as Ahmed's—questions that come from people who see the world in dramatically different ways than we do? Further, when Christians such as Jun develop answers to Ahmed's questions, how do we know if they are good answers?

As noted in the brief historical review of contextualization (chapter

1), ever since the fundamentalist-modernist split in the early part of the twentieth century American evangelicals have been concerned with these types of questions. However, we have focused not only on the answers to them but also on the assumptions we have that determine how we find those answers.

These premises—or presuppositions—ground and shape our search for answers. False premises inevitably lead to false answers, so evangelicals are interested in the presuppositions that missionaries bring to their ministries. We value the types of assumptions inherent in the things that characterize us, which we explained in the introduction to the book. To make it easier to keep them in mind, I summarize them in Table 2.1.

TABLE 2.1: CHARACTERISTICS OF EVANGELICALS				
	Conversion	**Activism**	**Biblicism**	**Crucicentrism**
Bebbington	the belief that lives need to be changed	the expression of the gospel in effort, especially evangelism and missionary work	giving special importance to the Bible	Christ's atoning sacrifice on the cross is central
Stott	The gospel...	is effective because it is revealed by God himself		
		comes from God and not human ingenuity		
		is Christological, biblical, historical, theological, apostolic and personal		

In light of these characteristics, it is not surprising that evangelicals highly value presuppositions in these areas (e.g., Driscoll and Breshears 2008). They are especially important when we evaluate contextual models.

Although evangelicals are not the only ones concerned with the issues discussed in chapters 2 and 3, we are *consistently* concerned with them. Whoever would understand evangelical models of contextualization must understand the things that are important to evangelicals. We turn our focus to those presuppositional concerns.

The Importance of Presuppositions

The simple fact is, we all bring a set of presuppositions to anything we do; we cannot avoid them (Nicholls 1979a, 40–43; Carson 1984, 12–15; Cortez 2005b, 348). While we include the types of presuppositions that are part of worldviews (see chapter 6), we will focus on presuppositions that evangelicals consider especially important (Table 2.1) to our theology and ministry.

Evangelicals did not develop the presuppositions I discuss because of contextualization. Many came from the theological and philosophical battles over the past few centuries concerning the importance of Scripture and what constitutes legitimate Christian ministry. However, from the earliest use of the term, evangelicals debated whether the underlying presuppositions used by those promoting contextualization aligned with evangelical values. David Hesselgrave succinctly states the connection of presuppositions to contextualization:

> . . . there can be no doubt that pre-understandings are of paramount importance. Consequently, in the consideration of any attempt to interpret or contextualize scripture-based religious faith, one is inevitably driven to a consideration of the contextualizer's epistemic pre-understanding—how he views the scripture text with which he is working. (1984, 696)

We may challenge or reinterpret the presuppositions mentioned below in a variety of ways, but together they contour the ways I constrain contextualization. In large measure, evangelical reaction to contextual approaches has been determined by the extent to which those approaches cohere with evangelical assumptions. By way of illustration, evangelicals care about "effectiveness" (see chapter 4), but we also *de*value highly successful contextual methods that violate presuppositions that we consider foundational to Christian faith. For example, many evangelicals react negatively to "prosperity" or "health and wealth" gospel approaches even though such approaches are "effective" in that they have large numbers of promoters and adherents around the world. To evangelicals, *truth* is a central presuppositional issue (chapter 3), and when success becomes more important than truth, we have lost our way (Corwin 2006).

The Bible

If there is one defining characteristic of evangelical models, it is the normative nature of the Bible (Lausanne 1978) in the contextualizing process—the "unchanging word in the changing world" (Espiritu 2001, 280). This is the orientation of the "canonical principle" behind Kevn Vanhoozer's approach to contextualization (2006, 112–15).

Evangelicals do not claim there are specific biblical passages that discuss every evil act or moral dilemma seen in the world. Rather, we believe that Scripture has all we need—teachings, historical events, poems, proverbs, prophecies, and the like—to determine how to live in a godly fashion in any circumstance of any culture at any time. This is not to say that evangelicals think we have already unpacked all of this; we only maintain that everything we need to know about life is present in the Bible.

Thus, evangelicals contend that "The goal of contextualization is not to create a new God, a new soteriology or a new gospel message. Rather it is simply to understand, teach, live and express the gospel in a way that is relevant to a particular context" (Meral 2005, 212).

Evangelicals see the Bible—rooted in God's own normative nature (Howell 2001, 31)—as central in all of our theological tasks.

> The primary vehicle used in this process has been the Bible, God's Word to and for humankind.
>
> Larry Caldwell (1987a, 3)

A Revealed Bible

Evangelicals unequivocally maintain that the Bible is more than simply the religious reflections of inspired human beings. We contend that, at the very least, God chose what he wanted to reveal, through whom he wanted to reveal it, and how he revealed it. Because God is who he is, we believe that he chose to reveal everything we need to know about life and living. Rodrigo Tano notes "a valid indigenous or contextual theology must uphold the supremacy of the biblical revelation as normative for faith and conduct" (1984, 99; see also Imasogie 1984, 72; Cortez 2005b, 359; Bautista 2005).

Evangelicals universally agree that the Bible is our record of God's special revelation for all humanity. Traditionally, we also have agreed that God's revelation to humankind through the Bible is both verbal (in language) and propositional (truths are revealed) (Vanhoozer 1986, 56–67; Larkin 1988, 223–24).

Recent challenges to this perspective have come from some evangelical missiologists such as Charles Kraft, who posits that we must separate the *informational content* of revelation (which he maintains is an important component) from the *dynamic process*. He takes what I call a "calculus" approach to revelation, which is "in the dynamic interaction within that world [*in which we live*] that the impactful, life-transforming revealing activity of God takes place" (2005c, 141). A summary of his most significant ideas includes the following (2005c, 133–52; 169–85):

- Revelation is best understood as a *process* not a product.

- Each revelational event, then, is an example of the interaction of the supracultural God and culturally embedded humanity. It is a balance of meaning and the activation of it in a person's life by God.

- Meaning is *information + personalization* (meaning is progressive in the Bible, but not evolutionary).

- God must activate "meaning" in person(s) before revelation can be said to have occurred.

- Because revelation is a process rather than a product, general and special revelation are not *qualitatively* different.

- Through general revelation, people have enough information to move their allegiance to God, though they infrequently (at best) do so.

- If we can find ways to allow God to "activate" this general revelation through receptor-oriented communication, people can shift their allegiance to God without having to know the specifics of special revelation. Ultimately, however, they need to experience the impact of both general and special revelation.

- The canon is closed—God has given us sufficient "case studies" to meet all human circumstances.

Thus, for Kraft, the most significant component of revelation is the dynamic process, not the information-focused and static content. Content *is* important but not central. Since God does not change, Kraft argues that the process of revelation today is no different than it was for the biblical authors (2005c, 147). Given this perspective, it should not surprise us that Kraft eschews tools built on static dissection of information, such as grammatical historical exegesis (2005c, 112–13). He advocates that they be subsumed to analytic tools which recognize the dynamic process of revelation—especially the tools of the social sciences.

He contends that models which focus on static information "turn living events into cadavers, capable of being dissected but no longer capable of life" (2005c, 141). Such turns of phrase certainly draw attention—and it is not surprising that evangelicals so accused of being theological coroners responded by dissecting Kraft himself. Carl Henry notes that Kraft departs from historical evangelical theology in his view of revelation and inspiration in ways that echo neo-orthodox clichés (Henry 1980, 163). Graham Cole notes that while Kraft seeks to be biblical he does not draw his model of revelation from biblical data (1981, 88). David Hesselgrave charges that Kraft's underlying epistemology is closer to the "writings of the enlightened" of Hinduism and Buddhism than to the "inspired writings" of Christian orthodoxy (1984; 722–23; 2005, 262). Daniel Hardin asked, using some of Kraft's terminology, "Is the closed conservative fearfully and wrongly clinging to outmoded forms, or is the author, overly influenced by third-world paganism, relegating God and Biblical theology to a common denominator somewhere behind cultural universals?" (Hardin 1981, 353)

Further, Kraft's orientation removes an important foundation for the evangelical belief that the biblical canon is closed. If revelation does not include the content and is identical today to revelation recorded in the Bible, on what basis can we say that today's revelation is not equal in all respects to that of the biblical writers? Left without a theological or rational justification for the closing of the canon, Kraft can only note that he has "no expectation that further Scripture will be written" . . . "because we don't need any more, not because there are no more inspired things happening" (2005c, 162; cf. Grudem 1988). Kraft's own colleagues warn that placing ourselves at the same revelatory level as Paul starts a process that puts us on a very slippery slope (e.g., Shaw and Van Engen 2003, 33).

Finally, Kraft's definition of "revelation" is what evangelicals have long called "illumination," in which God, through the Holy Spirit, "causes the letter of the Bible to become charged with life and to become the living voice of God to us" (Pinnock 1984, 163). Evangelicals agree that illumination continues, and focus on its dynamic nature (e.g., Shaw and Van Engen 2003, 15–16). However, conflating illumination with revelation weakens the latter, which evangelicals have always understood as God's specific inspiration in the lives of those who wrote the Bible.

Perhaps the most significant implication of the traditional evangelical view of revelation is that God was able to inspire the biblical authors in such a way that what they wrote was what he wanted them to write. In some places God actually dictated some of the content (e.g., the Ten Commandments; Harris 1971, 20). In other places the Bible indicates that God gives his word to his prophets (e.g., "The word of the LORD came" to or through them—see, e.g., Deut. 5:5; Isa. 1:10; Jer. 1:2; Ezek. 1:3; Hos. 1:1; Joel 1:1; Amos 7:16; Hag. 1:1). However, for much of the biblical text, evangelicals assert that "the human author freely wrote what he wanted while the divine author at the same time superintended and guided that writing" (Moo 1986, 187). Being thus inspired, what they wrote was true. This understanding has historically been framed using terms such as "infallibility" and "inerrancy" and has been the traditional staple of the evangelical diet concerning the truth of the Bible (Carson 1986, 10).

It is true that some evangelicals have challenged traditional understanding of biblical revelation as propositional (see discussion in Vanhoozer 1986, 56–75) and inerrancy (see discussion in Carson 1986, 22–24, 30–31 and Beale 2008), but evangelicals as a whole still value both such that any contextualizing efforts suspected of demeaning either will be carefully scrutinized.

Biblical Congruence

> Scripture itself as the Word of God written constitutes the
> most authentic and effective instrument of contextualization.
> This is so because its divine Author has so ordered history and
> so inspired certain human authors that the cultural settings,
> languages, literary genres, events and actors of the Bible—
> as well as the meaning of the text itself—bear the stamp of
> what I will call "transculturality."
>
> David Hesselgrave (1995b, 139)

In light of the centrality of the Bible for evangelicals, it is appropriate that we evaluate the extent to which all contextualized efforts "convey Christian meanings with minimum distortion to the message of the Bible" (Gilliland 2005, 509; see also Samuel and Sugden 1984, 161–63; Hesselgrave 1995a, 115; 2007; and Strauss 2006, 101–3). Kraft, for example, refers to the Bible as a "yardstick" (2005c, 147) and a "tether" (2005c, 150), both images conveying his concern for biblical congruence. Hesselgrave and Rommen insist, "The adequacy of an attempted contextualization must be measured by the degree to which it faithfully reflects the meaning of the biblical text" (1989, 201; see also Demarest 1983; see also Kirk 1979, 185–94; Tiénou 1984, 159; Nuñez 1985; Gnanakan 1994, 128; and Horrell 2005). In sum, since the Bible is transcultural, congruence with the Bible is not negotiable.

Simply declaring the centrality of congruence with the Bible is critical, but so is *discerning* the extent to which it is true for a particular contextualization model. While not all evangelicals agree how to do this, all do agree that determining whether a model or application of a model is congruent with the Scriptures is critical. This accords well with the Reformation concept of *sola scriptura* (Latin for "by scripture alone"), that the Bible alone is the final arbiter of theological doctrine. Evangelicals continue to use the concept of *sola scriptura* to evaluate contextualization models and practices (e.g., Asad 2009, 138).

Various evangelical missiologists suggest ways to evaluate congruence. Marc Cortez offers a method of maintaining appropriate congruence based on the level of discourse in both the model of contextualization and the Bible (2005a). Hesselgrave and Rommen propose an evaluative framework based on two types of conceptual validity: *categorical* and *principial* (1989, 172–74). *Categorical* validity refers to those aspects of the Christian message that are nonnegotiable. We can group them into two broad types: 1) Those aspects of truth necessary for justification by grace, such as the sacrificial death of Christ, faith, repentance, and conversion; and 2) Those which, by nature of their form or symbolism, cannot be altered without changing their meaning. The sacraments are a good illustration. Some type of correspondence between form and meaning underlies this orientation.

Principial validity, however, refers to those aspects of revealed truth that grow out of the implications of new life in Christ. These aspects fit into two broad subcategories. First are elements of the truth of the gospel that are explicitly stated and logically necessary for godly living, walking worthy of our calling, separation from the world, and keeping the moral law. Second are aspects of the gospel's truth which, although stemming from the believer's life in Christ, are not explicitly stated and for that reason allow considerable latitude of expression, such as goodness and faithfulness. We can change or determine the form or mode of expression of these according to the culture into which they are implanted.

Kraft is also concerned with biblical congruence, but he differs on how to achieve it. As I explained earlier in this chapter, Kraft argues that evangelicals over-focus on the information component of revelation and ignore the dynamic process. For Kraft, then, biblical congruence is not as much alignment with *truth* or *teaching* as it is with *process*. He maintains that we should focus our energy on understanding and attempting to reproduce the *impact* of God's revelation on others rather than simply give them information they can grasp. This will enable people to turn to God in allegiance and (as led by him) begin the process of transforming themselves and others in their culture (for application, see D. Priest 1990). In essence, in this "humanward" (though *not* human-powered) focus, Kraft wrestles with the *stimulus* revelation generates in the receptors more than with God's work of *illuminating* the Scriptures for their benefit (though he does not ignore the latter).

Kraft does not advocate *replacing* content with process. Rather, he wants to shift our focus away from an exclusive orientation on content. Other evangelicals have challenged this approach. Critics contend that Kraft's approach ignores the historical particularity of the text (Carson 1985, 202–5) and puts the Bible as subject to our understanding of ancient culture (McQuilkin 1980, 117) in a way that has the potential to develop "a biblical 'sound alike' that becomes a hermeneutical tool for rewriting biblical teaching according to a cultural consensus" (Inch 1984, 745–46). Hesselgrave goes even further, stating that Kraft's methods potentially lead to the "death of the apostolic Christianity which he proposes to champion" when his former students go beyond his own intentions (1984, 723).

The desire for congruence with the Bible means that evangelicals look to the Bible for methods of contextualization (Davies 1997; Hesselgrave 1995b). While finding examples from the Old Testament may be more difficult (e.g., Archer 1978; Niles 1980; Lind 1982; Glasser 1989; Peterson 2007b), the New Testament itself is a set of contextualized documents, and evangelicals regularly look to it for insights on contextualization (Van Allman 1975; Ericson 1978; Yego 1980; Inch 1982; Gilliland 1989c; Sanchez 1998; Poston 2000; Flemming 2005). We also look for examples from which we can draw lessons to use in contextualizing efforts (Fritz 1995; Hesselgrave 2000b; Culver 2000). Additionally, we warn against uncritical use of social sciences or other extrabiblical approaches as *primary* resources equal to Scripture (Hesselgrave 2000a).

Since "Models cannot be built on sources that are incompatible with the Bible" (Gilliland 2005, 514), evangelicals tend to look with suspicion on any contextual methodologies built on views that challenge or eschew biblical authority or fidelity. We are cautious in using the four models in Bevans's map (Table 1.2) which see Scripture (and tradition) as "culturally conditioned/incomplete" (Bevans 2002, 141–43). While the Bible does not always have to be the starting point for evangelicals, our very definition of an evangelical is someone who sees the Bible as the norm.

The "Eternal Word" in "Changing Worlds"

Evangelicals agree that God used the culture, times, circumstances, and personalities of the biblical writers in the inspirational process. Being a human *and* divine product, evangelical approaches to understanding the Bible are characterized by two interconnected issues. First, is there a "kernel" (supracultural core) that can be separated from a "husk" (cultural wrapping)? Bevans and Schreiter single out this approach as one of the distinguishing characteristics of the translation model (Bevans 2002, 40; Schreiter 1985, 7). Second, how do we distinguish normative (supracultural) commands from relative (culturally restricted) commands? I will approach these as a single question.

William Smalley called this concept "superculture" in 1955. For several decades evangelicals struggled over whether it is possible to separate the supracultural "kernel" from the relative cultural "husk" (Conn 1984) and how to determine whether any particular command is transcultural and normative or cultural and relative (e.g., McQuilkin 1984; Eitel 1987, 135; Osborne 1991, 326-36). For example, clearly the command to love God with all our heart, soul, mind, and strength is transcultural. However, it is far more difficult to distinguish which of the many Old Testament dietary laws apply today.

William Larkin identified five methodologies for separating supracultural from cultural that evangelical scholars proposed from 1971 to 1982. In 1983, Krikor Haleblian summarized the confusion:

> Although this question is integral to the problem of contextualization, missiologists and theologians are obviously divided in their answers. Some (McGavran, Kato, Athyal, Fleming) believe that there is a gospel core and that it is identifiable, albeit in general terms. Others (Nicholls, Marshall, Packer, Loewen) seem to contend that there is no gospel core, and even if there is such a thing, it would be difficult to separate it from the cultural forms in which it is given. Those who believe the core can be separated from the form give several answers as to its precise context. (1983, 101)

Larkin noted that no consensus was reached on the issue by the late 1980s (1988, 107–13), which is not surprising given that "every attempt to systematize the biblical data or to extrapolate the most essential, unchanging elements of the Gospel is itself a product of changing cultural forces" (Blomberg 1993, 226). In 1988, Harvie Conn pointed out that this type of distinguishing is tantamount to developing a "canon within the canon" with potentially dangerous consequences

(1988, 196–97). Hesselgrave and Rommen declared, "Little is to be gained by attempting to identify supracultural elements of the gospel and its culturally bound parts" (1989, 172). By and large, evangelicals concluded that it is the "whole counsel of God" (Nuñez 1985, 285) that we must "reclothe" (Winter 1995) in new settings and trying to separate supracultural from cultural is inappropriate in the contextualizing process (Carson 1987, 249; also Dyrness 1990, 28).

More recently evangelicals have explored the difference between "deep-level structures of meaning (including cultural symbols and manifestations) and surface-level structures of meaning (including cultural themes and metaphors)" (Shaw and Van Engen 2003, 84). Kraft posits three levels: 1) culture-specific, 2) general-principle, and 3) basic-ideal. He notes that the culture-specific level (parallel to Shaw and Van Engen's surface-level) structures are so context specific that they must be changed (Kraft 2005c, 108–12). While Shaw and Van Engen advocate differentiating the levels and moving from deep-level of the Bible to deep-level of the receptor culture, they also note that the deep-level and surface-level are "dynamically and intimately interconnected" within a culture (Shaw and Van Engen 2003, 85) and so separation might be a difficult task.

If this more sophisticated approach is to escape the orientation of kernel and husk, it must hold all layers as truly biblical revelation and not simply discard any because they are more localized. The recognition by Shaw and Van Engen of the interconnection of layers is an important step in that direction. Evangelicals need to continue developing constructive approaches that acknowledge differences between deep-level and surface-level or culture-specific level structures of meaning. But they should not do so in ways that essentially attempt to separate them into kernel and husk. For example, Cortez discusses layers of biblical and theological discourse and the relative scope of each layer in a way that keeps each in its proper place without separating them from each other (Cortez 2005a). Despite the complexities involved, it is appropriate to conclude this presuppositional discussion on the Bible with Bernard Adeney's apt declaration, "The entire canon of the Bible . . . is constitutive of what it means to be a Christian in every time and place" (Adeney 1995, 79; see also Gener 2004, 151; Horrell 2005).

General Revelation

Evangelicals recognize that the Bible teaches that God reveals himself in the order of the cosmos. The adage "All truth is God's truth" captures it in one sense. However, that saying does not mean that extrabiblical truths are always *revealed* by God. We recognize that in some areas (e.g., science) truths that God has established are *discoverable* by humans rather than directly revealed by God. While we often speak of general and special revelation separately, Bruce Nicholls notes that both play an inseparable role in conversion:

> Effective cross-cultural communication requires a clear theological distinction between God's general revelation and his special revelation, though in the process of conversion and re-creation they can never be separated. Revelation is unitary. The former without the latter is powerless, and the latter without the former lacks the basis of the knowledge of God as Creator. (1979a, 67)

In contextualization, evangelicals are less concerned with the type of general revelation seen in scientific discoveries. Rather, they are concerned with what can be called religious general revelation seen in every part of the world. While we recognize that God continues in a variety of ways to call people to himself through general revelation, we maintain that this type of revelation is preparatory for the gospel rather than salvific by itself.

Applications of the ways evangelicals see general revelation are numerous. For example, many evangelical contextualizers look for biblical truth in other religions in order to use it as bridges to introduce special revelation. As Kraft articulates,

> I assume, . . . that we should (1) take seriously those passages of Scripture (e.g., Acts 14:17; 17:22–31; Rom. 1, 2; Gen. 14:18–20) that indicate that God has been at work with every people at every time; (2) that, therefore, Christian witnesses need to be diligent in discovering such workings (e.g., in redemptive analogies). (1982, 140)

Evangelicals believe that God uses general revelation as a type of preparation for the special revelation of the Bible. This shows up in evangelical contextualization models in several ways, though not all evangelicals agree on each of these uses.

First, some evangelicals use the scriptures of other religions as bridges to the gospel (e.g., the Camel Method discussed in chapter 11). Not all evangelicals agree on this point, however (e.g., Schlorff 2000, 306–7).

Similar to that is the recognition by some evangelicals that general revelation results in indirect components in a culture that provide bridges for understanding religious truths found in the Bible (Strom 1987). For example, Rick Brown compares selected terms in contemporary Muslim worldviews with some of the same terms (or ideas) found in the Bible in order to "highlight those elements of the Biblical worldview which Muslims already share and those which they are likely to misunderstand or reject" (e.g., Brown 2006a, 6; 2006b; 2006c).

Evangelicals also use general revelation as a means of "redemptive analogies." Don Richardson posits that within cultures are beliefs, rituals, or other practices that enable people to understand one or more facets of the redemptive truths of the Bible (Richardson 1981; we return this in chapter 6).

Finally, evangelicals use general revelation to help new Christians connect truths they already know from their own cultures to biblical truths or teachings (e.g., proverbs; Moon 2009). Another way this is seen is when the contextualizer grasps biblical truth in new ways as a result of learning another language or culture (e.g., Moon 2009, 110–18) such that "the Christian message becomes more appropriate and comprehensible to both those to whom it is proclaimed and to those who proclaim it" (Anderson 2000a, 377).

While evangelicals use general revelation in contextualization, certain limitations are important to us. We tend to be suspicious of any contextual model that equates or puts general revelation on par with special revelation (see "Characteristics of Evangelicals," Table 2.1). As a rule of thumb, evangelicals are more willing to look positively on contextual models in which general revelation in the context *illuminates, illustrates,* or *enhances our understanding of* special revelation. At the same time, barring some type of special consideration, by virtue of the characteristics of evangelicals we will reject contextual models when we sense that using them will in some way allow general revelation in the context to *negate, contradict, or supplant* special revelation. Thus, for example, the reaction of fellow evangelicals to Charles Kraft's proposals on special revelation noted above.

Conclusion

Evangelicals value both special and general revelation. Of the two, however, we assign to special revelation a normative role in determining religious truth. Evangelicals more likely reject out-of-hand contextual methods that we perceive to deviate from biblical norms as we understand them. How do evangelicals know when contextual methods deviate from biblical norms? This can happen only when we adequately understand special revelation. In chapter 3, I turn to the presuppositions related to the process of doing that.

Keywords for Review

Activism: one of the characteristics Bebbington identified of evangelicals, namely, the expression of the gospel in effort, especially evangelism and missionary work

Biblicism: one of the characteristics Bebbington identified of evangelicals, namely, the importance they give to the Bible as foundational to Christian faith

Conversion: one of the characteristics Bebbington identified of evangelicals, namely, the belief that lives can (and must) be changed through Christ

Crucicentrism: one of the characteristics Bebbington identified of evangelicals, namely, the belief that Christ's atoning sacrifice on the cross is central to Christian faith

General revelation: the idea that God reveals important truths (such as his existence) to all people everywhere

Presupposition: a pre-understanding that is assumed to be true

Special revelation: the particular revelation of God about his character and plan for humankind as given in the Bible

QUESTIONS FOR REFLECTION

1. Why do evangelicals consider presuppositions so important?

2. What presuppositions about the Bible do you consider the most important? Why?

3. In what ways does Bebbington's fourfold characterization of evangelicals fit your experience? In what ways does it not fit your experience?

4. What limitations do you think there should be on using the scriptures of other religions as bridges to the gospel?

5. What do you understand the phrase "all truth is God's truth" to mean?

FOR FURTHER STUDY

Bebbington, David W. 1989. *Evangelicalism in Modern Britain: A History from the 1730s to the 1980s.* London: Unwin Hyman.

Conn, Harvie M. 1984. *Eternal Word and Changing Worlds: Theology, Anthropology, and Mission in Trialogue.* Grand Rapids: Zondervan.

Hesselgrave, David J. 1984. "Contextualization and Revelational Epistemology." In *Hermeneutics, Inerrancy, and the Bible*, ed. Earl D. Radmacher and Robert D. Preus, 693–738. Grand Rapids: Zondervan.

Kraft, Charles H. 2005. *Christianity in Culture: A Study in Dynamic Biblical Theologizing in Cross-Cultural Perspective.* 25th Anniversary Edition. Maryknoll: Orbis.

Shaw, R. Daniel, and Charles E. Van Engen. 2003. *Communicating God's Word in a Complex World: God's Truth or Hocus Pocus?* Lanham, MD: Rowman and Littlefield.

Presuppositional Concerns

in Contextualization 2:

Interpretation

CHAPTER OVERVIEW

We have seen that evangelicals anchor faith in the biblical text, so biblical congruence plays the central role in evangelical contextual models.

In this chapter we explore the underlying presuppositions evangelicals hold that enable them to safeguard congruence with Scripture. It is critical to start the discussion by noting evangelical presuppositions about the staining effect sin has on everything in the process—from agents to receptors to the structures both construct.

Then we shift to foundational philosophical considerations. What do evangelicals assume about "truth" and "knowing" and how do these assumptions guide our contextual efforts? What do we assume about language and logic when we choose among alternatives or evaluate the efforts of others? How might these assumptions frame what we consider legitimate in contextualization? What approaches do evangelicals take to understand how form (e.g., the word *God*) and the meanings people attach to these forms are connected? What paths do our assumptions open for experimenting (e.g., "Behold the Ox of God," Anderson 1998) and what paths do they close?

In the final two sections we focus on what evangelicals assume about connecting the "forms" of the Bible with the meanings of the text. What do we assume about the number of viable meanings, and what do we assume about how we can derive appropriate meanings?

CHAPTER OUTLINE

1. The Ongoing Reality of Sin
2. Truth and Knowledge
3. Logic
4. Language
5. Form and Meaning
6. How Many Meanings?
7. Hermeneutics

Evangelicals are aware that sin affects all human endeavors, including contextualization (Feinberg 1982; Larkin 1988, 293–99). Sin is part and parcel of every society in which contextualization takes place. Sin also is pervasive among the agents of contextualization themselves, as well as the organizations and societies from which they come (Moreau 1995a).

The Ongoing Reality of Sin

Individual, agency, or denominational agendas driven by such things as ambition, revenge, and anger are easily disguised as objective or servant-oriented. Evangelicals have recognized that sin all too often dominates and drives our lives as individuals and members of organizations. We have not done as well in seeing the depth and reality of structural sin and its constraining and dehumanizing impact on societies as well as individuals. This reality pervades and impedes all of our contextualizing efforts, as Marc Cortez notes:

> We must account for sin as one of the overriding realities of the human situation in any attempt to make the context a serious part of the theological task. The fact that "all have sinned and fallen short of the glory of God" (Rom 3:23) should be a serious reminder that all theologizing is done with a significant handicap. This should cause us to be theologically aware of at least three realities: the need for suspicion, the problem of oppression, and the inequality of cultures. (2005b, 356)

The recognition by evangelicals such as William Larkin (1988, 293–99) and Cortez of how pervasive sin is in our own hermeneutical orientation and the resulting need for suspicion of our hermeneutical methods is one of the reasons why evangelicals have slowly been moving away from a naïve realist epistemology to a critical realist one. To that we now turn our attention.

Truth and Knowledge

At the outset, we must acknowledge that contemporary discussion of truth and epistemology is so complicated that our cursory review cannot adequately convey the issues. That said, there are certain irreducible approaches to truth that evangelical contextualizers highly value. For example, we hold that God himself is the ground of truth (Cortez 2005b, 348–49), so that truth is objective and absolute. We also believe that we can convey truth through ordinary human language (see below) from one culture to another (Davis 1981, 57–65; Nicole 1983; Carson 1986, 35–36; Vanhoozer 1986, 95–103; Fudge, 1987; Larkin 1988, 231–41; Brown 2006d). As one missionary working in South East Asia noted, "The goal in contextualization is not to make the gospel as Islamic as possible. Rather it is to communicate the unchanging truth to an Islamic audience so that it makes sense to them" (Woods, 2003, 189).

> While contextualized *communication* is worthy of applause, attempting to contextualize *faith content* is a disaster.
> —Gary Corwin (1998, 145; emphasis mine)

While evangelicals hold to these ideas, they hold to them in important ways. Paul Hiebert explains three approaches to epistemology (1994, 19–51; see also a synopsis in Moon 2009, 114–18). The first approach, not characteristic of evangelicals, is instrumentalism. This position holds that all knowledge is subjective since it is constrained by culture, language, and the particular perspective of the individual. Contextualizers who hold to this position maintain that the Bible may contain truth, but it is *subjective* truth constrained by those who wrote, collated, and collected it. At best, it is only one version of that truth among many possibilities. Those who hold this position go to another culture looking only for truth as seen within the culture, since every culture has its own grasp on the truth and there is no need to introduce a different version of truth. Evangelicals reject any contextual model that takes this approach.

The second approach is naïve realism, the belief that knowledge is objective and that we can know reality as it is in all of its fullness. Those who approach contextualization with this orientation believe that the Bible teaches truth and that they can know biblical truth completely and without distortion. Contextual models built on this position frame the task as simply bringing biblical truth to another setting and inserting it. The only reason to learn the culture, therefore, is to find out how best to insert biblical truth, since the culture will have little at best to add to the contextualizers' understanding of the Bible. They downplay the value of insights from the culture, since they already know all they need to know. This has been the position of evangelicals in the past, and many continue to hold to it in some form. This position has been the basis of critique of evangelical contextualization models, since naïve realist evangelicals often convey a type of "epistemological arrogance."

The third position, which Hiebert argues is the most viable epistemological approach, is critical realism. Like naïve realists, advocates of this position uphold the truth of the Bible. The difference is that *critical* realists recognize our inability to grasp truth without constraints. To understand some of the debates among evangelicals, it is crucial to understand that there are two distinct approaches to critical realism that result in different contextual approaches.

Hiebert's perspective exemplifies one approach. He recognizes that our grasp of truth is imperfect but believes that we can grow in our understanding. Even if our grasp is only "a poor reflection as in a mirror" (1 Cor. 13:6), we can check its correspondence to the truth revealed in Scripture (Hiebert 1985b; 1988; 1989; Nagasawa 2002; Cortez 2005a, 89; Horrell 2005, 476; Vanhoozer 2006). Those who follow Hiebert will go to another culture and work to understand it in an effort to find ways to make the biblical message understandable. Recognizing that they do not comprehend the whole message of the Bible, they study their new host culture 1) to learn how to convey biblical truths in the new culture and 2) to discover insights from the culture that will help them better understand the message of the Bible (see, e.g., Moon's portrayal of this, 2009, 110–18). Further, they recognize the need to do this in a "hermeneutical community" where diverse people struggle together to discern truth in particular texts and learn how to apply those truths in specific contexts (see Padilla 1979b, 104; Hiebert 1994, 91; Moreau 1997, 129–32).

Charles Kraft offers a modified version of critical realism with the following main tenets (see Kraft 1991a, 92–93; 2005c, 18–34; 2005h, 162–63; 2008, 55–74):

- There is a REALITY that exists, but only God knows this RE-ALITY perfectly and completely.

- Each person interprets her or his experience of REALITY to create a personal reality (small "r").

- Persons try to communicate their understanding of REALITY to others by encoding what they "mean" into "messages" that they send to others through a variety of channels.

- These "messages" and the "forms" through which they are transmitted have no inherent "meaning." Meanings are in people, not in the messages. "Messages" and "forms" are simply codes and cultural structures that people imperfectly share and use to communicate.

- Receptors receive the "messages" and "forms" but create their own meanings and construct their own reality based on their personal interpretation of the "message."

Like Hiebert, Kraft recognizes that our grasp of truth is imperfect. Unlike Hiebert, however, he argues that "messages" do not contain "meaning." He is concerned that evangelicals put too much focus on the REALITY (which is static and never perfectly understood) and not enough on the process by which people construct their own realities. Therefore it is a mistake to give so much attention to the adequacy of the correspondence of our perceptions of reality with REALITY—that is too much like naïve realism. Kraft argues that since people construct their realities from messages, and the messages do not contain meanings (or REALITY), we should shift focus away from the *content* of REALITY to the *process of God's ongoing revelation* of REALITY among people today. Critical realist contextualizers who follow Kraft's lead will go to another culture hoping to participate in God's revelation of himself to the people of the host culture. For example, they will learn the culture so that the effect of their Bible translations will parallel the effects of the original Bible on original audiences. They will experiment with ways to help people change faith allegiance, sometimes using traditional religious forms (e.g., Christian shrines in Japan) and other times bringing in new ones. Kraft argues that the forms, while very important, are in and of themselves neutral. Thus we can use forms—even religious ones—already found in societies to help people construct faith allegiance to God by using their own forms rather than importing new ones (see, e.g., Parshall 1980, esp. 55–61).

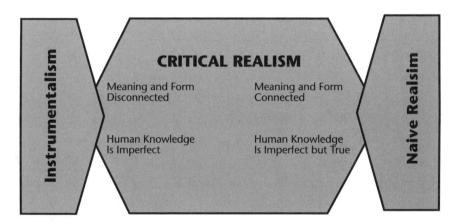

Figure 3.1: Critical Realist Continuum

I illustrate the differing interpretations of critical realism (Figure 3.1) as a continuum of views on our ability to know REALITY (Table 3.1). Traditionally, evangelicals have leaned toward naïve realism, with the attendant dangers of becoming static and mistakenly thinking we have a complete "photograph" of reality. Kraft, however, articulates a critical realist position that leans toward instrumentalism, with the dangers of unrestrained experimentalism and the possibility that we can never really know whether the meanings we construct truly correspond to REALITY. Both perspectives are within the critical realist continuum, but they are on different ends of the continuum.

81

TABLE 3.1: ALTERNATE EVANGELICAL VIEWS OF CRITICAL REALISM	
Kraft's Critical Realism	**Hiebert's Critical Realism**
Realism	
True REALTY exists; God is the only one who knows REALITY in its fullest sense.	True REALITY exists; God is the only one who knows REALITY in its fullest sense.
Critical	
Humans experience Reality but cannot experience or understand REALITY as God experiences or understands it.	While we cannot experience or understand REALITY as God experiences or understands it, *being made in God's image, we can grasp REALITY adequately and sufficiently.*
Human experience and understanding of REALITY is always subjective; we generate our own reality from our perceptions of REALITY.	While our experience and understanding of REALITY is always subjective and we generate our own reality from our perceptions of REALITY, *our understanding of reality corresponds with REALITY such that 1) we have a benchmark against which to test our reality and 2) our reality is still true even though limited.*

In summary, both critical realist positions affirm that truth (or REALITY) exists and is beyond complete human understanding. Hiebert, following a traditional evangelical approach, focuses on the content of that reality. Kraft argues that the traditional approach focuses exclusively on static content and in contextualizing we must add a focus on the process of constructing meaning (especially God's ongoing work of revelation in the people). Content is important to Kraft, but he argues that we are wrong to focus exclusively on content and ignore process. Critics respond that he focuses so much on process that he overlooks content. To help distinguish these approaches, I call Kraft's perspective *"dynamic critical* realism," and Hiebert's perspective *"correspondence* critical realism." We will return to this important difference in our discussion on form and meaning later in the chapter.

Logic

Evangelical missiologists (and theologians) wrestle with what it means that different cultures have differing systems of logic. Are we to build our approach to truth on the logical foundation of the law of non-contradiction (something cannot be true and not true at the same time and in the same way)? Is that "law" no more than a Western invention or is it a universally applicable concept? Herb Hoefer's questions and examples (see Sidebar) illustrate the type of contextualization implications that evangelicals consider.

SIDEBAR: QUESTIONS ABOUT LOGIC AND THEOLOGY (HOEFER 2007B, 135)

[I]n India, the most common form of persuasive logic in religious matters is what I have termed "evocative theology." The theologian/philosopher uses analogies and metaphors to evoke insight into a particular truth. When this illustration evokes an "Aha!" experience in the listener/reader, it is persuasive.

For another example, we use the typical Western form of logic in doing Western theology. Western logic assumes clear categories and distinctions. One thing cannot be another. However, in other forms of logic around the world, reality is viewed as much more porous and fluid.

Think of the "yin/yang" worldview of traditional Taoist philosophy. Reality is in flow and interpenetrating. One thing is part of another and indistinct. In Western theology, concepts such as the Trinity and the two natures of Christ and the bread and wine of the Eucharist as also the Body and Blood of Christ are logically absurd. However, in the yin/yang view of reality, such complexities are perfectly acceptable.

Clearly, our Western form of logic may not be suitable for doing theology and apologetics in different cultures. It may not even be the best form of logic for religious discourse at all.

As Hoefer illustrates, evangelical missionaries and missiologists struggle to understand how or whether to use other systems of logic. Peter Chang asked similar questions about the dominance of inductive logic in theological education in Asia (1984). Along similar lines, Charles Taber noted:

> . . . there is no *a priori* reason to suppose that the philosophically oriented western approach to theologizing is the best approach for everyone; rather, approaches should be developed by these people themselves that take with great seriousness and make full use of their problems, their categories, and their methodologies. (1978, 10)

Evangelical missiologists are open to consider alternative logic systems as part of contextualizing. This is important in contextual decisions such as choosing a local ministry leader. A person may be the best qualified in terms of leadership skills, administrative abilities, and vision casting. A logical analysis confined to skills and abilities might clearly indicate the best "qualified" person for the job. However, if that person does not have the relational networks, or is perceived by others as too young, or does not have the approval of certain elders in the community, or simply does not "feel" right to others, her or his skills will be negated by other "logical" considerations (such as relational logic). There can be advantages to using other logical systems. Hiebert offers helpful thinking along these lines, noting that we have tended to rely on abstract algorithmic logic, but there are analogical, topological, and relational logics used by peoples around the world that we need to attend to as well (2008, 39–45).

This does not mean that all such logical systems are equally valid or helpful. Having noted that there is no a priori reason to suppose that Western logic is the best for theologizing, Taber offers this qualification: "And all theologies, western or nonwestern, must be continually brought into subjection to the inspired Scriptures, responsibly interpreted" (Taber 1978, 10). Taber's assertion resonates with biblicism that evangelicals value.

It makes sense to look for Scriptural guidelines to answer contextual theological questions whatever the favored contextual logic. Consider, for example, the test of a prophet:

> If a prophet, or one who foretells by dreams, appears among you and announces to you a miraculous sign or wonder, and if the sign or wonder of which he has spoken takes place, and he says, "Let us follow other gods" (gods you have not known) "and let us worship them," you must not listen to the words of that prophet or dreamer. (Deut. 13:1–2)

The logic that frames the test of such a prophet is in comparing the content of the prophet's message with the content in Scripture calling us to follow God alone. Note the similarity to Paul's statement to the Galatians, "But even if we or an angel from heaven should preach a gospel other than the one we preached to you, let him be eternally condemned!" (Gal. 1:8).

The logical test in both cases is not the strength of the miracle, the experience of an "aha" moment, the counterbalancing yin and yang, or our relationship to the messenger. In both cases, we are exhorted to measure the content of the message against standards that have been set, and the best way to do this is through analytical logic. Evangelical theologians and missiologists conclude from these types of examples that jettisoning analytic tools such as the law of non-contradiction would undermine epistemological foundations as well as the hermeneutical process as we currently understand it (e.g., Carson 1983, 80; Moo 1986, 179–81).

Given this foundation, however, we can still use alternate logical systems. The challenge is to determine the best logical system to use for the case at hand, and Scripture offers more than one possibility. Recent applications have been seen in contextual issues ranging from the use of binary versus fuzzy logic (see Brown's response in Corwin 2007, 13; and Brown 2007b) and bounded and centered set theory in church planting and growth (see chapter six; Hiebert 1994, 107-36; Brown 2007b). Hiebert states:

> Mathematicians have shown that we can construct many non-Euclidean geometries, each of which is internally consistent. More recently they have shown that fuzzy sets ("fuzzy algebra" and "fuzzy logic") provide us with a system of reason in which the Western notions of either/or-ness and the law of the excluded middle do not hold.

If there are mental universals, and there certainly are, they reside at a deeper level of thought than we once believed. Anthropologists have found different systems of logic used in different societies. (1994, 28)

In summary, while we are open to using alternative logics as tools in contextualization, evangelicals still view with suspicion any hermeneutic that relativizes biblical teaching or opens the door to multiple meanings of a biblical text (see below).

Language

Evangelicals build their models on the recognition that God created language and used it from the very beginning in his relationship with humans (Larkin 1988, 224). Thus, language is an appropriate vehicle for God's revelation to humankind. Further, as Kevin Vanhoozer notes, biblical language is ordinary language: "We have seen that the Bible is eminently human—not in the sense that it errs, but in the sense of communicating to ordinary people in ordinary language and ordinary literature" (1986, 92). Thus, the Bible is not loaded with special language that somehow mandates that it remain in the original Hebrew, Aramaic and Greek. Ordinary language is translatable, though care and precision in the translation process are important to observe (see, e.g., Hill 2006).

As Andrew Walls points out, it was God who first "translated himself" through the incarnation, and Bible translation is parallel to incarnation: "As the Incarnation took place in the terms of a particular social context, so translation uses the terms and relations of a specific context" (1990, 26). The incarnation, then, indicates that there is no single language that is somehow "God's language." Vinay Samuel and Chris Sugden assert from a philosophy of language orientation that "it is impossible to formulate propositions that are timeless and universally true regardless of their context" (1984, 147), a challenge to traditional evangelical framing of a supracultural truth.

Evangelicals, however, recognize that God does not confine himself to a language or even a family of languages. Instead, every human language can adequately communicate God's revelation of himself. The Bible and the Christian faith are "infinitely culturally translatable" (Bediako 1995, 173), and *all* languages have the capability of conveying the message of the gospel adequately to those who speak it (Hesselgrave 1978, 239–42, 258–70; Bediako 1998b, 65; Escobar 2002, 173; Cortez 2005b, 351).

Form and Meaning

Missionary anthropologist Alan Tippett explains that the "problem of meaning"—"how a supracultural gospel could be communicated and manifested in meaningful 'cultural forms'" (1975, 130)—is a fundamental problem for us in communicating the gospel across cultural boundaries. Differences among evangelicals make it necessary to explain the two main camps in regard to the relationship between form and meaning.

As we saw in the discussion on critical realism, Charles Kraft follows a particular branch of communication and linguistic theory in maintaining that *meanings* are located within people rather than in the *messages* sent from one person to another (Kraft 1991a, 82-85; 1991b, 22). He describes the communication process as the exchange of messages, not meanings:

> Meanings, therefore, do not pass from me to you, only messages. The meanings exist only within me or within you. . . . The messages, then, serve as stimulators rather than as containers. Receptors, in response to the stimulus of messages construct meanings that may or may not correspond to what the communicator intended. (Kraft 1979b, 34–35)

The implications of this orientation are at the heart of his approach to contextualization. It appears that he divorces meaning from REALITY since meaning is something each person constructs:

> Meanings lie within people, not in either the external world or in the symbols we use to describe that world. Meaning is a personal thing, internal to persons rather than either a part of the world outside or of the symbols people use. Meanings, being personal, are attached by people to message symbols according to cultural rules in their minds. (Kraft 2005h, 162)

Traditionally evangelical missiologists realize that we construct our own versions of reality but moderate the possibility of full relativism by noting that we can *truly* apprehend REALITY even if we can never fully understand it. We believe it is dangerous to posit personally constructed realities without ensuring some means by which we can affirm or deny the correspondence of those realities to REALITY. The ability to affirm or deny such correspondence has been critical to evangelicals historically. We perceive a denial of biblical authority when Kraft argues that affirming or denying correspondence is not as important as the process of God's revealing himself to people. We fear that Kraft's de-linking of meaning and form or message removes a safeguard and opens the door to the relativism seen in anthropology and theological neo-orthodoxy (e.g., Henry 1980; Heldenbrand 1982). Kraft himself emphatically rejects this as a misinterpretation of his position (1982, 141; 2008, 61–62).

Table 3.2 summarizes the different approaches (see also Nishioka's perceptive comparison of Kraft and Hiebert in relation to meaning and form; 1998, 464–66).

TABLE 3.2: ALTERNATE EVANGELICAL VIEWS ON THE CONNECTION OF MEANING AND FORM (OR MESSAGE)	
Meaning *Disconnected from* **Form and Message**	**Meaning** *Corresponding to* **Form and Message**
"Meaning"	
Meaning exists only in the hearts and minds of people.	Meaning exists in the correspondence between reality and Reality. While constructed in the hearts and minds of people, "meaning" that corresponds well to Reality is sufficient and adequate for human needs and purposes.
"Forms" (or "Messages")	
Messages can be transmitted in linguistic and other symbolic form; they have no inherent "meaning."	Messages can be transmitted in linguistic and other symbolic form; the "meaning" of the "message" is in the correspondence of that "message" with Reality.
Like "messages," forms have no inherent "meaning" and are by definition neutral "vehicles" of communication.	Like "messages," forms have meaning in the way they correspond to Reality; they can be, but are not by definition, neutral.

As the last row indicates, Kraft's position is that religious cultural structures are in and of themselves neutral. It is the meaning that people attach to the forms, their basic faith allegiance, which is not neutral (Kraft 1979a, 115). Kraft, like all evangelicals, remains concerned that we guard against syncretism. False religions, or syncretism, happen when people construct meanings of faith allegiance to someone or something other than the Christian God. The danger lies in the *meanings* they construct, not the *forms* or *religious structures* they use. This orientation enables him to state that what the church has historically called "heresies" (e.g., Modalism) "can validly be classed as cultural adaptations rather than as theological aberrations" (Kraft 2005c, 233).

While forms are important, Kraft maintains that we do not need to change the forms (or religious structures) themselves, only the meanings people ascribe to those forms. As a result, he can ask a Japanese seminary student about making "Christian shrines" (Nishioka 1998, 457). Other missionaries have applied this approach, distinguishing religious structures from faith allegiance in their contextualization efforts (e.g., McCurry 1976; Parshall 1980, 55–61; Spielberg and Dauermann 1997; "A Different Kind" 1997).

Other evangelicals are not comfortable with this approach. We recognize that there is no single relationship between forms and meanings, that there is an external reality to which meanings refer. We also recognize that both communicator and receptor can communicate ideas across the barriers that divide them because of the messages or forms they use to correspond to reality (see Lausanne 1978; Osborne 1991, 319–23).

As D. A. Carson notes, Kraft's assertions are too dichotomistic (1985, 207–8). Fuller graduate Krikor Haleblian, in noting a weakness in Kraft's translation model, asserts that "in no way can we assume that form is less significant [than meaning] or that the two can easily be separated like oil and water" (1983, 105). Kraft's critics maintain with David Hesselgrave that "meaning is to be found in the relationship between signs/forms and reality; that it is discoverable by a careful examination of context; and that, insofar as possible, the people of the receiving culture context must contribute to that process" (1995b, 140).

> I believe we must move beyond dynamic-equivalent translations, at
> least when it comes to cultural practices other than language that
> tend to divorce form from meaning completely. To push dynamic
> equivalence too far is to overlook the message in the media, and to
> overlook the fact that in future years second and third generation
> students in a new church will be reading the Bible in its original lan-
> guages and wonder why translations of the Bible in their native lan-
> guages diverge from the original texts. (Hiebert 1979, 65)

In summary, the criticisms of Kraft from fellow evangelicals stem
from the implications of 1) his radical dichotomy of meaning and
form, 2) his focus on meanings as what people themselves generate,
and 3) relegating the "content" of revelation to a relatively less important role than the process (discussed in chapter two). Because he poses
his version of critical realism in an instrumentalist direction, fellow
evangelical critics have associated him with cultural relativism (e.g.,
Henry 1980, 154–55) and instrumentalism (Hesselgrave 1984; 2005,
243–77; and Osborne 1991, 322) even though he insists he is a critical
realist (Kraft 2008, 55–74).

As a final note, I find it ironic that Kraft asserts "And you (not I)
will have the final say as to what I mean. Your part, then becomes at
least as important as mine in determining the reality of what I intend"
(2008, 63). This assertion is incongruous with his insistence that those
who criticize him misunderstand him (e.g., Kraft 1982; 1995). Kraft's
own long-term focus on the need for communicators to be receptor-
oriented makes it even more ironic. Either Kraft has failed to follow
his own guidelines or he does not completely disconnect meaning
and message in his thinking, despite the contraindication of the proposals themselves.

How Many Meanings?

Western evangelical theologians and missiologists maintain that there
is essentially a single meaning for the biblical text. This meaning is
the intent of the original author as superintended by God's inspiration (Larkin 1988, 70–76, 242–63; Hesselgrave 1978, 38–50; Nida
and Reyburn 1981, 7–9). The following sections from the Chicago
Statement on Biblical Inerrancy explain this idea:

WE AFFIRM that the meaning expressed in each biblical text is single, definite and fixed.

WE DENY that the recognition of this single meaning eliminates the variety of its application.

The Affirmation here is directed at those who claim a "double" or "deeper" meaning to Scripture than that expressed by the authors. It stresses the unity and fixity of meaning as opposed to those who find multiple and pliable meanings. What a passage means is fixed by the author and is not subject to change by readers. This does not imply that further revelation on the subject cannot help one come to a fuller understanding, but simply that the meaning given in a text is not changed because additional truth is revealed subsequently.

Meaning is also definite in that there are defined limits by virtue of the author's expressed meaning in the given linguistic form and cultural context. Meaning is determined by an author; it is discovered by the readers.

The Denial adds the clarification that simply because Scripture has one meaning does not imply that its messages cannot be applied to a variety of individuals or situations. While the interpretation is one, the applications can be many. (Chicago Statement on Biblical Inerrancy 1982)

Hermeneutics

In 1979, Kraft stressed "the importance of going beyond the 'grammatico-historical' method to a 'culturo-linguistic' or 'ethnolinguistic' method of interpretation" (see also Kraft 2005c, 104), which he called "ethno-theological hermeneutics." Larry Caldwell later coined *ethnohermeneutics* to indicate a receptor-oriented hermeneutical method (Caldwell 1999; 2000). Fellow evangelicals sharply criticized both proposals (e.g., Carson 1985; Tappeiner 1999; Whelchel 2000; Espiritu 2001), concerned that each opened doors to relativized hermeneutical approaches.

These proposals and the strong responses demonstrate one of the ways evangelicals have wrestled with how to best interpret the Bible.

As biblicists, evangelicals consider this important. We want to know how to best "integrate the horizons" of text, its context, and our context without compromising either God's sovereignty or the implications of Christ's incarnation.

A second case study further illustrates the challenges. In 1984, Vinay Samuel and Chris Sugden responded to several areas in which evangelicals faced contextualization challenges. One focused on hermeneutics. (See sidebar: Deciding the Meaning of the Text.)

SIDEBAR: DECIDING THE MEANING OF THE TEXT (VINAY SAMUEL AND CHRIS SUGDEN 1984A, 147–51)

Samuel and Sugden present four general approaches on how to determine the meaning of the Bible. The first focuses on the existential experience of the biblical authors. A major weakness is that this does not help contemporary people who do not share the existential moment of the authors.

The second approach takes the stance that *how* we interpret is not important, but *who* interprets is. Proponents tend to maintain that only those with a commitment to seek justice for the poor can interpret the Bible correctly. This approach depends on the whim of whatever paradigm is in vogue.

Since both positions lean toward relativity in ways that ultimately demean biblical authority, evangelicals generally do not take them seriously.

The third and fourth approaches more clearly build on biblical authority and so are more amenable to evangelicals. According to Samuel and Sugden, the third approach on "how to decide the meaning of the Bible is to deny that the meaning is in any substantial doubt" (149). This position builds on God's sovereignty in revelation such that the meaning of Scripture is clear (traditionally the term is "perspicuous") and readily discernible by people. Samuel and Sugden indicate that a weakness of this approach is that it appeals to God's sovereignty to "overcome the precise difficulties of interpretation from a different culture" (150). They argue that this approach leads people to confirm their own theological pre-understandings or traditions and thus promote a fourth approach.

They build this fourth approach on the incarnation of Christ rather than God's sovereignty:

> This position seeks to retain that objectivity and authority without identifying it with any one theological formulation of what the Scripture teaches. On the other hand, it seeks to interpret the Scripture with relevance to each context, and with acknowledgement of the cultural factors impinging on that process, not as a barrier, but as a vehicle for interpretation. This position begins from the incarnation as the climax of God's revelation to man. (150)

Samuel and Sugden note three implications of using the incarnation rather than God's sovereignty as the starting point of hermeneutical method. First, it calls us to examine Jesus in his complete context (socioeconomic, political) and to start with the Gospels rather than the epistles. Second, it holds that "the Bible can only be interpreted faithfully to its intention by people committed to their contexts in the same way that Jesus was committed to his" (151). Third, we do not study the Bible for abstract truths but to "seek by word and deed to incarnate in our contexts the words and work of Jesus" (151).

The sidebar illustrates the types of hermeneutical questions with which evangelical missionaries struggle. Even biblicists struggle to determine the best ways to understand the implications of "biblical authority," appropriate ways to express it, and how to integrate the implications into the world's many cultures. As this case study illustrates, additional questions remain. For example, should our approach to interpreting Scripture be based on God's sovereign oversight of its development, the incarnation, or on some other key event in biblical or human history?

Despite Samuel and Sugden's critique, evangelicals still hold to the idea that the meaning of Scripture is clear because God superintended the revelatory process. Rather than taking a positivist approach in our discussion, we have shifted toward critical realism (discussed previously) and the understanding that our grasp on biblical truth is not as clear as the truth itself. We are learning to look through the lenses of cultural perspectives for guidance without drifting into relativist hermeneutics in the process.

As an example, Harvie Conn's model of guidelines (1988, 197–207) is a way to "aid in our human search for meaning and significance." Conn's approach has two sides of the hermeneutical spiral: God's work in tutoring us to understand the text (the "Godward side") and our work in determining its meaning (the "humanward side"). Table 3.3 explains both.

TABLE 3.3: GODWARD AND HUMANWARD SIDES OF HERMENEUTICS (ADAPTED FROM CONN 1988)	
Godward Side of Hermeneutics	**Humanward Side of Hermeneutics**
The most obvious is our recourse to Scripture for hermeneutical stability. Wherever we begin in the [hermeneutical] spiral, the only proper control for our judgments remains the original intent of the biblical text.	Before a proper "fusing" of the two or three horizons can take place, a "distancing" must also take place.
Another Godward side to hermeneutics aids in our search for what have been called universals. We speak of the dynamic process of the self-revelation of God in recorded Scripture. There is a history of redemption that sweeps us in unity from the first promise of the gospel in the garden to its fulfillment in the New Jerusalem.	Most of our discussion has concentrated on the distortions that our presuppositions bring to understanding. We also need to recognize that there are times when those same assumptions may aid us in the task.

The Holy Spirit is an active participant in the hermeneutical spiral. He brings into being the first horizon of the text (2 Peter 1:20–21). He opens our mind to understanding (John 14:16–17, 26).	It will also help to acknowledge that there are levels of cultural particularity in both horizons and therefore levels of particularity in interpretation. Much of the biblical material, for example, is presented in cultural forms that are specific to cultural practices quite different from ours. In fact, because of their specificity to the cultural agreements of the first readers, these materials communicated with maximum impact. But they have minimum impact on us.

Numerous evangelical missiologists and theologians propose models of hermeneutics that are faithful to the text and deal appropriately with the contemporary context (Conn 1988, 197–207; Nicholls, 1979a; Padilla 1979b; Osborne 1991; Shaw and Van Engen 2003; Redford 2005; Schlorff 2006). I offer the following as a synopsis of core ideas. The fact that they do not all cohere with each other indicates that the discussion will continue.

First, from a critical realist orientation, evangelicals believe that God superintended the authors of the Bible in such a way that what he wanted to be written was in fact written, even though it was written through the style, personality, and mood of the particular author or compiler.

Additionally, evangelicals have several core ideas about *how* interpretation should take place. We have moderated and refined them over the past several decades and will continue to do so for the foreseeable future, but they still are foundational to evangelical ideals:

- We apply the normal rules of the grammar of the language of any biblical text in light of the literary style.

- We interpret texts in light of the historical setting at the time of writing. This includes not just the setting *per se* but especially the personal history and narrative tendencies of the author or compiler, the way the author or compiler perceived the intended audience, and the way the author intended to convey the message or story being communicated.

• We consider the type of literature of the text in determining which types of interpretive rules to use in its interpretation (Vanhoozer 1986; thought we again note Kraft's critique of grammatical-historical exegesis; 1979e, 118).

> The prime objective of any theological methodology is to evolve a message that will be relevant to real men and women in life situations and faithful to the Scriptures and Church historical development.
>
> Ken Gnanakan and Sunand Sumithra (1995, 43-44)

• We argue that hermeneutics should be a dialogue between text and context in an ever-refining spiral (see, e.g., Kraft 2005c, 113). Rene Padilla offers a concise and powerful description of this complex process:

. . . the interpretative process involves a continuous mutual engagement between the horizons of the text and the horizons of our historical context. Neither our understanding of the text nor our understanding of our concrete situation is adequate unless both of them constantly interact and are mutually corrected. When that is done, the interpreter progressively approaches Scripture with the right questions and from the right perspective, and his theology is in turn more biblical and more relevant to his situation. He goes from his concrete situation through his (increasingly biblical) world-and-life view to Scripture, and from Scripture through his (increasingly relevant) theology to his situation, to and fro, always striving for a merging of his own horizons with those of Scripture. Hermeneutics may thus be conceived as having a spiral structure in which a richer and deeper understanding of the Bible leads to a greater understanding of the historical context, and a deeper and richer understanding of the historical context leads to a greater comprehension of the biblical message from within the concrete situation, through the work of the Holy Spirit. (1979b, 101–2)

In addition to these four core ideas, evangelicals from the Global South add hermeneutical concerns that might surprise Western evangelicals. For example, *who* interprets can be just as important to them as *what* the interpretation is (e.g., Samuel and Sugden 1984, 148). As they rightly note, they are not simply recipients of Western knowledge; they too bring important voices to the table (see Tennent 2007). They also point out ideological underpinnings of hermeneutics that ignore issues such as justice, oppression, and poverty. Further, they see the missiological nature of the whole of the Bible (e.g., see Wright 2006) and judge any theological interpretation that omits missiological consideration as invalid.

> The domestic tasks of Third World theology are going to be so basic, so vital, that there will be little time for the barren, sterile time-wasting by-paths into which so much Western theology and theological research has gone in recent years. Theology in the Third World will be, as theology at all creative times has always been, about doing things, about things that deeply affect the lives of numbers of people. . . . There is no need to go back to wars of religion when men shed blood for their theologies: but at least there is something to be said for having a theology about things which are worth shedding blood for. And that, Third World Theology is likely to be.
>
> Andrew Walls (1982, 100-101)

Conclusion

In summary, over the past two chapters we have seen that evangelicals work to identify the presuppositions we hold and to ensure that they are worth holding. At the same time, we recognize that we hold and apply them imperfectly (see Hiebert 1994). Thus, evangelicals share the presuppositions discussed in this chapter and use them as standards to compare and ultimately judge every approach to contextualization.

As biblicists, evangelicals are passionate that congruence with biblical thinking and methods characterize contextualization. We accept that the entire canon is inspired, and so do not pursue the idea of separating kernel from husk as we previously did. However, we continue to recognize that certain layers in biblical discourse are for all peoples, times, and places while other layers, which are just as much part of biblical revelation, are more restricted in their scope.

Knowing that we do not have a full grasp on the entire scope of biblical revelation, we want to learn more about our own faith from the insights of those from other cultures and ways of thinking. We believe that we, as diverse members of the body of Christ, dig together for the meaning of biblical stories and texts based on normal uses of language. We are leery of methods or orientations that open the interpretive doors so wide that everyone can find whatever they want. We realize both the limitations *and* the appropriateness of all human languages for conveying God's revelation.

We also realize that sin pervades everything we do, so that humility through the entire process of contextualization is valued, even though not always demonstrated in the way we would like it to be. In fact, this presents something of a conundrum for evangelicals. We are convinced that Christians do truly have God's revelation of himself for all humankind. Among some evangelicals (Americans in particular), a naïve realist approach inevitably leads to shallow triumphalism. However, many evangelicals recognize that such triumphalism is a form of sin that mucks up the process, like poison in bread. We trust that we will continue to grow in grace as well as truth in this area.

With the presuppositional foundations established, I turn to what evangelicals use as indicators to discern what is appropriate and inappropriate contextualization.

KEYWORDS FOR REVIEW

Critical realism: epistemological position that truth exists and, while our grasp of it is imperfect, we can grow in our understanding of truth by comparing our grasp to the truth revealed in the Bible

Epistemology: philosophical study of the nature of knowledge

Form and meaning: relationship between forms (words, artifacts, rituals) and their meanings; various evangelicals posit answers ranging from *arbitrary* to *correspondence* to *equivalence*

Hermeneutics: the process of interpreting Scripture, including the rules, the methods, the agents, and the conclusions involved in that process

Instrumentalism: epistemological position that all knowledge is subjective because it is constrained by culture, language, and the perspective of the individual

Law of non-contradiction: logical argument that something cannot be both true and not true at the same time and in the same way

Naïve realism: epistemological position that knowledge is objective and that we can know reality as it is in all of its fullness

Structural sin: the ways sin pervades the structures of society, including such things as cultural values, laws, and the ways these are used as instruments to oppress or marginalize segments of a society

QUESTIONS FOR REFLECTION

1. What are the strengths and weaknesses of the critical realist positions?

2. Evangelicals agree that there is one actual meaning for the biblical text. However, we do not agree on what the "one meaning" is for multiple passages. What are the consequences of this?

3. For some evangelicals, *who* the interpreter is can be just as important as *what* the interpretation is. Why do think this is so?

4. What are the consequences of choosing an instrumental approach to understanding Scripture?

FOR FURTHER STUDY

Conn, Harvie M. 1978. "Contextualization: A New Dimension for Cross-Cultural Hermeneutic." *Evangelical Missions Quarterly* 14.1 (January): 39–48.

_____. 1988. "Normativity, Relevance, and Relativism." In *Inerrancy and Hermeneutic: A Tradition, A Challenge, A Debate*, ed. Harvie M. Conn, 185–209. Grand Rapids: Baker.

Hiebert, Paul G. 2008. *Transforming Worldviews: An Anthropological Understanding of How People Change*. Grand Rapids: Baker

_____. 2009. *The Gospel in Human Contexts: Anthropological Explorations for Contemporary Missions*. Grand Rapids: Baker.

Kraft, Charles H. 2008. *Worldview for Christian Witness*. Pasadena: William Carey Library.

Nishioka, Yoshiyuki Billy. 1998. "Charles Kraft's and Paul Hiebert's Approaches to Worldview: Why Don't You Build a Christian Shrine?" In *Footprints of God: A Narrative Theology of Mission*, ed. Charles Van Engen, Nancy Thomas, and Robert Gallagher, 174–86.

Samuel, Vinay, and Chris Sugden, eds. 1983. *Sharing Jesus in the Two Thirds World*. Grand Rapids: Eerdmans.

Walls, Andrew. 2002. *The Cross-Cultural Process in Christian History*. Maryknoll: Orbis.

Discerning the Good from the

Bad in Contextualization

CHAPTER OVERVIEW

I start this chapter with a case study of two early evangelical taxonomies that illustrate how we distinguish appropriate from inappropriate contextualization and what we consider significant in grouping models together. Bruce Nicholls, British missionary in India, split his map into categories: 1) models that are "dogmatic" in being anchored in Scripture and theology, and 2) models that are "existential" in being anchored in the times and circumstances of the context (1979b). David Hesselgrave , American missionary in Japan prior to joining the faculty at Trinity Evangelical Divinity School, developed a threefold taxonomy: 1) models anchored in faithfully accommodating Scripture in local settings, 2) models focused on the agent of contextualization expressing God's response to cultural injustice, and 3) models that combine the best of multiple religious teachings and developing a faith that goes beyond any of them (1979).

However, much has happened since these pioneering efforts. In the remainder of the chapter I describe the indicators evangelicals have identified that mark good contextualization. I arrange the indicators into four categories, namely, markers related to 1) the *grounding* for contextualization, 2) the *agents* of contextualization, 3) the *processes* of contextualization, and 4) the *products* of contextualization.

CHAPTER OUTLINE

1. Early Evangelical Maps
   a. Bruce Nicholls
      i.   Dogmatic Contextualization
      ii. Existential Contextualization
   b. David Hesselgrave
      i.   Apostolic Accommodation
      ii. Prophetic Accommodation
      iii. Syncretistic Accommodation
2. Evangelical Markers of Good Contextualization
   a. Marks of Good Contextual Grounding
   b. Marks of Good Contextual Agents
   c. Marks of Good Contextual Processes
   d. Marks of Good Contextual Products

Sunand Sumithra, an Indian missiologist, tells the following story from the life of the great twentieth-century Indian evangelist Sadhu Sundar Singh.

> Once when I was travelling in Rajputana, there was a Brahman of high-caste hurrying to the station. Overcome by great heat, he fell down on the platform. The Anglo-Indian stationmaster, anxious to help him, offered him water in a western cup. But the Brahman would not take the water, although he was thirsty.
>
> "I cannot drink that water. I would prefer to die."
>
> "I am not asking you to eat the cup," the station master said to him.
>
> "I will not break my caste," he said, "I am willing to die."
>
> When, however, the water was brought to him in his own brass vessel, he drank it eagerly. It is the same with the Water of Life. Indians do need the Water of Life but not in the European cup. (Sumithra 1984, 230–31)

If Singh were alive today, what characteristics do you think he would indicate are good contextual practices? Simply stated, Singh likely would have noted that contextualized faith is faith in an Indian cup. This is a wonderful metaphor, and one that raises many questions. In this chapter I offer evangelical perspectives on how we determine what characterizes "Indian cup" contextualization.

Early Evangelical Maps

For the first decade after the coining of the word *contextualization*, evangelicals were in flux as to how to respond to the ferment it generated. Because the term was coined in ecumenical circles and framed in relation to humanization and justice rather than evangelism and church planting, evangelical missionaries and agencies were initially skeptical. As the term gained traction in all types of Christian circles, however, missiologists felt pressure to respond in ways that helped missionaries and agencies decipher the rhetoric and separate the "wheat" from the "chaff." They developed early taxonomies with specific purposes in mind. They did not intend the taxonomies to be descriptive. Rather, they were prescriptive to help fellow evangelicals sort through the confusion.

At the time, there were far fewer examples to categorize than today. In looking at these historical taxonomies (Table 4.4), remember that the taxonomers' focus was to help missionaries and agencies who were confused about contextualization and were trying to determine how to respond to methods, models, and proposals generated. Given evangelical focus on congruence with the Scriptures, it is not surprising that both maps take that as their central criterion for determining the propriety of the contextualization models. It is also not surprising that they used this as a boundary marker to separate one type of model from another.

Bruce Nicholls

In developing his binary taxonomy, Nicholls (1979b) followed the lead of William Horden (1966, 141–54) and separated models into the "dogmatic" (Horden's "translators") and "existential" (Horden's "transformers") categories (see discussion in Cortez 2005a, 86–87).

Dogmatic Contextualization

According to Nichols, those who use the dogmatic or Scripture-controlled model begin "with a concern for biblical theology as a fixed and authoritative orientating point for contextualization" (Nicholls 1979b, 70). Their goal was to translate and communicate the authoritative biblical message in such a way that the receptors will understand it. Thus, the Scriptures anchor this approach.

Existential Contextualization

Those who practice existential (or context-controlled) models, according to Nicholls, seek "to develop a dialectical interaction between questions of man in history and an existential understanding of the word of God." They start with these two relative sets of data and "expect to find tentative theological formulations in a progression to synthesis of understanding" (1979b, 69–70).

Given the biblicist orientation of evangelicals (Bebbington 1989), it is not surprising that the criteria Nicholls chose for his categorization is what controls the process: Scripture (dogmatic) or context (existential). Nicholls offered a divide that enabled evangelical use of the word *contextualization* while holding to the models built on an absolute rather than a relative foundation.

Years later evangelicals criticized this simple binary map. Stanley Grenz expresses concern that both the dogmatic and existential approaches have problems and proposes that "the two approaches must be 'held in tandem' employing 'an interactive process that is both correlative and contextual'" (Grenz 2000, 44). Following the lead of Grenz, Marc Cortez proposes a third category of models that draws from both approaches (2005a, 87; see Appendix B).

David Hesselgrave

Hesselgrave developed a threefold map with categories based on how each handled "truth": apostolic accommodation (truth *revealed*), prophetic accommodation (truth *proclaimed*), and syncretistic accommodation (truth *in process of being discovered*) (1979).

Several evangelicals strongly critiqued Hesselgrave's contextualization continuum when he introduced it in 1979, noting that it was too simplistic and too neatly categorized (Barney et al. 1979, 12–22). Even so, the model appeared essentially unchanged a decade later in *Contextualization: Meanings, Methods, and Models* (Hesselgrave and Rommen 1989).

Historically, the term *accommodation* has been used by missionaries to describe how we bring the biblical text to a new context (Luzbetak 1988, 67). Since Hesselgrave developed his taxonomy, some evangelical missiologists have eschewed the use of *accommodation* because of its association with a one-way flow (from *us* to *them*) rather than the two-way flow that more properly characterizes contextualization (e.g., Whiteman 1997, 4; Moreau 2006a, 327).

Apostolic Accommodation

By *apostolic accommodation*, Hesselgrave meant models in which the agents of contextualization changed the *form* of the message so that receptors can understand its *content*. In these models, the agents of contextualization *accommodate* the absolute and authoritative biblical truth revealed by God in the receptor culture so that it is understandable in their categories of thought and thought processes. Contextual efforts that strayed from this concern at best weakened biblical authority and at worst destroyed it altogether.

Prophetic Accommodation

Hesselgrave used *prophetic accommodation* for approaches based on the prophetic insight of the contextualizer. This approach "entails entering a cultural context, discerning what God is doing and saying in that context, and speaking and working for needed changes" (Hesselgrave 1989, 150).

Hesselgrave split this category into two subcategories: neo-liberal and neo-orthodox. The neo-liberal models put greater emphasis on the insights gained by the struggle in the setting. The neo-orthodox models put greater emphasis on the insights gained from reflection on Scripture and history. Hesselgrave believed that there was limited space in the neo-orthodox approach that evangelicals could engage. However, the weaker view of Scripture implied in such models made it a method that evangelicals should generally avoid (ibid., 154–55).

Syncretistic Accommodation

The label "syncretistic accommodation" shows Hesselgrave's evaluation of the third type of contextualization practices in his continuum. Championed by people such as M. M. Thomas, John Hicks, and Wilfred Cantwell Smith, this position, according to Hesselgrave, is one in which people seek "to accommodate various cultures, religions and ideologies by selecting the best insights of all of them and evolving a faith that goes beyond any one of them" (Hesselgrave and Rommen 1989, 153).

Evangelical Markers of Good Contextualization

In the years since the two maps in our case study appeared, evangelicals have proposed numerous ways to identify "best practices" in contextualization (e.g., Poston 2000; Whiteman 2005; Moreau 2005, 324–25; Woodberry 2008). Most of these identifiers or markers reflect evangelical values and beliefs (Table 2.1). I have organized these markers into four broad categories: the *grounding* of contextualization;

the *agents* of contextualization, the *processes* of contextualization, and the *products* of contextualization.

TABLE 4.4: PRESCRIPTIVE MAPS COVERING ALL MODELS	
Nicholls **Classified by** *controlling source*	**Hesselgrave** **Classified by** *theological orientation*
Dogmatic	Apostolic Accommodation
Existential	Prophetic Accommodation
	Neo-orthodox Neo-liberal
	Syncretistic Accommodation

Marks of Good Contextual Grounding

Contemporary evangelicals agree with Nicholls and Hesselgrave that ultimately the only viable grounding for good contextualization is Scripture (Moreau 2005, 324; discussed more extensively in chapter 2).

To this grounding we also add *scope* as a factor. While most of the literature deals with theological contextualization (see Moreau and O'Rear 2004b for examples), good contextualization is broader than that. It is concerned with the whole of the Christian faith, including the existential realities of those among whom the faith is being contextualized (Moreau 2005, 324-25), and including their historical and cultural contexts (Hiebert 1994, 47).

Marks of Good Contextual Agents

Evangelicals are concerned that we contextualize not only our faith but also ourselves (e.g., Massey 2004b; Steffen and McKinney-Douglas 2008). Larry Poston identifies three helpful actions that should identify proper contextual cross-cultural workers:

Adapting to a specific cultural context by immersion.
1. Adapting one's manner of thinking, speaking, and acting to a specific context.

2. Demonstrating to one's audience what a Christ-centered life would look like in their culture—deliberate cultural adaptation, knowledge of the revealed Word of God, and the dynamic internal working of the Holy Spirit together produce a "contextualized" individual. (Poston 2000; see also Parshall 1982b, 34)

Another significant mark of good contextualization is careful attention to the effect of human sinfulness on contextual processes—including the sinful habits and perspectives of the missionaries themselves (Moreau 2005, 324). For example, in training people for cross-cultural service, evangelicals often give those being trained mixed messages. We want people to go as learners (e.g., Elmer 2006). At the same time, however, the missionary is an ambassador of Christ delivering a message that requires repentance and conversion. Further, there are ideals of missionary "heroism" that evangelicals hear about in churches and other Christian settings (e.g., Moreau, Corwin and McGee 2004, 17–22). Finding how to combine the "servant" or learner attitude while simultaneously being a bearer of a message of repentance can lead to a type of schizophrenia between rhetoric and reality. The juxtaposition of these two elements with the mythic ideals of the "missionary hero" results in stressors that contribute to an environment where sinful attitudes and habits can lodge and fester.

Marks of Good Contextual Processes

Perhaps the most significant marker for good contextual processes is the guidance of the Holy Spirit (Flemming 2005, 304). Unfortunately, criteria by which to judge this are very subjective, depending on such things as existential setting and theological orientation of the agents.

One important check in this regard is the extent to which we incorporate diverse voices into the process—including living voices in the community and in other communities as well as historical voices of the world church (Hiebert 1994, 48; Flemming 2005, 304). Flowing from that, a third marker of good process is that it flows in multiple directions and is not a one-way process from "expert" to "community" (Moreau 2005, 325).

A fourth identifier of good process is that it is interdisciplinary or systemic in its approach to culture (Moreau 2005, 324) and theology (Hiebert 2008; 2009). No single discipline can avoid the danger of reductionism. Contextual process will incorporate voices and perspectives from a variety of disciplines in healthy dialogue. As Darrell Whiteman notes:

> Contextualization . . . transforms the local community and it connects us to the larger global community. In this way it enlarges our understanding of how Christianity shapes people and their cultures. It expands our understanding of the gospel and the Kingdom of God. (2005, 64).

Together, these indicate that good contextual processes will be marked by dynamic change (Moreau 2005, 324). Human cultures constantly change, so that today's contextual expressions—if left in stasis—will inevitably calcify into tomorrow's anachronism. We do not *make* the gospel relevant; it is *always* relevant in all human settings at all times. However, without ongoing contextualization in response to cultural shifts, future generations likely will not understand its relevance in ways that make sense to them.

One result is that evangelicals look for and evaluate practices or models that *work* (Richard 2001; "History Reveals" 1998; Parshall 1998b; Terry 1998). For example, we develop tools that help us understand the process of conversion (Engel and Norton 1975; Lausanne 1978; Conn 1979a; 1979b; Costas 1979; Jacobs 1979; Meral 2006) so that more people come to Christ (Kraft 1982; Otis 1980; Haines 1983; Netland 1988). We try new ways to form churches (Stutzman 1991; Hesselgrave 2000b; Dixon 2002; Garrison 2004a) or mobilize them for outreach (Parshall 2001).

Marks of Good Contextual Products

An important indicator of a good contextual product is that it addresses local needs in local sensibilities; we "communicate the gospel in such a way that people will understand in their own terms from their own worldview" (Whiteman 2005, 64). Mack Harling succinctly notes, "Contextual theology is incarnational in utilizing cultural forms and transformational in sanctifying their meanings" (2005, 164; also Imasogie 1984, 79–84; Lam 1984, 339).

However, a challenge in contextualizing a universal Christian faith in thousands of cultural settings involves handling the theological inconsistencies—and contradictions—that inevitably arise. Good contextual theologies "may differ and yet be complementary; they may address different needs and situations while resolving contradictions by examining the Scriptures" (Hiebert 1994, 48).

The Christian message of human sin stands as a critique that applies to all human cultures. Thus, a third identifier for evangelicals is that we communicate Christ's critique of all human societies in such a way that "we offend people for the right reasons, not the wrong ones" (Whiteman 2005, 64).

Finally, following the characteristic belief of evangelicals that the gospel is effective because God gave it (Table 2.1), we use effectiveness as a marker of good contextual products. Ultimately, "Authentic theology bears fruit in the furtherance of the Christian mission and the transformation of individuals and the community" (Flemming 2005, 304).

Thus, we look for better ways to understand the hardest areas for outreach—especially Muslim (Bell 1974; Moreau and O'Rear 2005; Parshall 1980; 1983a; 1994), Hindu (Richard 1998), and Buddhist (Lim, Spaulding, and De Neui 2005) settings. We look for practices that were successful in one locale so that we can use or adapt them elsewhere (Woodberry 2008). However, our emphasis on effectiveness is subordinate to our emphasis on truth, and replacing truth with effectiveness as a criterion of good contextualization is not appropriate (e.g., Corwin 2006).

Conclusion

The case study of two historical taxonomies illustrates that evangelicals are passionate about safeguarding biblical congruence in contextualization and that we appreciate prescriptive taxonomies that can guide us in turbulent times. The ongoing development of markers that help us distinguish good contextualization from bad has given evangelicals criteria by which we can evaluate contextual models and practices. These criteria also guide evangelicals as we seek to contextualize our faith in new settings. Over the next two chapters, I consider additional ideas and tools that evangelicals use to frame and guide our contextual practices.

KEYWORDS FOR REVIEW

Apostolic accommodation: contextual models in which the contextual agents change the form of the absolute and authoritative message of the Scriptures so that its content may be understood by the receptors

Dogmatic Scripture-controlled contextualization: contextualization that is anchored in the Scriptures as a fixed and authoritative orienting point for contextualization

Existential or context-controlled contextualization: models that practice a dialectical interaction between local questions with an existential understanding of the word of God

Marks of good contextualization: criteria that evangelicals use to identify good contextualization practices

Prophetic accommodation: contextual models in which the contextual agents discern what God is doing and saying in that context and then speak and work for needed change

Syncretistic accommodation: contextual models in which the agent selects the best insights from various cultures, religions, and ideologies and develops a faith that goes beyond any one of them

QUESTIONS FOR REFLECTION

1. Nicholls and Hesselgrave are both from prior genera-
    tions, and prescriptive maps fit them well. If you were to
    construct a map for your generation, what might your
    approach be?

2. Compare Hesselgrave's approach with Schreiter's (from
    chapter 1). What concerns appear to have been impor-
    tant to each in their respective approaches?

3. In what ways might the generational difference of the
    agents of contextualization drive them to value differing
    markers of good contextualization?

4. With which marks of good contextualization do you
    most resonate? Why?

5. With which marks of good contextualization do you least
    resonate? Why?

FOR FURTHER STUDY

Flemming, Dean. 2005. *Contextualization in the New Testament: Patterns for Theology and Mission.* Downers Grove: InterVarsity.

Harling, Mack. 2005. "De-Westernizing Doctrine and Developing Appropriate Theology in Mission." *International Journal of Frontier Missions* 22.4 (Winter): 159–66.

Hesselgrave, David J., and Edward Rommen. 1989. *Contextualization: Meanings, Methods, and Models.* Grand Rapids: Baker.

Moreau, A. Scott. 2006. "Contextualization That Is Comprehensive." *Missiology* 34.3 (July): 325–35.

Nicholls, Bruce J. 1979. "Towards a Theology of Gospel and Culture." In *Gospel and Culture. The Papers of a Consultation on the Gospel and Culture, Convened by the Lausanne Committee's Theology and Education Group,* ed. John R. W. Stott and Robert T. Coote, 69–82. Pasadena: William Carey Library.

Concepts That Shape and

Constrain Contextualization

CHAPTER OVERVIEW

In this chapter, I explore important conceptual ideas that evangelicals use to shape and constrain how we view contextualization. The first term is *indigeneity*, which has more than a century of use by evangelical missionaries and missional thinkers. An indigenous church is one that is fits the local setting, using local resources and local patterns in all it does.

Next I discuss *transformation*, a biblical term that is used in a bewildering variety of ways by evangelicals to guide contextualization.

One of the most challenging concepts evangelicals struggle with is *syncretism*. I introduce the challenges and illustrate them through a case study of the debate over some of the practices employed by those ministering among Muslims.

The fourth term is *incarnation*, and I explain how evangelicals react to the Christ's incarnation as the historical and theological imperative for contextualization.

From there I turn to *holism* as a concept with a mixed history among evangelicals. I use a brief historical excursus to place the major issues in context, indicating the role it currently plays in our thinking. Finally, I introduce *praxis*, a term embodying a particular orientation toward contextualization and gradually gaining ground in evangelical circles.

While missiologists of all theological stripes utilize these six conceptual guides in varying degrees, evangelicals in particular use them to shape and constrain how they contextualize.

CHAPTER OUTLINE

1. Indigeneity
2. Transformation
3. Syncretism
4. Incarnation
5. Holism
6. Praxis

After a significant pastoral ministry in an urban setting in the United States, a former student of mine returned to his home country of India to minister. When visiting him, I asked, "What is the most significant obstacle you face?" He paused and then said, "The biggest I've seen recently has been working to overcome the impression left by some well-intentioned American short-term missionaries. When they came to my village, they gathered and marched around a temple in the village, asking God to tear it down in the name of Jesus. Later one of the priests at the temple told me, 'You Christians are no different than we Hindus. We practice Hindu magic, and Christians practice Christian magic. I know because I saw those American Christians walking around our temple seven times praying. That's no different from what we do.'"

Was this prayer-walk an example of contextualization or syncretism? I am sure they thought they were engaging in appropriate spiritual warfare and would likely cite the Old Testament story of Joshua marching around Jericho (Josh. 6) to confirm it. The Hindu priest, however, read their actions as a "Christian" version of a Hindu magical practice. The long-term worker was left to sort through the mess after the short-termers returned home.

These and other contemporary practices of evangelicals deserve understanding and explanation. What ideas guided the short-term workers, and how do we respond to their actions? In this chapter I discuss several concepts that evangelicals use to shape and constrain our contextual landscape.

Indigeneity

In the height of the colonial era, when churches planted in various colonies around the world were largely dependent on Western leadership and financing, missionary leaders Rufus Anderson and Henry Venn utilized "indigenization" to promote the idea of planting national churches that were 1) self-propagating, 2) self-governing, and 3) self-financing.

> When the indigenous people of a community think of the
> Lord as their own, not a foreign Christ; when they do things
> as unto the Lord, meeting the cultural needs around them,
> worshipping in patterns they understand; when their con-
> gregations function in participation in a body which is struc-
> turally indigenous; then you have an indigenous church.
> —Alan Tippett (1987, 136)

In 1958, in what Charles Kraft calls "a major breakthrough in our thinking about indigeneity" (Kraft 2005d, 19), William Smalley challenged the way indigenization was being practiced. He argued correctly that churches with autochthonous leaders but still Western in leadership style and organization were not truly indigenous. His vision of an indigenous church was "a group of believers who live out their life, including their socialized Christian activity, in the patterns of the local society, and for whom any transformation of that society comes out of their felt needs under the guidance of the Holy Spirit and the Scriptures" (Smalley 1958, 55). Thus began a journey of rethinking indigenization among evangelicals.

In 1973 Alan Tippett suggested a truly indigenous church would have six "selfs," adding to the existing three-self formula (i.e., [1} "self-image" [seeing itself as independent of its founding mission]; [2] "self-functioning" [capable of carrying on all of its own functions]; and [3] "self-giving" [knowing the needs of its local community and be able to assist in meeting those needs]; 1973; also 1987). In 1979, Alfred Krass rightly noted that indigenization could not adequately handle social change (1979). Kraft reminded fellow evangelicals in 1980 that a genuinely indigenous church would be no different from the rest of the culture (1980), clearly not a goal for which evangelicals strive.

In 1982, Andrew Walls pointed out that the indigenizing principle will always be in tension with what he labels the *pilgrim* principle—that we are part of a church which is universal and no human culture will ever completely be our home. The indigenizing principle is rooted in the gospel and associates Christians with the particulars of their culture and group. The pilgrim principle, equally rooted in the gospel, associates Christians with things and people outside their culture and group and is in tension with the indigenizing principle. The loyalty to

124

the faith family links Christians to those in groups opposed to their indigenous groups (1982, 98–99).

TABLE 5.1: INDIGENIZATION AND CONTEXTUALIZATION COMPARED (SOURCE: KWAN 2005, 240)		
Criterion	**Indigenization**	**Contextualization**
Understanding of contexts	Emphasis is placed on 'culture,' which is narrowly understood as socially rooted ideas people hold about a certain set of questions. It almost always excludes considerations of concrete ecological, social, political, or economic conditions.	Local context is to be understood multi-dimensionally. Besides, it rejects the limiting of interest to what happens internally within a single social group, but demands that relations between groups, including nations, also be considered.
Views of culture	Tends to be static and backward-looking.	Tends to be present-and-future oriented. It often seeks to work towards sociocultural changes.
	Culture as closed and self-contained.	Insists on considering [sic] relations between cultures and social groups right up to the global scale.
Locus of concern	Focuses on what is going on 'out there' on the foreign mission field.	Focuses also on what is going on in the sending countries.
View of gospel	The substance of the gospel is universal and timeless. Only the presentation of it has to be changed in order to have it intelligible to other cultures.	The gospel is not even known until a proper analysis and critique of the context have been done, because for gospel to be good news it must address the specifics of each context.
Role of the missionary	Assumes a fairly critical and even definitive role for the missionary in shaping the entire process.	Places the burden of initiative and authority squarely on Christians of the local context.

In 1985 Paul Hiebert noted that indigenous communities must also be able to develop theologies that are biblically derived but framed in vernacular thought patterns as well as language (1985a, 195–96; 216–19). Self-theologizing is now widely accepted among evangelicals as an appropriate addition to the three-self formula; certainly it fits well into current discussion on contextualization, though the hidden assumptions behind Western understanding of "self" as a construct of independent individualist thinking still need to be challenged (e.g., Moreau 2001; 2005).

Despite these modifications and challenges, indigenization is still valued as "a term describing the 'translatability' of the universal Christian faith into the forms and symbols of particular cultures of the world" (Conn 2000). Thus, as far as most evangelicals are concerned, given appropriate qualifications the indigenous church model is still an appropriate orientation for mission (Van Engen 2005a) and continues to have wide and positive use among evangelical missiologists (e.g., Ekka 2007). Samuel Kwan, building on the work of Charles Taber (1991, 175–76), compares the orientations of indigenization and contextualization (Table 5.1) as evidence that the movement from the one to the other is more of a change in discursive practice than a paradigm shift (Kwan 2005).

The fact that evangelical missiologists continue to generate proposals framed by indigenous principles (e.g., Bill Taylor's addition of self-missiologizing; 2000, 6) demonstrates the continuing vitality of indigeneity as a guiding concept for evangelicals in contextualization.

Transformation

Historically, evangelicals used transformation to refer to the changes that happen in an individual who converts to Christ. Donald McGavran called this "redemption and lift" (1980, 297).

Certainly its popularity is anchored in both the biblical metaphor of transformation (e.g., Romans 12:2) as well as in the way it captures and expresses the conversionist and activist hopes that characterize evangelicals. Evangelical contextual practices have as a goal some type of transformation of the individual. At the very least, this includes conversion and worldview change. Paul Hiebert's admonition summarizes this type of transformation as

> both a point and a process; this transformation has simple beginnings (a person can turn wherever he or she is) but radical, lifelong

consequences. It is not simply mental assent to a set of metaphysical beliefs, nor is it solely a positive feeling toward God. Rather it involves entering a life of discipleship and obedience in every area of our being and throughout the whole story of our lives. (Hiebert 2008, 311)

In the first half of the twentieth century, evangelicals reacted negatively to just about anything perceived to be aligned with the "social gospel." As such, *social* transformation was not part of our mental landscape, despite the prior history of evangelical engagement in social reform such as the abolition of slavery (Wilberforce). However, by the 1950s evangelicals began to re-incorporate social transformation into our missional rhetoric (e.g., Smalley 1958, 55).

In evangelical missiological circles, the ongoing debates over the relationship of evangelism and social concern fueled ongoing expansion of what we intend by transformation. For example, the World Evangelical Fellowship, with joint sponsorship from the Lausanne Committee for World Evangelization, convened Wheaton '83 to consider ways in which evangelism and social concern are both part of mission. This conference resulted in the initiation of the journal *Transformation* (1984) and *The Church in Response to Human Need* (Samuel and Sugden 1987).

Today evangelicals use the term to mean a variety of things (Bush 2004). It can indicate almost any positive change (e.g., reduced corruption) seen at any societal level (church, local community, people group, an entire nation). In contextualization discourse, evangelicals use *transformation* of reductions in crime rates or corruption (e.g., the *Transformations* videos; http://revivalworks.com), public demonstrations for Christ (e.g., massive March for Jesus rallies; http://www.gmfj. org/), declarations by public officials (e.g., the 1991 declaration by Zambia's President Chiluba that the country was a Christian nation; http://www.christianitytoday.com/ct/2000/januaryweb-only/24.0b. html) and approaches to community development (Myers 1999). It is clear that evangelicals use transformation as a guiding idea as well as a goal in our contextual approaches.

Syncretism

Phil Parshall tells the following story to introduce concerns he has about the practices of some evangelicals engaged in Muslim ministry:

Recently I was speaking to a group of young people who are highly motivated about Muslim evangelism. They excitedly told me of a missionary who had shared a "new" *modus operandi* for winning the Sons of Ishmael to Christ. This strategy centers around the Christian evangelist declaring himself to be a Muslim. He then participates in the *salat* or official Islamic prayers within the mosque. The missionary illustrated the concept by mentioning two Asian Christians who have recently undergone legal procedures to officially become Muslims. This was done to become a Muslim to Muslims in order to win Muslims to Christ.

Actually taking on a Muslim identity and praying in the mosque is not a new strategy. But legally becoming a Muslim definitely moves the missionary enterprise into uncharted territory. I address this issue with a sense of deep concern. (1998a, 404)

Parshall's concerns, and the numerous responses and counter-responses in the years since, aptly illustrate evangelical concerns. Both contextualization and syncretism are processes of faith and culture (Van Rheenen 2006b, 3), so it is inevitable that they are interconnected. Given the evangelical commitments to biblical congruence and appropriate hermeneutics, it is not surprising that evangelical missiologists regularly explore the realities of syncretism in contextual work (Beyerhaus 1975; Yamamori and Taber 1975; Kim 2006; Nicholls 1979a, 20–36; Parshall 1980, 43–53; Conn 1984, 176–79; Asad 2009, 137–38).

We see this when evangelicals explain how their contextual approaches guard against syncretism (e.g., Hiebert 1987, 110; 1991; 1994, 91; Connor 1991). We also see it when evangelicals identify syncretism in contextual practices and question their validity (e.g., Racey 1996; Parshall 1998a; Ma 2000; Flemming 2005, 303–5; Van Rheenen 2006a; Owens 2007). Gary Corwin facetiously notes one of the inherent difficulties for us: "What's the rule-of-thumb definition for the difference between contextualization and syncretism? Simple: it's contextualization when I do it, but syncretism when you do it!" (2004, 282).

In its most neutral form, syncretism is the blending or interpenetration of two differing systems. Contemporary missiological scholarship, drawing from this definition, has been gradually rede-fining syncretism as a neutral or even a good thing (see Gort 1989; Schineller 1992; Schreiter 1993). Because biblical congruence is non-negotiable for evangelicals, it is natural for us to retain the traditional definition of syncretism as "the replacement or dilution of the essen-tial truths of the gospel through the incorporation of non-Christian elements" (Moreau 2000b; see also Shaw 1995, 159; Olsen 2002, 117).

However, syncretism can be exceedingly complex to distinguish from contextualization, as the differences between them are often more fuzzy than binary (see, e.g., Anderson 2000; Corwin 2004; Johnson 2006). It is even more complicated when we realize that shifts in culture make syncretism a moving target; what is "seeker-oriented" contextualization in one generation becomes "market-driven" syncre-tism to the next generation if society has shifted while Christianity has not (Connor 1991, 28).

> Almost from the beginning of the evangelical deliberations on contextualization, a deep fear of syncretism has been evi-dent in the discussions about theologizing.
>
> —Harvie Conn (1984, 176)

Evangelicals have identified issues that are foundational to on-going conversations about syncretism. First, contextualizers cannot neglect the possibility that they themselves may be the source of syn-cretism (Hesselgrave 2006), and that syncretism is not just an issue in the Global South but everywhere, including Western churches (Lausanne 1978). At the same time, however, Kraft argues that fear of syncretism may be the major reason that evangelicals refrain from or do not go far enough in contextualization (Kraft 1978, 35–36; 2005f, 77). Too much fear can be paralyzing!

Second, syncretism often results from pragmatic rather than theo-logical issues. When a person converts from another religion to Christ, he or she has two sets of solutions to draw on when facing a crisis, and that person may simply choose the one that "works" as needed (Droogers 2005, 465). Contextualizers should realize that one way to help avoid syncretism is to ensure that faith in Christ provides real an-swers to the problems people face, not simply theological formulations that have no "feet" in daily life. They can do this only by developing a deep understanding of the social and cultural context, ensuring they know what they are dealing with rather than condemning it outright (see, e.g., Clark 2001; Johnson 2006).

Another important issue is the temptation to use pronouncements about syncretism (or even a threat of it) as a cover for an issue of power. Those who are in control have the power to assign the label and, when threatened, they are the most likely to use it (Heideman 1997; Moreau 2000b; Droogers 2005). The ability to develop trust so that we all work as a community is an important part of overcoming the too-quick application of negative labels (Cortez 2005b, 361; Hiebert 2006, 44–45).

CASE STUDY: BECOMING MUSLIM TO WIN MUSLIMS?

In this case study we illustrate the difficulty of identifying syncretism through debates among evangelicals in contextual practices. Building on Paul's model of acting like a Jew to win the Jews (1 Cor. 9:23–24), Kraft, in the early 1970s, advocated "that we encourage some Christians to become Christian Muslims in order to win Muslims to Muslim Christianity" (1974, 144; see also Woodberry 2006; 2007). Practitioners hoped that by adapting Christian practices they would be less offensive to Muslim sensibilities and thus could communicate Christ more effectively. Bill and Jane (pseudonyms) exemplify this approach, explaining their adaptation:

Within the first few months of our arrival I asked a friend to teach me how to pray in Muslim fashion and how to do the preliminary ablutions. With this information and the assistance of a booklet on the subject entitled *Elementary Teachings of Islam*, we proceeded to write a Christian version of the prayer routine (which is more accurately thought of as a liturgy or worship service). We followed the basic format of body postures; substituted quotes from the Bible for the Arabic words; and eliminated the repetition that is involved in Muslim prayer by organizing the quotes around the themes of God's holiness, God's justice and God's love. We then memorized the prayers and used them ourselves, being careful to do the necessary ablutions first, and to pray with the head covered and feet unshod on a clean surface and to face in the direction of the Ka'ba in Mecca (1990, 88).

Table 5.2 illustrates the increasingly radical experiments in contextual practices. The scale is not absolute; some will arrange the practices differently. In any event, the table shows both *what* experiments are happening and the *range* of those experiments.

TABLE 5.2: RANGE OF EXPERIMENTAL PRACTICES
←Less radical--More radical →
Worship in Muslim style (e.g., barefoot; ritual washings, bow to Mecca)
Keep Ramadan (annual Muslim fast)
Participate in Mosque worship
Claim modified Muslim identity (e.g., "Muslim follower of Isa")
Recite a modified form of the Creed
Recite an unmodified Creed
Claim unmodified Muslim identity
Legally convert to Islam

Given these experiments and the multiple warnings in Scripture against intermingling faiths (1 Kings 18:21; 2 Kings 16:10; Zeph. 1:5; see Greenspahn 2004; Moreau 2006b, 49–51), it is not surprising that debate over experimental practices in Muslim settings has heated up significantly over the past two decades. Perhaps the most direct way to explore what advocates on both sides of the debate say is to peruse recent editions of *International Journal of Frontier Missions* (www.ijfm. org) and *St. Francis Online Magazine* (www.stfrancismagazine.info/ ja/).

More recently, some evangelicals propose distinguishing various forms of social or cultural syncretism (impossible to avoid in a globalized world and seen as generally acceptable) from religious or worldview syncretism (seen as generally unacceptable; see Jacobs 2000; Brown 2006d; Hiebert 2006). Those who separate (religious) form from meaning (spiritual allegiance) and maintain that cultural structures are neutral will agree with John and Anna Travis:

As Kraft has stated (1996:212–213), once this principle of true spiritual allegiance versus formal religion is grasped, "we begin to discover exciting possibilities for working within, say, Jewish or Islamic or Hindu or Buddhist or animistic cultures to reach people who will be culturally Jewish or Muslim or Hindu or animist to the end of their days but Christian in their faith allegiance." (Travis and Travis 2005b, 14)

Those who do not separate meaning and form as radically, however, are far more cautious on the separation of religious forms from religious meanings (e.g., Tennent 2006; Corwin 2007). Harvie Conn presciently expressed his concerns thirty years ago:

We fear the simplism of the past that has reduced the conflict to primarily one of a purely "religious" sort and the simplism of the present that can reduce the conflict to primarily one of a purely sociological or cultural sort. Religion is never that pure and neither is sociology. Both interact constantly on one another in a cultural continuum. And in many situations, the sociological dimension of the continuum may be the more important as the "real" barrier to the gospel. The traditional evangelical approach, by its view of culture, inhibits us from seeing that continuum. How may this insight help us in correcting our understanding of the barriers? (Conn 1979b, 101)

Ultimately, evangelicals recognize that we must acknowledge that every church is in some sense syncretistic. The reality of sin, the dangers of cultural idolatry, and the fact that none of us has a complete grasp on truth are so much a part of our lives that syncretism is in some sense inevitable. Even groups such as the Amish who have withdrawn from the larger societies in which they live face these issues. We can never escape the fact that we are fallen and subjective human beings.

In Table 5.3 I list two sets of issues that evangelicals face in syncretism. Gary Corwin's five questions help us understand the subtleties and difficulties of distinguishing contextualization from syncretism. I address five potentially dangerous "hidden assumptions" that we too often make in relation to syncretism—each exposing an underlying naïve realist perspective. We must attend to both as we struggle over how to identify and address syncretism in our contextual efforts.

TABLE 5.3: QUESTIONS AND ASSUMPTIONS ABOUT SYNCRETISM	
Questions to Ask (Corwin 2004)	**Hidden Assumptions We Make (Moreau 2006b, 48)**
1. What biblical practices or mandates are often overemphasized to either good or bad effect? 2. What cultural assumptions significantly impact for good or ill the gospel's incarnation? 3. Is the gospel's essence, as the Bible presents it, fully embraced by the church? 4. Is anything added to the gospel? 5. Does the typical church and believer remind people of Jesus or simply of any good citizen?	1. It is syncretism when I do not like what they are doing. 2. It is my job to determine what is syncretistic. 3. I always take the only correct biblical approach. 4. It is possible (and necessary) to eliminate all syncretism. 5. It is always easy to identify syncretism.

Incarnation

It did not take long for evangelicals to connect the incarnation with contextualization (e.g., Kraft 1973c). It is central to both the possibility and the necessity of contextualization (Walls 1990; Howell 2001, 35; Campbell 2005; Cortez 2005b, 349). God initiated this "translation" of himself (Walls 1990, 26) and it not surprising that Dean Gilliland labels it "God's Ultimate Act of Contextualization" (2005, 513). He argues that it is impossible for us to contextualize the meaning and depths of the incarnation because the incarnation is itself God's paradigm ("matrix") for contextualization (2005, 505; see also 1989a; 2000b). The incarnation proves that God "desires to be visible in every people and community" (2005, 495) and, as a result, "the task of contextualization is to help everyone, regardless of race, religion, or life situation, to know that God can be 'at home' with him or her" (2005, 496).

> The incarnation is the ultimate paradigm of the translation
> of the Text into context. . . . In his life and teaching he [Jesus
> Christ] is the supreme model of contextualization.
> —(Nicholls 1987, 101, 106)

In view of the unique nature of the incarnation, some challenge whether it should be a model at all (Hill 1990; 1993; contra McElhanon 1991). This is true in that no one who crosses cultural boundaries as an adult can "incarnate" into the new cultural setting, though the example it sets certainly challenges us to set aside paternal attitudes as we contextualize.

However, that does not change the truth that the incarnation is the historical fact from which we take our contextualization cues (Whiteman 2004a; 2004b; 2005). These cues include the following:

- The gap between human cultures is so miniscule in comparison to the gap between God and humanity that incarnation establishes the infinite translatability of the gospel (Van Engen 2005a, 187).

- We imitate the model provided by Jesus and "discover anew, . . . how to express and embody the gospel *in each context*" (Taber 1983, 122; emphasis his).

- We imitate Jesus' humility in the contextual task (Wells 1985; Billings 2004; Frost 2006, 55).

- We identify with those among whom we serve (Shaw and Van Engen 2003, 80), for "When God became man, Christ took flesh in a particular family, members of a particular nation, with the tradition of customs associated with that nation" (Walls 1982, 97).

Holism

Despite the stereotypes, over the past one hundred years, evangelicals as a whole never truly doubted that evangelism and social engagement are both responsibilities of the church. It is true that we debate how to best articulate the holistic relationship between the verbal proclamation of the gospel and the varieties of social engagement. Certain types of social engagement are not debated, such as the work of rescue missions or the call to live socially responsible lives. Among American evangelicals of the boomer generation, the deeper we move in the direction of social justice the sharper the debates over propriety become. However, among evangelicals of the millennial generation— who resonate with issues of justice and social engagement—these debates have less traction.

A significant part of the issue is the larger context of each generation in American culture. Thus, a brief excursus to gather historical perspective will indicate the amount of energy evangelicals have expended on considering holism.

When we dig below the rhetorical surface issues, we find that evangelicals have always considered evangelism and some form of social engagement as non-negotiable components of the ministry of the church. Despite popular stereotypes, evangelicals never quit social engagement, as evidenced by the founding of numerous evangelical relief and development agencies from the 1940s on, including World Relief (1944), World Vision (1951), Compassion International (1952), Map International (1954), and Mission of Mercy (1954). At the same time, existing evangelical agencies initiated and sustained uncounted ventures to minister to the physical and social needs of those among whom they worked (e.g., see http://www.mislinks.org/developing/relief-and-development/ for links to Christian relief and development agencies).

It is also clear, however, that evangelicals do not see evangelism and social engagement as equal in immediate urgency or ultimate concerns. At the Berlin Congress in 1966, some evangelicals complained that they did not come to any clear consensus on the relationship between evangelism and social responsibility. When Lausanne Congress convened in 1974, evangelical discussion about the relationship of evangelism and social engagement was in full swing (see, e.g., Padilla 1979c; 1985). The Lausanne Covenant states in the section entitled "Christian Social Responsibility":

[W]e express penitence both for our neglect and for having sometimes regarded evangelism and social concern as mutually exclusive. Although reconciliation with other people is not reconciliation with God, nor is social action evangelism, nor is political liberation salvation, nevertheless we affirm that evangelism and socio-political involvement are both part of our Christian duty. (Lausanne 1974)

In the decades since Lausanne, evangelicals have organized numerous international gatherings to promote or discuss holism in one form or another. Notable examples include the International Consultation on the Relationship of Evangelism and Social Responsibility (1982), the Consultation on the Church in Response to Human Need (1983), the International Consultation on Children at Risk (1997), Integral Mission and the Poor (2001), Globalisation and the Poor (2003), Integral Mission in a World of Conflict (2006), and Churches Living with HIV (2008).

Additionally, evangelicals produced numerous statements and declarations on holistic mission, such as the Chicago Declaration of Evangelical Social Concern (1973), Transformation: The Church in Response to Human Need (1984), the Manila Manifesto (1989), the Micah Declaration on Integral Mission (2001), the Lausanne Occasional Paper on Holistic Mission (2004).

By and large, evangelicals affirm a holistic focus for contextual work. Even so, the bulk of evangelical contextual examples over the past several decades have attended to issues of spiritual ministry rather than holistic ministry. While the historical excursus indicates that it is inappropriate to characterize evangelicals over the past century as being concerned only with "souls," the examples evangelicals offer of contextualization indicate we still have far to go in being intentionally holistic in our contextual efforts.

Praxis

Of Greek origin, *praxis* means to work or execute. It is used in the New Testament as the title for the book of *Acts*. It has an impeccable biblical heritage.

However, in larger missiological circles (e.g., Bevans's map from chapter 1), it typically refers to transformative social engagement rather than spiritual ministry. Liberation theologians popularized it to indicate work directed toward transforming oppressive and unjust political, social, and economic structures (e.g., workers' rights, land rights, etc.).

From an evangelical vantage point, this is not the central intent of Luke's account of the early church, so it is not surprising that the liberationists' use of the term caused many evangelicals to initially resist using *praxis* as an important concept for contextualization.

However, evangelicals from Global South settings who live in oppressive environments helped their (largely Western) colleagues see that theology (and contextualization) could not be limited to reflective exercises lived out in academic ivory towers. They challenged Western evangelicals to see that our *praxis* includes living our lives in Christ's name on behalf of victimized and marginalized people.

Because of this interplay, *praxis* has slowly been gaining traction as a guiding idea in evangelical contextual rhetoric. While today it undergirds several evangelical contextual approaches, especially for those in the relief and development area, it is not yet fully integrated within contextual work.

Conclusion

We now have marks that evangelicals consider necessary for appropriate contextualization and concepts that we use to shape and constrain how we contextualize. In the next and final chapter in this section, I describe the analytic tools evangelicals use as well as how we use them in contextualization.

KEYWORDS FOR REVIEW

Holism: on an individual level, ministry attending to the whole person (body and soul); on the societal level, ministry attending to all areas of society (religion, politics, economics, education, and so on)

Incarnation: conceptual framing for contextualization on the basis of God coming as Jesus Christ which gives us a foundation for "incarnating" the gospel in new cultural settings

Indigeneity: concept that churches fit naturally into their environment, incorporating such things as self-financing, self-propagating, self-governing, and self-theologizing

Praxis: to work or execute, often refers to action by Christians that engages the society around them in order to transform it

Religious or worldview syncretism: the replacement or dilution of the essential truths of the gospel through the incorporation of non-Christian elements

Social or cultural syncretism: the reality of cultural diffusion that takes place in a globalized world; this is inevitable and can be good or bad, depending on what is being diffused

Syncretism: inappropriate blending of non-Christian religious ideas or practices with Christian faith

Transformation: change in person, church, community, or country as a result of engagement with the gospel on Christ

QUESTIONS FOR REFLECTION

1. What kinds of things do you think of when you hear the word *transformation*?

2. What steps might Christians from any setting take to guard against syncretism?

3. If Christians are concerned with people's eternal destiny, why should we engage in holistic ministry?

4. What are the limits on your ability to "incarnate" in a new cultural setting?

5. What types of *praxis* do you identify within churches in your community? In what ways is it contextual? In what ways it not contextual?

FOR FURTHER STUDY

Bush, Luis K. 2004. *Transformation: A Unifying Vision of the Church's Mission.* Foreword by Paul Cedar. Thailand: 2004 Forum for World Evangelization.

Hiebert, Paul G. 2008. *Transforming Worldviews: An Anthropological Understanding of How People Change.* Grand Rapids: Baker.

Lausanne Committee for World Evangelization. 2004. *Holistic Mission.* Lausanne Occasional Paper No. 33. Online: http://www.lausanne.org/documents/2004forum/LOP33_IG4.pdf.

Kwan, Simon S. M. 2005. "From Indigenization to Contextualization: A Change in Discursive Practice Rather Than a Shift in Paradigm." *Studies in World Christianity* 11.2: 236–50.

Van Rheenen, Gailyn, ed. 2006. *Contextualization and Syncretism: Navigating Cultural Currents.* E MS 13. Pasadena: William Carey Library.

Tools for Analysis

and Application in

Contextualization

CHAPTER OVERVIEW

In this chapter I explore several conceptual tools that evangelicals use to operationalize contextualization. I start with *worldview*, which evangelical use widely in relation to contextualization. I explore two examples of how worldview thinking drives contextualization (orality and redemptive analogies) and conclude with challenges inherent in the idea of worldview.

Perhaps no other single framing for contextualization has been utilized—and fought over—more than that of *dynamic* (or meaning) *equivalence*. I explain the idea and the tensions it has generated.

The third and fourth tools were developed by Paul Hiebert. Those who contextualize in folk religions or spiritual warfare often cite his *flaw of the excluded middle* as an analytic tool that turned their thinking in a fresh and helpful direction. Just as important in evangelism, discipleship, and church planting is his connecting of *set theory* and contextualization

In the past several years the idea of *insider movements* has been identified and promoted as people who come to Christ within other religious settings remaining in those religious settings as insiders rather than leave their social settings.

John Travis captured the imagination of evangelicals with a scale he initially developed to help him understand the various types of contextual churches and Christian fellowships that were being reported in Muslim settings. Since this initial scale, similar *scales of contextualization* for Hindu and Buddhist settings have been proposed.

Even though evangelicals do not all agree with how or even whether these tools should be used, they are so embedded in evangelical models that it will be almost impossible to explain the models without understanding these tools. With that, I turn my attention to them roughly in the chronological order in which they were developed.

CHAPTER OUTLINE

1. Worldview
   a. Using Worldview: Orality, Storying, and Narrative
   b. Using Worldview: Redemptive Analogies
   c. Challenges to "Worldview"
2. Dynamic (or Meaning) Equivalence
3. The Flaw of the Excluded Middle
4. Set Theory and Contextualization
5. Insider Movements
   a. Introduction
   b. Development of the Concept
   c. Questions Evangelicals Consider
6. Scales of Contextualization

Yoshiyuki Billy Nishioka begins an article to explain two differing perspectives on worldview with this fascinating account:

> I come from Japan where Christian churches in general have not grown since the revival movement after World War II, even though most Japanese Christians are very committed and pastors are striving to stimulate church growth. The problem is not that the Japanese are not open to Christianity, but rather that the culture of the churches in Japan unconsciously excludes outsiders, "non-Christian" Japanese. One of the major tasks of missiology in this situation is to analyze the approaches of the church in the society and to find new directions for Japanese Christian leaders.
>
> This difficult issue has challenged me to study missiology in the United States. In a class called "Worldview and Worldview Change," at Fuller Theological Seminary, I met missiologist Charles H. Kraft. I often asked what seemed to be unanswerable questions, both in the class and in his office. One day he said to me, "Why don't you build a Christian shrine?" (1998, 457)

What is your response to Kraft's question? Some see it as an illustration of why contextualization is dangerous. Others see it as the type of question we need to ask if we are to contextualize.

How we respond to the question reveals things that are central to our understanding of contextualization. Our responses expose concerns about the Christian faith each of us brings to the contextual task. This story introduces the types of tools evangelicals use to understand and apply contextualization today—and shows why there is tension over the use of those tools.

Worldview

Conservative missiologists have been integrating *worldview* into their discussions of culture for fifty years (e.g., Luzbetak 1963; Loewen 1965). Even today, however, "It is one of those fascinating, frustrating words that catches our attention. Its ambiguity generates a great deal of study and insight, but also much confusion and misunderstanding" (Hiebert 2008, 13). This ambiguity has not stopped evangelical missiologists from using worldview to explain contextual approaches (Hiebert 2008; Kraft 1999; 2008; see Table 6.1) or communication strategies (e.g., Hesselgrave 1978).

TABLE 6.1: PAUL HIEBERT'S AND CHARLES KRAFT'S DEFINITIONS OF WORLDVIEW	
Hiebert (2008, 25–26)	**Kraft (2008, 12)**
As a preliminary definition, let us define "worldview" in anthropological terms as "the foundational cognitive, affective, and evaluative assumptions and frameworks a group of people makes about the nature of reality which they use to order their lives." It encompasses people's images or maps of the reality of all things that they use for living their lives. It is the cosmos thought to be true, desirable, and moral by a community of people.	I define worldview as the totality of the culturally structured images and assumptions (including value and commitment and allegiance assumptions) in terms of which a people both perceive and respond to reality. These assumptions are structured in relation to each other and in relation to the surface-level structures to form the deep level of culture. We call this deep level of culture "worldview."

Our worldviews are buried, but they constrain our every observation, reaction, and action. Something this central to a person (or society) necessarily plays a major role in contextualization. Discovering the "rules" that govern the relationship between worldview and responses offers this tantalizing possibility: that we may devise forms of communication that receptors will intuitively grasp at the deepest level. Evangelicals use the concept in pragmatic ways.

Using Worldview: Orality, Storying, and Narrative

Building on the work of Walter Ong (1982), evangelical contextualizers have begun working through the implications of how *orality* affects the worldviews of those who are oral. Orville Boyd Jenkins notes, "The insights of Ong's perspective have led to a broad re-evaluation of the role and validity of literacy in the deep worldviews of most societies" (2007). At the risk of oversimplification, at the root is the contention that the worldviews of people shaped by orality are framed around *sound* in contrast to the worldviews of people who are shaped by literacy, which are framed by *sight* (see, e.g., Colgate 2008a and 2008b; Koehler 2009).

Since most of the world's societies are oral, how we contextualize and communicate among oral people needs to be reconsidered from the ground up. Toward that end, leaders from major evangelical mission organizations formed the International Orality Network (http://www.oralbible.com/) in 2005, "seeking to radically influence the way oral preference learners are evangelized and discipled in every people group." Two examples illustrate the importance.

The first is how orality influences Bible translation. Though the Bible is a written document, the audiences throughout biblical times were oral people. Thus, contemporary translators need to understand and translate the Bible in light of oral performance orientation rather than a written one (Maxey 2009).

The second example is how orality affects discipleship. In *African Proverbs Reveal Christianity in Culture: A Narrative Portrayal of Builsa Proverbs Contextualizing Christianity in Ghana* (2009), Jay Moon constructs an engaging series of discussions over Builsa proverbs among Builsa Christians as a means of confronting complex religious and ethical issues. Proverbs are "sweet talk" to the Builsa (Moon 2004), and taking advantage of this as a means for discipleship clearly illustrates how evangelicals utilize worldview thinking in contextualization (International Orality Network 2007).

Using Worldview: Redemptive Analogies

A second practical use of worldview in contextualizing is the idea of redemptive analogies—specific cultural beliefs, rituals, or artifacts that come from worldview and can act as bridges for the gospel message. It stems from the experience of Don Richardson as told in the best-selling book and subsequent movie *Peace Child* (1974).

Richardson and his family lived and worked among the Sawi in West Papua (formerly Netherlands New Guinea). The Sawi value treachery, and Richardson's moving to live among them resulted in an increase in number of the killings. Distraught, Richardson announced his intention to leave. The leaders, anxious for him to stay, tell him they will perform a ceremony that will bring peace among them. Richardson stayed to see how a society that values treachery and killing so highly could possibly ensure peace. The peace ritual involved opposing villages exchanging infants, each of whom then carry the title "Peace Child." As long as the Peace Child lives, peace lives with him. Richardson realized that this gave him a key to communicate the gospel, and he explained to the Sawi that Jesus is God's Peace Child for us. Since Jesus will never die, God will always be at peace with us—as long as we accept his Peace Child.

In subsequent works (1977; 1981), he buttressed redemptive analogy thinking with examples such as John's identification of Jesus as the "word" of God (John 1) and Paul's equating God with "the unknown God" of the Greeks (Acts 17) and asserted that redemptive analogies are cultural catalysts that God often uses to spark people movements (2000).

Given the popularity of Richardson's works, numerous evangelical missionaries searched for redemptive analogies among the unreached peoples they served. Some have been more successful (e.g., Garrison 2004a, 319-30) than others. Les Hensen—working among the Momina of West Papua–related that in looking for the one key analogy, a colleague working among a different language group lamented she had overlooked numerous potentially helpful but less significant bridges in searching for a single key (2008, 224). The fact that such articles are published indicates that evangelicals continue to resonate with the assertion that God has planted redemptive analogies in the cultures of peoples, and this view continues to shape our contextual efforts today.

Challenges to "Worldview"

Despite the success of specific examples, such as orality and redemptive analogies, there are formidable challenges to using the broad construct of "worldview" as a significant tool in contextualization. One is that the very hiddenness of worldview makes it extraordinarily difficult—perhaps impossible—to grasp well enough to use as an analytic tool. We may instinctively resonate with its viability, but once we try to articulate concretely what comprises "worldview," we discover it to be impossible. For example, Hiebert lists *worldview* as a subcomponent of *world maps,* which are themselves components of *worldview* (2008, 335)!

Further, it is nearly impossible to speak of a single worldview for most societies. However, confining worldview analysis to that of an individual reduces the viability of using it to construct contextual approaches to groups, let alone cultures. As I note elsewhere:

> Christians across a variety of academic disciplines such as education (Thiessen 2007), psychology (Blanton 2008), philosophy (Naugle 2002), and theology (Wright 2007) regularly use worldview as a key for understanding culture. However, many Christian anthropologists have distanced themselves from using worldview in this way, and anthropological discourse largely jettisoned the conceptual framework of worldview as a central base for cultural investigation decades ago (Howell 2009; Priest 2009a, 2009b). (Moreau 2009, 230).

Despite the challenges, Hiebert postulates, "If behavioral change was the focus of the mission movement in the nineteenth century, and changed beliefs its focus in the twentieth century, then *transforming worldview must be its central task in the twenty-first century*" (2008, 11–12; emphasis mine). Even though we have no coherent consensus on how to understand it, engage it, or transform it, it seems clear that the *concept* of worldview will continue to serve as a foundational and guiding idea for innumerable evangelical contextual efforts.

Dynamic (or Meaning) Equivalence

The School of Intercultural Studies at Fuller Theological Seminary has graduated more missiologists than any other U.S. seminary. Charles Kraft, considered by many to be one of the leading evangelical missiologists, has served on the faculty of Fuller's School of Intercultural Studies (formerly School of World Mission) since 1969 (full time since 1973; De Carvalho 1999, 63).

Students who studied under Kraft over the past four decades learned the concept of dynamic equivalence, and many of them carry the concept with them into their spheres of influence and intercultural service. His influence has been so significant that some mission agencies expect their members to use dynamic equivalence contextualization (e.g., Bill and Jane 1990, 85). It was this approach that Stephen Bevans used as the exemplar of the "translation" model (1992; 31–33; 2002, 38–39).

Eugene Nida first coined "dynamic equivalence" as a linguistic theory for use in translation (North 1974, xii). Borrowing from the linguistic and communicational frames, Kraft's goal through dynamic equivalence in contextualization is "to see expressed in the lives of the receptors the meanings taught in Scripture" (Kraft 2005h, 168).

> [A] dynamically equivalent church (1) conveys to its members truly Christian meanings, (2) functions within its own society in the name of Christ, meeting the felt needs of that society and producing within it the same Christian impact as the first century Church in its day, and (3) is couched in cultural forms that are as nearly indigenous as possible.
>
> —Charles Kraft (1973a, 40)

As I noted in chapter 2, Kraft is essentially proposing a dynamic type of "calculus" approach to revelation and contextualization. This approach motivated him to ask his Japanese student, "Why don't you build a Christian shrine?" related at the beginning of this chapter. The most significant implications of the *dynamic* nature of contextualization are as follows (adapted from Kraft 2005c):

- Contextualization is a process not a product.

- Learning is best done by self-discovery rather than impartation of information.

- Since revelation is the same now as then, the Bible is a case book of divinely inspired classic cases (2005c 154–58; "an inspired record of significant events," Kraft 2007) for us to learn from and apply to today's varied contexts.

- Understanding revelation today (hermeneutics) requires the best of sciences (especially communication; 2005c, 134) and theology.

- The goal of a dynamic equivalence approach is the transformation of lives—individuals and groups; God accepts people where they are and leads them in a process of transformation (e.g., 2005c, 270–96).

In chapter 3, I described Kraft's approach to the relationship between form and meaning, contrasting it with the more traditional perspective of evangelicals (summarized in Table 3.2). In Table 6.2, I expand the contrast, indicating some of the ways Kraft's disconnection of form and meaning (or message) changes how we understand communication and contextualization.

TABLE 6.2: CONNECTION OF MEANING AND FORM OR MESSAGE IN COMMUNICATION AND CONTEXTUALIZATION	
Meaning *Disconnected* from Form and Message (Kraft's perspective)	**Meaning *Corresponding* to Form and Message (adapted from Hiebert's perspective)**
"Communication"	
To communicate, a person tries to transmit his/her view of reality to another person by creating a "message" or using a "form"—both of which are essentially neutral.	To communicate, a person tries to transmit his/her view of reality to another person by creating a "message" or using a "form"—both of which are often in some way connected to underlying REALITY such that the forms can be inherently good, neutral, or evil.
We transmit "messages" or "forms," but they do not have inherent "meaning." The receptor constructs "meaning" by interpreting the "message" or "form" so the communicator has the responsibility of being receptor-oriented in all aspects of composing his or her "messages."	We transmit "messages" or "forms," which often have inherent "meaning" based on their connection to REALITY. The receptor can understand (fully or partially) or misunderstand (fully or partially) the meaning, so the communicator has the responsibility of being receptor-oriented in all aspects of composing her or his "messages."

TABLE 6.2: CONNECTION OF MEANING AND FORM OR MESSAGE IN COMMUNICATION AND CONTEXTUALIZATION	
Meaning *Disconnected* from Form and Message (Kraft's perspective)	**Meaning *Corresponding* to Form and Message (adapted from Hiebert's perspective)**
Religious "Forms" and Contextualization	
Religions have two components: 1) the "given cultural system made up of cultural structures that are seldom evil in and of themselves" and 2) "the basic faith allegiance of the people who employ them" (Kraft, 1973d, 117; emphasis his). Result: If we can change the meaning people give to the religious forms, then their basic faith allegiance can change as well. This gives us flexibility to experiment with traditional religious forms in ways that allow new meanings to be generated in the people who use them.	The components of a religious cultural system are not inherently neutral. The meaning of each is in its correspondence (or lack thereof) to REALITY —and the value (positive, negative, or neutral) of that meaning in addition to the "meaning" as the basic faith allegiance of the adherents. Experimentation with traditional non-Christian religious forms can only be done after proper understanding of the meaning of the forms is evaluated and the local community decides whether the forms should be rejected, modified, or accepted.

Kraft does not intend that *equivalence* refer to equivalence *of form*. For example, he does not mean that the goal is to recreate the form of a poem in translating it from one language to another. Rather, drawing from the disciplines of linguistics, translation, communication, and anthropology, he focuses on the *equivalence of impact*. Using the same example, he would advocate a translation of the poem that produces the same impact on receptors that the original poem had on its receptors. To summarize (adapted from Kraft 2005c):

- Equivalence is in impact not in information transfer;

- Equivalence is ever changing (as cultures are ever changing);

- Equivalence is focused on the deeper meanings of the forms seen in the Bible. For example, the greater the specificity the command or instruction (the form), the more culture-bound it is and the greater need to discover the underlying framing (the basic-idea level) rather than the surface-level form for proper contextualization;

- Since all cultures are "adequate and equal in potential useful-ness as vehicles of God's interaction with humanity" (2005c, 43) we focus on methods that present to people the signifi-cance of Christ and invite them to align their allegiance with God through a minimum of worldview shift.

As noted in previous chapters, Kraft's approach has been both widely utilized *and* widely criticized among evangelicals. The example critics cite most often is Kraft's approach to handling Paul's list of qualifications for an elder (1 Tim. 3). Kraft argues that in the New Testament we see "not a single leadership pattern set down for all time, but a series of experiments with cultural appropriateness" (1973b, 51). Therefore, Paul's list is surface-level, not a universal (deeper-level) one. At the deeper level, the New Testament focus is "constantly on ap-propriateness of function rather than on the standardization of form" (1973b, 51).

Thus, Paul's elder qualification list is effectively a culturally appro-priate experiment expressing qualities that demonstrate unimpeach-able social maturity to Paul's readers (surface-level). The dynamic equivalent of this list in another cultural setting will be those qualities that demonstrate unimpeachable social maturity *in that setting*. Thus, we should look for what people in the new setting consider to be traits of impeccable social maturity and use those traits as qualifications for elders so that our new list will have the same impact in the new setting as Paul's list had in Timothy's setting. If in the new setting a quality of social maturity is being a polygamist, then the dynamic equivalent list will incorporate polygamy as a requirement for eldership (Kraft 1973b and 2002b, 415–26). The responses of other evangelicals to this sug-gestion were sharp (e.g., Carson 1985, 206; Hesselgrave and Rommen 1989, 67; Osborne 1991, 328; and Hesselgrave 1995b, 143).

Building on the idea that cultural forms are important but essentially neutral (and thus variable), Kraft calls for an "experimental" attitude in contextualization that is very broad. Two examples illustrate why other evangelicals are uncomfortable with the open experimental approach of dynamic equivalence contextualization.

First, as seen in the introduction to the chapter, *allegiance* to God is the primary factor, not the *forms* that such allegiance takes. Thus, Kraft's suggestion to build Christian shrines in Japan fits dynamic equivalence (Kraft 2005h, 161), though, in personal correspondence he notes the following caveat:

> [M]y suggestion that shrines can be used within Christianity is cou-
> pled with the need to disempower them and to make major changes
> in the interior of the shrines so that though they are recognizable
> by the people as places of power because of their traditional appear-
> ance, they convey God's power and the meaning that Christianity is
> powerful in contrast to the powerless appearance (from an ordinary
> Japanese person's perspective) of the churches in Japan." (Kraft 2007)

Second, other evangelicals are concerned with Kraft's experimen-
talist approach when applied to techniques of spiritual warfare. Kraft notes that he expects to see "the kinds of regularity in the spirit realm that scientists have found in their studies of the physical and human worlds" (Kraft 1995, 89). As a result, he advocates that "there may be greater insight for all of us if we are venturesome, risking in faith in God to perhaps discover some of that additional truth that He promised us (John 16:13)" (1995, 91). The Lausanne Committee for World Evangelization statement on spiritual warfare (from the Deliver Us from Evil Consultation held in Nairobi in 2000 in which Kraft partici-
pated) notes disagreement among evangelicals over experimenting in spiritual warfare:

> Tension exists concerning the extent to which we can learn and verify
> things from the spiritual realm from experiences not immediately
> verifiable from Scripture in contrast to limiting our understanding
> of the spiritual realm from Scripture alone. Some have maintained
> that experience is crucial to understanding spiritual conflict; this is
> a point to be explored in ongoing dialogue. (Lausanne 2002, xxvi)

Others are not so neutral in their response (e.g., see Lowe 1998 and Reid 2002 for critiques of the pragmatic orientation that comes from an experimental grounding). They express deep concern that Kraft's particular application of his experimental approach in spiritual warfare practice leads to new doctrines or practices that are not simply extrabiblical but even anti-biblical (e.g., Priest, Campbell, and Mullen 1995; though note Kraft's strong 1995 response).

It is clear that Kraft carefully, creatively, and often brilliantly articulates his ideas. It is also clear that he does not hide his agendas as he challenges those he calls "closed evangelicals and fundamentalists" (1979d, 187) to be more open to fresh insights and ideas. It should not be surprising, then, that the same "closed evangelicals" vigorously respond to his "open evangelicalism."

Even so, it seems apparent that many who received training under Kraft carry on the dynamic equivalence approach in contextualization, though often with their own take on what dynamic equivalence means (see, e.g., Kraft 2005a).

The Flaw of the Excluded Middle

Paul Hiebert provided one of the most widely used analytic tools for evangelical contextualization when he published "The Flaw of the Excluded Middle" (1982). Many consider it one of his most significant legacies to evangelical missions (see Anana-Asane et al. 2009). David Hesselgrave, for example, noted that it was "published, reviewed, and acclaimed in a great variety of contexts" (2005, 194).

Hiebert argues that Western missionaries readily identified with a two-tiered universe. The top tier was of the ultimate (unseen) powers that govern the universe. For Christians, this is the realm of God. Other religions would include their deities as well as powerful cosmic forces, such as karma. This was the realm of formal religion, and it is the one that Western missionaries were taught to take to places where Christ was not yet known. The bottom tier was that of earthly (seen) powers, including such things as human powers as explored by the social sciences. This, too, missionaries understood and took with them, especially when working in developmental areas.

However, as Hiebert looked at the understanding of the universe among the Indians where he worked, he realized that their perspective included a realm between the ultimate and unseen powers and the immediate and seen ones, namely, *unseen powers of this world*, including such things as curses, ancestral spirits, objects of power, blessings, and the like. This was the area that local people handled through a variety of local beliefs that we call *folk religions*. Hiebert recognized that he did not receive training in this area—it was an "excluded" (or overlooked) area—due to worldview issues. The flaw of many Western agencies and schools, then, was to exclude consideration of this realm in training missionaries. Workers on assignment who ignored it tended to see a type of "split-level" Christianity develop—people appealed to God for some problems, appealed to people such as medical doctors for others, and turned to folk religious practitioners and practices for things in the middle realm.

Hiebert's idea gained wide acceptance among evangelical missionaries and missiologists who were trying to explain things they had faced and wrestled with but had no reference in their training or textbooks (Love 2000, 70–88). Some used the excluded middle to justify approaches to spiritual warfare that Hiebert had not anticipated, at times expanding this middle realm so that the flaw of the *expanded* middle became a problem (Moreau 1995b; Love offers an example in 2000, 71–72). Others used the concept to explain the split-level Christianity seen in places where Christianity as offered by missionaries meets some needs, but folk religious practices continue to meet other needs that the expatriate workers do not see because of their own worldviews (Hiebert, Shaw, and Tiénou 2005, 15–20; see, e.g., Moon 2009).

Set Theory and Contextualization

When I was a freshman in high school, I had to submit to an interview by our minister prior to confirmation to establish that I was ready for the process. At the interview, I stated that I was not sure that God even existed. The minister commended me for my honesty and chose to allow me to proceed. I went through the confirmation ritual the following week—and then stopped going to church altogether. Three years later, I asked Christ to come into my life in a rush of emotions after a stirring presentation at a summer camp—even though I knew that my emotions were driving me. Six months after that emotional experience, with greater clarity of the message of the gospel through a ministry working at my high school, one night before going to bed I knelt in prayer and quietly committed my life to Christ. Four years after that, after being challenged repeatedly by friends, I was baptized in the Fox River west of Chicago at a weekend church retreat.

When did I "really" become a Christian? My story illustrates questions missionaries often face in ministry. What criteria do we use to determine if someone is really a follower of Christ? When should we baptize someone?

Hiebert realized that by applying the basic concepts of set theory to these questions we could better examine the types of assumptions people make in answering them. He hoped to help missionaries better understand how we categorize people into sets ("Christian" or "non-Christian") and how that affects our entire orientation toward evangelism, discipleship, and church planting (1994, 107–36; 2008, 33–37, 308–10). Subsequent use of his ideas clearly demonstrates that their impact on evangelical missions has been significant (Yoder et al., 2009).

TABLE 6.3: FOUR OPTIONS IDENTIFYING THE SET OF "CHRISTIANS"		
Type of Boundary / *Basis of Inclusion*	**Binary**	**Fuzzy**
Intrinsic	People who have "intrinsic Christian qualities"; they are either completely in or completely out.	People who have "intrinsic Christian qualities"; they may be partially in or out.
Centered	People who have Christ as their center; they are either completely in or completely out.	People who have Christ as their center; they may be partially in or out.

Drawing on his background in math, Hiebert explained that we form categories, or sets, based on two types of decisions—each with two options (Table 6.3). The first decision involves the *basis* of including something in the set. One option is to include things based on an *intrinsic* quality shared by every member of the set. For example, in a set of "Christians" we might include only people who we consider to have changed on the inside (using whatever criteria we think demonstrate such a change). Sets we form on the basis of fundamental qualities are *intrinsic* sets. The other option we have is to include things in the set based on an *identified relationship* shared by every member of the set. For example, in a set of "Christians" we might include only those people who have a relationship with Christ (using whatever criteria we think demonstrate such a relationship). We call these types of sets *centered* sets because who or what they are related to (in this case, Jesus) is the "center" of the set.

The second decision involves the *type of boundaries* we choose for the set. One option is to choose a boundary that is *binary*—having only two possible options. For example, we might consider our "Christian" set to have such tight boundaries that people are either completely in the set or completely out. We call sets with such binary boundaries *bounded* sets. The other option is to choose an imprecise boundary— like shades of gray or steps of a ladder (Taber 1975, 246). For example, we may decide to allow for a "partial" inclusion in our "Christian" set. We call sets with multiple levels of inclusion *fuzzy* sets.

When we combine these two decisions used to form sets, four types of sets result. Our sets can be 1) *intrinsic bounded* on the basis of intrinsic qualities with a tight boundary, 2) *intrinsic fuzzy* on the basis of intrinsic qualities with a fuzzy boundary, 3) *centered bounded* on the basis of the relationship to the "center" with a tight boundary, or 4) *centered fuzzy* on the basis of relationship to the "center" with a fuzzy boundary.

Hiebert's insight was in applying the various sets to our understanding of what belongs in the set we label "Christians," which is why I shared part of my journey. Hiebert recognized that more conservative Christians—especially evangelicals—answer the question of when I "truly" became a Christian based on intrinsic inclusion and a binary boundary. Christians who are more liberal tend to see the boundary as more fuzzy (whether using intrinsic or centered inclusion).

Hiebert argued that the Bible portrays "Christian" on the basis of a relationship to Christ that, while not always clear to us, nonetheless has a binary boundary. Thus, the biblical idea of a "Christian" is *centered bounded* rather than *intrinsic bounded*. Centered sets do not require definitions of the intrinsic qualities necessary for inclusion— qualities we too often derive from particular doctrines or cultural values. Instead they focus on relational qualities, and people do not have to look or act like us to have Christ as their "center." This frees us from the rigidity and idiosyncrasy inherent in an intrinsic orientation.

Darrell Whiteman called Hiebert's approach "one of the most liberating and powerful missiological concepts students have encountered" (2006, 56). Rick Brown uses centered-set thinking to explore the boundary markers for Muslims who come to Christ (Brown 2007b, 65–74), and Abdul Asad uses it to help us better understand the growth of the African church (2009, 139–40). Michael Frost and Alan Hirsch use it to help us better understand church in contemporary secular settings (2003). It has become a common point of reference in Western missional and contextual church thinking (Yoder et al. 2009, 184).

Insider Movements

Evangelicals often use "movement" to refer to the process of large numbers of people coming to faith over a short time period through widespread means. They are so important in the church that some mission historians trace the ebb and flow of mission (and church) history through the lens of Christian movements (Pierson 2009, 5).

Movements are simultaneously exciting and messy. They are exciting because God is doing things beyond our imagination; they are messy because they shift and sway with great vigor in unanticipated directions and fray at the edges in ways we cannot anticipate. They have great power for positive change as well as great potential for social upheaval and chaos. Steve Addison identifies five historical characteristics of movement: 1) white-hot faith; 2) commitment to a cause; 3) contagious relationships; 4) rapid mobilization; and 5) adaptive methods (2009, 23–25). He notes, "Movements change people and changed people change the world" (28). Evangelical attention to movements is evidence of our activist and conversionist character (Table 2.1).

Evangelicals wrote about religious movements (Barrett 1968) and people movements (McGavran 1963, Tippett 1971) prior to the adding of contextualization to our lexicon. Recently we have written about contextual movements (Richard 2002), church planting movements (Garrison 1999; Register 2000), house church movements (Zdero 2005), church strengthening movements (Cantrell 2006), and the correlation between contextualization and movements (Brown et al. 2009). Evangelicals anticipate that successful contextualization can result in movements of people coming to Christ. Over the past decade, however, discussion on what are called "insider movements" has moved to the forefront of evangelical reflection and controversy (e.g., Brown 2007a; Corwin 2006; 2007; 2008; "An Extended Conversation" 2006; Garrison 2004b; Higgins 2006; 2007; Lewis 2009; Madany 2009; Mallouhi 2009; Nikides 2006a; 2009; Peterson 2007a; Steele 2009).

Introduction

When a person comes to faith in Christ from a different religious background, how much religious change is necessary? The form and meaning discussion from chapter 3 frames our options (see Table 3.2). If forms are neutral and people construct meaning only in their minds, then we have enormous freedom to experiment with non-Christian religious forms. Our hope is that by transforming how new believers construct meaning, they may use their non-Christian forms to worship our living God. If, however, forms are *not* neutral and meaning exists in the *correspondence* between reality and Reality, then we must approach such experimentation with caution, attending carefully to the possibility of syncretism.

The differences between these two orientations are at the heart of the debates over some of the practices of those promoting insider movements. Debate is vigorous because of the recognition by all parties of what is at stake. Due to space, I limit the discussion here to some of the more significant questions and developments that have brought evangelicals to where we are today (see also http://www.mislinks.org/understanding/contextualization-for-islam/ for resources).

Development of the Concept

Stressing that Islam is a social as well as a religious term (similar for Hinduism and Buddhism), there has been considerable debate on whether or how to avoid "extracting" a new convert to Christ from her or his former community setting. Evangelicals on both sides agree that extraction is not a good option (e.g., Parshall 1980; Richard 1994; Tennent 2005). Even though in reality the Muslim community *expels* new converts far more than missionaries *extract* them (Schlorff 2000), the question remains: How can Muslims come to Christ without leaving their own community?

Similar questions, together with dissatisfaction with the results of traditional missions in such settings, propelled evangelicals to look for new ways of contextualizing ministry. Those trained in dynamic equivalence contextualization (with the attendant separation of form and meaning) considered new possibilities. For example, perhaps Muslims may, "while committing themselves to God through Christ simply remain *culturally* Muslim" (Kraft 1979a, 119; McCurry 1976; the same can be said for Hindus: Richard 2001).

Another consideration was to retain Muslim worship forms and traditions but invest the old forms with new (Christian) meanings (Kraft 1973b). Dudley Woodberry, Islamicist at Fuller Theological Seminary, provided historical support by showing that most Islamic religious forms were themselves originally borrowed from Christians and Jews living in the Middle East when Islam developed (1989). Thus, advocates contend, "when we contextualize to so-called 'Islamic forms' we are actually 'reusing' many of the forms formerly found in the faith of our ancestors" (Travis and Travis 2005a, 398).

If true, then Muslims who come to faith could worship Christ using Muslim forms of worship. That opens up the possibility that they could stay in their communities and could form "a new social entity . . . , which followers of Christ would feel at home. When this occurred, believers would cease to be lost, and the movement would gain further momentum" (Wilder 1977, 309). Over the next several decades, the idea was refined until today:

Insider movements can be defined as movements to obedient faith in Christ that remain integrated with or *inside* their natural community. In any insider movement there are two distinct elements:

1. The gospel takes root within *pre-existing communities* or social networks, which *become* the main expression of "church" in that context. Believers are not gathered from diverse social networks to

create a "church." New parallel social structures are not invented or introduced.

2. Believers *retain their identity* as members of their socio-religious community while living under the lordship of Jesus Christ and the authority of the Bible. (Lewis 2009, 16; see also Lewis 2007a, 75)

Questions Evangelicals Consider

The questions raised and debated are numerous. I catalogue specific questions in two categories in Table 6.4 (see also Oksnevad 2007), along with people on both sides of the debate. While I frame the questions for Muslims, they equally apply to Hindus and Buddhists.

TABLE 6.4: DEBATED QUESTIONS IN INSIDER MOVEMENT CONTEXTUALIZATION		
Advocates	**Question**	**Cautious**
Biblical/Theological/Hermeneutical Questions		
Travis 2000, 55; Effa 2007, 311; Higgins 2009	Can we use Elijah's response to Naaman ("Go in peace"; 2 Kings 5:17–19) as a parallel for today's insiders going to the mosque?	Nikides 2009, 106
Massey 2004c; Higgins 2009	Does 1 Corinthians 7:17–24 indicate that Muslims can "stay where they are" once they come to Christ?	Dixon 2009, 18; Grafas 2007; Tennent 2006; Smith 2009
Travis and Travis 2005a; Higgins 2007	Does Acts 15 justify not forcing Muslims to act like "Christians" in conversion?	Grafas 2007, 10–11
Massey 2004c; Peterson 2007b; Woodberry 2006; 2007	Can we render Paul's statement in 1 Corinthians 9:19–23 ("I became as a Jew in order to win the Jews") as "I became as a Muslim in order to win Muslims"?	Waterman 2007; Back 1999; Grafas 2007; Poston 2000; Smith 2009

Jameson and Scalevich 2000	To what extent are Judaism and Islam parallel and what are limits on how we can use this? (a related question: "Is there such a thing as a 'Messianic Muslim'"?)	Wilder 1977; Guthrie 2004; Waterman 2007; Bourne 2009; Nikides 2009; Span 2009
Brown 2000; 2002; 2005a; 2005b; 2007c; Gray and Gray 2008; Al Kalima 2009	Is it appropriate to produce Bible translations that eliminate offensive terms or that are "Muslim friendly"?	Dixon 2007; Nikides 2006b; Phil 2009; Smith 2009
Socio-Cultural Questions		
Parshall 1982a; Dutch 2000; Travis 2000; Richard 2001; Hoefer 2001a; 2001b; 2008; Winter 2003b; Chandler 2007; Peterson 2007a	Do Muslim followers of Christ have to become "Christians" or join churches?	Heldenbrand 1982
Kraft 1973b; Kraft 1996; 212–213; Travis 1998b; Winter 2003a; 2003b; Travis and Travis 2005b; Higgins 2006; 2009; Brown 2007b	Is religion primarily (or even exclusively) a cultural construct? Must "Muslim" be only religious? Can it be purely cultural? Is it possible to be both Muslim and Christian at the same time? *Alternate 1*: Is it possible to separate religious and social/cultural identity? If so, to what extent can we do this? *Alternate 2*: Can we separate Muslim cultural forms from their religious meaning and infuse them with Christian meanings? If so, to what extent can we do this?	Taber 1979b; Parshall 1985a; 2003; Eenigenburg 1997; Schlorff 2006; Corwin 2006; Waterman 2007; 2008; Tennent 2006; Nikides 2009; Bourne 2009
Brown 2006d	To what extent can MBBs continue to pray in the mosque facing Mecca, perform the fast, give alms, or other Islamic forms of piety?	Heldenbrand 1982; Parshall 1994; Speers 1991
Brown 2006d; 2007b	Is it viable for an MBB to say the creed? (Parallel: to what extent is Muhammad a prophet?)	Chastain 1995; Parshall 1998b; Waterman 2007; 2008; Asad 2009

Goal/Transformational/Kingdom: Hoefer 2001a; 2001b; Peterson 2007a; Gray and Gray 2009a; 2009b	Is C5 (see below) a *goal* or final destination (advocates) or a *means*—a transitional stage that may take years (cautious)? *Alternate 1*: do we "plant churches" (attractional model) or transform social networks (transformational model)? *Alternate 2*: Are we "church" focused or "kingdom" focused?	Transition/ attractional/ church: Travis 2000; Asad 2009
Kraft 1982; Weerstra 2000; Woodberry 2008	To what extent should success/failure drive our ministry methods in difficult settings?	Schlorff 2006; Waterman 2008; Phil 2009; Smith 2009

The chart shows that missionaries and missiologists are talking to themselves and to each other. However, it is also true that those pushing the boundaries are meeting on a regular basis, but not necessarily inviting others to the discussion (Smith 2009). Security is a critical issue; open debate on these questions likely will endanger the lives of people who live in sensitive areas. Closed debate is happening, but in small gatherings and without dissemination of the discussion.

Could it be that we are witnessing the development of a type of evangelical missionary "insider movement"—with the more radical experimenters investing new meaning in traditional evangelical forms without being transparent about what they do? At one level, this is understandable. I learned as a missionary while on furlough that missionaries must handle some things that would take so long to explain to American Christians that it is not worth the time; it was better to say nothing than to arouse suspicion. At another level, however, this *modus operandi* separates practitioners from the normal set of checks and balances that operates in the larger body of Christ. Rumors of evangelical missionaries practicing contextualization by changing official religious affiliation or denying cardinal Christian teaching (including the deity of Christ) generate great suspicion for the entire contextualization enterprise.

Perhaps most tragic is the appearance that evangelical church historians, religious scholars, theologians, and biblical scholars are not participating—often for the same reasons that I did not discuss everything I faced when I knew how long it would take to explain. An unfortunate result is that we lose valuable input from outstanding resources. Or worse, when word does get to an expert, it is about an extreme case, generating suspicion rather than simple curiosity.

Exceptions exist (e.g., Roger Dixon's correspondence with D. A. Carson; Dixon 2009), but the fact remains that evangelical missionaries have not brought into the discussion the resources and insights of those with appropriate expertise. As long as this is the case, clarity and consensus will likely remain out of reach. Evangelical missiologists on their own have not reached consensus in more than thirty years of debate, and without something (or someone) to jar us loose, it seems unlikely we will reach one in the foreseeable future.

Scales of Contextualization

As evangelicals have experimented with contextual approaches in Muslim settings, Travis came up with a six-step spectrum to describe the types of gatherings of those who follow Christ in Muslim settings (Travis 1998a; see also Massey 2000; Travis and Travis 2005a; Lewis 2007b). Called "The C–1 to C–6 Spectrum" (Table 6.5) in the 1998 publication in *Evangelical Missions Quarterly*. This scale is now the standard that evangelical missionaries and agencies use to indicate which type of Christian community they prefer. The scale is so widely used that Christians published parallel scales for Hindu (Anonymous 2004; Richard 2004) and Buddhist (DeNeui 2002) as well as Web-based evangelistic sites (The X Spectrum, n.d.).

	C1	C2	C3	C4	C5	C6
TABLE 6.5: THE C1 TO C6 SPECTRUM (ADAPTED FROM TRAVIS 1998A; TRAVIS 2000; TRAVIS AND TRAVIS 2005A)						
Christ-Centered Community Description	Traditional church using a language different from the mother tongue of the local Muslim community	C1 in form but using the mother tongue of the local Muslim community	Contextualized Christ-centered community using the mother tongue and some non-Muslim (non-religious) local cultural forms (dress, music, diet, etc.)	Contextualized Christ-centered community using the mother tongue and biblically acceptable socio-religious Islamic forms	Community of Muslims who follow Jesus yet remain culturally and officially Muslim	Secret or underground Muslim followers of Jesus with little or no community
Self-Identity	"Christian"	"Christian"	"Christian"	"Follower of Isa"	"Muslim follower of Jesus"	Privately: "Christian" or "Follower of Isa" or "Muslim follower of Jesus"
Muslim Perception	Christian	Christian	Christian	A strange kind of Christian	A strange kind of Muslim	Muslim

The major point of contention among evangelicals is over the C4 and C5 approaches, though distinguishing the two in actual settings is not as clear as the scale indicates. However, the C1 to C6 scale is useful to those on all sides of the debate for identifying ministry approaches and establishing common nomenclature.

Figures 6.1 to 6.3 show how evangelical missiologists have tried to find ways to clarify their perspectives on the various models. From our set theory discussion, each attempts to clarify either or both: 1) the basis of inclusion and 2) the type of boundary. Timothy Tennent, former missionary to India and now president of Asbury Theological Seminary, uses as his basis of inclusion the extent to which each model identifies most closely with the Christian community or the Islamic community and draws binary boundaries around each model (Figure 6.1). Mark Williams, working among Muslims in the Philippines, uses as his basis of inclusion the underlying theology behind each model as well as how that theology determines praxis (Figure 6.2). His boundaries are fuzzier than Tennent's, but his diagram clearly indicates his judgment that C5 approaches cross the line into theological and praxeological syncretism. Finally, Rick Brown, working in the Muslim world since 1977, also uses identity as the basis of inclusion. However, he gives primary consideration on identity as the people of God and secondary consideration on identity within the local Christian or Muslim communities (Figure 6.3). He also indicates that the boundaries between C4 and C5 are fluid and fuzzy rather than settled and binary and indicates that Tennent is wrong to indicate binary boundaries among the models.

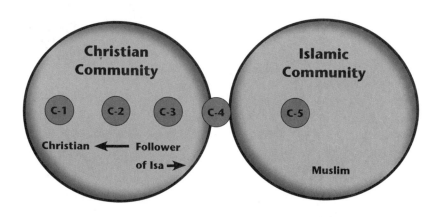

Figure 6.1 Tennent (2006, 102)

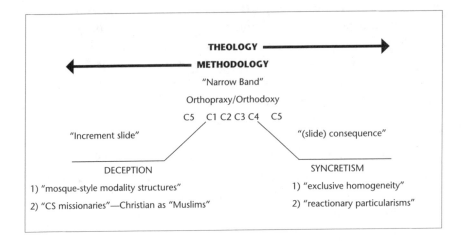

Figure 6.2: Williams (2003, 88)

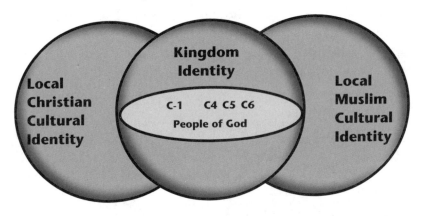

Figure 6.3: Brown (in Corwin 2007, 13)

Some recognize C5 as a goal for insider movements (e.g., Woodberry 1996; Travis 1998b; Gilliland 1998; Massey 2004a, Higgins 2006; Brown 2007b). Others insist it can only be a transitional point (e.g., Parshall 1998a; Woods 2003; Corwin 2006; 2007; Tennent 2006; Waterman 2007). Some say it is an illegitimate reality that new believers must move beyond as quickly as possible (Poston 2006; Schlorff 2000; 2006).

Most who are against C5 are not against what C5 describes *per se*, but against C5 as a goal or permanent position of converts from Muslim backgrounds. Dixon, former missionary to Indonesia, posits that we need to move beyond the scale because of the shadowy nature of how it is being used and supported: "It creates the illusion of offering insight to ministry while only giving a cursory view" (Dixon 2009, 9).

However strong the disagreements, evangelicals use this and other scales to identify their approach to contextualization—and to defend their thinking as to why the scale is either the best or at least a viable approach.

Conclusion

The wide variety of approaches taken by evangelicals and the vigor of debates that are going on demonstrate the energy we have for contextualization. Throughout this section, I have shown that evangelicals are committed to the Bible, to understanding the Bible well, to communicating the message of the Bible in ways that receptors will understand, and to identifying marks that indicate good contextualization. We have developed theological and anthropological concepts that shape good contextualization, and we have devised tools that help us analyze what we are doing and find better ways to do it.

I have also presented cursory overviews of the more significant areas of disagreement and ongoing debate among evangelicals on issues such as revelation, hermeneutics, and the relationship between form and meaning. Each of these debates plays out in the ways evangelicals choose to approach contextualization.

With these foundations in place, I turn next to the task of deciding how to catalogue these approaches in a usable conceptual map.

KEYWORDS FOR REVIEW

Dynamic (or Meaning) equivalence: Christians *expressing* in their lives the *meanings* taught in Scripture so that by using local forms they have the same *impact* in a local setting as the early church did in its setting

Bounded (or binary) sets: sets formed with sharp boundaries—something is either in or out of the set

Centered sets: sets formed on the nature of the members to a defined "center" of the set

Flaw of the excluded middle: the Western tendency to ignore the "middle" realm of spirits, angels, demons, and other invisible spiritual powers that affect people in real ways in our world

Fuzzy sets: sets formed without sharp boundaries—something can be in or out of the set, as well as partially in or partially out

Intrinsic sets: sets formed on the intrinsic nature of the members of the set

Insider movements: movements to obedient faith in Christ that remain integrated with or inside their natural community

Movements: the process of large numbers of people coming to faith over a short time period through widespread means

Orality: orientation of an oral-based worldview, which significantly shapes how people think and act

Redemptive analogies: specific cultural beliefs, rituals, or artifacts that come from worldview and can act as bridges for the gospel message

Scales of contextualization: Scales developed to describe the spectrum of what we observe in contextualization from non-contextualization to radical contextualization in various religious settings (notably Muslim, Hindu, Buddhist).

Worldview: the foundational (and hidden—or unconscious) perspective on life that constrains human observation, reaction, and action

QUESTIONS FOR REFLECTION

1. What metaphors, values, or beliefs in your culture could serve as types of redemptive analogies to contextualize the gospel?

2. Since worldview is such a difficult idea to define and identify, why do evangelicals continue to use the concept?

3. How might we see contemporary forms found in American Christianity (such as the Christmas tree and the Easter bunny) as examples of dynamic equivalence?

4. Describe what you think might characterize an insider movement in a U.S. public university.

5. Develop a "scale of contextualization" to describe the ministry models and methods of organizations working in campus ministries across the United States (e.g., Baptist Student Union, Campus Crusade for Christ, Campus Life, Fellowship of Christian Athletes, International Students Incorporated, InterVarsity, Navigators, and so on).

FOR FURTHER STUDY

Corwin, Gary. 2007. "A Humble Appeal to C5/Insider Movement Muslim Ministry Advocates to Consider Ten Questions." *International Journal of Frontier Missions* 24.1 (Spring): 5–20.

Hiebert, Paul. 1994. *Anthropological Reflections on Missiological Issues.* Grand Rapids: Baker.

_____. 2008. *Transforming Worldviews: An Anthropological Understanding of How People Change.* Grand Rapids: Baker

Kraft, Charles H. 2005. "The Development of Contextualization Theory in Euroamerican Missiology." In *Appropriate Christianity,* ed. Charles Kraft, 15–34. Pasadena: William Carey Library.

_____. 2008. *Worldview for Christian Witness.* Pasadena: William Carey Library.

Mapping Evangelical Models of Contextualization

In this section, I develop a new way to map contextual terrain. To do this, I chose the criteria and rules for categorizing each model, which is my *rubric*. Undergirding this process are three important considerations.

First, the rubric should result in categories that are capable of including *all* the approaches evangelicals use to contextualize. Second, the rubric should result in categories that can be distinguished from each other with little overlap. Though true binary boundaries are impossible (life is too messy), I want them as clear and sharp as possible. Finally, the rubric should allow me to fit new contextual methods into the map. I need the flexibility to create new categories, and the rubric must enable this development.

In chapter 7, I explain how I developed the rubric and overview the resulting map. Through the rest of the section, I explore each initiator role in alphabetical order (facilitator, guide, herald, pathfinder, prophet, and restorer). To do this, I:

1. Describe characteristics of the initiator role seen in the examples
2. Offer biblical and geographic exemplars of contextual practices of the role
3. Discuss selected examples from the database in greater detail
4. Identify strengths and weaknesses inherent in each role

After surveying the entire map and explaining each initiator role, I close by discussing some of the issues—from trends to tensions—that I anticipate evangelicals will see in the near future in relation to contextualization.

There are three considerations to keep in mind when reading the chapters on the initiator roles. First, the initiators of contextual practices do not consciously attend to the initiator roles and do not limit themselves to any single role. They may, and usually do, take on a variety of roles over the course of their ministries. As you will see, Jesus himself took on each of the initiator roles at various times in his ministry. However, this does not mean that these six roles were the only ones he took on. Indeed, perhaps one way for evangelicals to expand our map of approaches would be to explore in greater depth Jesus' own contextual roles.

In light of this, I need to clarify that when I identify an individual or method in any of the 249 examples as portraying a particular role, I do not imply that the individual never takes on other roles or that the method is constrained by that role. Rather, I indicate the role of the initiator(s) *that the particular example portrays.*

Second, in each chapter I clarify the initiator role under consideration. I do this by comparing the criteria for one initiator role with the same criteria for other initiator roles.

For example, in 36 percent of the 249 examples, initiators act as guides. Therefore, all other things being equal, we should expect that in 36 percent of all examples for which a particular criterion applies the contextual initiator would be a guide.

To illustrate, one of the 77 fields in the database is whether the example includes *theological development* within its scope. This is true for 80 of the 249 examples in the database. All other things being equal, then, we would *expect* that in 36 percent of these 80 examples—or 29 of them—the initiator would be a guide. However, the initiator acts as a guide in 41 (or 51 percent) of the 80 examples. This is far *more* frequently than expected. Thus, in a disproportionate number of examples, when the initiator has the role of a guide, the example includes theological development in its scope.

By contrast, in 122 of the 249 examples the scope of the contextual effort includes spiritual outreach. All other things being equal, then, we would expect that in 36 percent of these 122 examples—or 44 of them—the initiator would be a guide. However, the initiator acts as a guide in only 31 (or 25 percent) of these 122 examples. This is far *less* frequently than expected. Thus, in a disproportionate number of examples, when the initiator has the role of a guide, the example does *not* include spiritual outreach in its scope.

In some sense, all of us stand on the shoulders of others. We learn from what they offer in the hope of using the knowledge on behalf of the body of Christ. In the process of developing the map, I explored the maps of fellow evangelicals, constructed a composite map of their works, and constructed a visual semantic domain indicating emphases and foci that are important to evangelicals. To spare readers the tedium of the work that guided my thinking but ultimately did not integrate into my own map, I placed the information in Appendices A to E.

Mapping Evangelical Models

of Contextualization

CHAPTER OVERVIEW

Those who have mapped contextualization have developed their maps from theological or theoretical perspectives. Further, they include the entire spectrum of Christianity and tend to lump evangelical models into a single category. Such *deductive* approaches do have great value but are not helpful for my purposes. They do not attend exclusively to evangelicals and are not necessarily in touch with what evangelicals are doing. This leads me to conclude that an *inductive* map drawn from the living examples will be more helpful. Fortunately, evangelicals regularly write about what they do, and there are hundreds of examples in print. They include case studies, practices, methods, and models in almost every area of life.

In this chapter, I explain the means by which I develop the map I use. I introduce the process of selecting examples, choosing criteria to catalog them, and organizing the criteria into categories. From there, I describe five potential categories for the map and explain why I settled on the two that I use. I conclude the chapter with an overview of the resulting map for orientation prior to examining each category through the rest of the book.

CHAPTER OUTLINE

1. Categorizing Evangelical Contextual Examples
    a. Category 1: What the Examples Are
    b. Category 2: What the Examples Indicate about the Scope and Life-cycle Stages of the Church
    c. Category 3: What the Examples Indicate Is Being Addressed
    d. Category 4: What the Examples Indicate about the Methods of Contextualization
        i.   Linear Flow
        ii.   Dialogical Flow
        iii. Cyclical Flow
        iv.   Organic Flow
        v.   Unclear Flow
    e. Category 5: What the Examples Indicate about the Initiators of Contextualization
        i.   Guide
        ii.   Pathfinder
        iii. Herald
        iv.   Facilitator
        v.   Restorer
        vi.   Prophet
2. Categories for the Map Delineated: Initiator Roles and Flow of the Method

To identify evangelical contextual models and practices to put into a map is a challenging task. The "universe" of evangelical examples in my analysis comes from a combination of what I could find by a thorough search of publications, what I've done myself, and the things I've heard about or personally observed through travel or correspondence. Of course, any person's "list" will be incomplete, no matter how widely read or traveled or networked the person is. Enterprising missionaries who develop a new method or approach don't write about it unless it succeeds. Practitioners often are too busy doing the work to take the time to write about what they do; they are more concerned with implementing their ideas than writing about them. They may talk with colleagues, friends, and former professors about their work, but the discussions often go no further. Entrepreneurial practitioners who try things that are controversial, or those who work in areas where security is an issue, may try to ensure that what they are doing is not passed on to others. All of that is to say this: I recognize that the examples available to me, while many in number, are not even close to the complete picture.

In deciding what to include for analysis, I focused on examples available in print, primarily because the processes of writing and publishing increase the likelihood that it will be coherent. In total, I limited my analysis to 249 examples (see Appendix A for the complete list). Seventeen of them are not explicitly described by the initiators or promoters as contextual but were used on a multinational scale, such as Rick Warren's P.E.A.C.E. Plan (http://www.thepeaceplan.com), Evangicube (E3 Resources, www.e3resources.org.), Evangelism Explosion (Kennedy 1997; Ellenberger 1997), Truth Encounter (Anderson 1990), and Walk Thru the Bible (Dinkins 2000).

Finally, I needed some title to identify each example. I used names given by the initiators when possible. When such a name did not exist, I chose one that best described the example by using terminology found in the example itself.

Categorizing Evangelical Contextual Examples

I walked through several steps in developing the initiator role categories. For each example, I located enough published sources (both print and Web-based) to identify and explain it. I then culled the sources and developed an extensive annotation that summarizes the example (the annotations are roughly double the length of this book). As I added examples and examined each in detail, I began building a list of criteria that characterized the example. Ultimately, I used seventy-nine criteria for each example. Seventy-seven of the criteria are binary (True/False) indicating whether the example meets a certain qualification or not (e.g., Is it a *proposal*? Is it a *method*? Does it focus on contextual *theology*?). The final two criteria came from repeated patterns in the examples. In many cases, authors identified a specific issue or need (such as brokenness, development, health, marginalization, secularization, spiritual bondage, urban realities, and so on), so I included those when identifiable. I developed the other after observing that the initiators could not have accomplished their work without some characteristic or skill (character, competencies, faith, orientation, strategies, training), and I included them when it was clear or specifically identified as important for the initiators if they were to succeed.

As I continued to add examples and criteria, I began experimenting with various ways to group them in clusters that coalesced around a specific characteristic. By the end of the process, I had identified thirteen clusters, each a dimension of the example. For example, the *demeanor* for every example fit into one of four possibilities: analysis, advocacy, defense, or critique. Another cluster identified whether the *initiators* were insiders, outsiders, or both.

Finally, after many false starts, I grouped these thirteen clusters into five major categories:

1. What the example *is*
2. What the example indicates about the *scope* and *life-cycle stage of the church*
3. What the example indicates is *being addressed*
4. What the example indicates about the *method*
5. What the example indicates about the *initiator of contextualization*

Robert Schreiter observed (2002, vii) that contextualization always involves four significant realms or spheres: 1) the *contexts* where it happens; 2) the *addressees* or *recipients* of the process; 3) the *agents* who engage it; and 4) the *methods* those agents use. Table 7.1 indicates the correspondence of my categories to Schreiter's realms.

TABLE 7.1: SCHREITER'S REALMS AND CATEGORIES FROM 249 EVANGELICAL EXAMPLES	
Schreiter's Realms	**Evangelical Example Clusters**
	What the example *is*
The *addressees* or *recipients* of the process	What the example indicates about the *scope* and *life-cycle stage of the church*
The *contexts* where it happens	What the example indicates is the *area being addressed* for change or impact or attention
The *methods* the contextualizing agents use	What the example indicates about the *method*
The *agents* who engage it	What the example indicates about the *initiator of contextualization*

Category 1: What the Examples Are

Five of the clusters help identify the nature of each example. Table 7.2 identifies three of the clusters that I used to sort the examples and the percent of examples of each field: 1) what type of example it is; 2) what does the example offer; and 3) what is the demeanor of the example? Just over half of the examples offer proposals about contextual methods rather than case studies or reports.

TABLE 7.2: DIFFERENTIATING THE EXAMPLES					
What type of example is it?		What does the example offer?		What is the demeanor of the example?	
Proposal	52%	Method/Means	55%	Advocacy	82%
Case Study or Example	44%	Framework	23%	Analysis	16%
Report or Synopsis	4%	Guidelines	10%	Defense	1%
		Model	7%	Critique	1%
		Application	4%		

Given the activism of evangelicals, it is not surprising that more than half of the examples (55 percent) comprise a method or means of contextualizing, and about one-third (33 percent) incorporate either a particular conceptual framework or a set of guidelines for the relevant aspect of contextualization. It is also not surprising that most of the examples promote or advocate (82 percent) what they offer.

I was able to separate the examples into four categories (Table 7.3). Most attended to the activity in and of itself (47 percent)—fitting the activist orientation of evangelicals. The second most common area was how the contextualizer or method was to "lean into" contextualization (29 percent), by which I mean an underlying motivation or orientation that was driving how contextualization can or should be done. The remainder focused on either particular factors in the context that needed to be handled well (e.g,. religious sensitivity) (13 percent) or the primacy of the initiator (12 percent).

TABLE 7.3: FOCUS OF EXAMPLES					
To what does the example primarily attend?		On whom does the example primarily focus?	Exclusive	Named	Totals
Activity in-and-of itself	47%	Local Christian ad-dressees	45%	16%	61%
The "lean into" of example	29%	Cross-cultural worker	12%	29%	41%
Factors in the context	13%	Local non-Christian addressees	10%	5%	16%
Initiator	12%	Both local addressees	4%	8%	11%

Category 2: What the Examples Indicate about the Scope and Life-cycle Stages of the Church

Differences in the contexts and the people within each context can be significant. Throughout the examples in the dataset, as well as the broader literature, evangelicals use a variety of ways to separate one context (or set of addressees) from another. For example, there is significant rhetoric among evangelicals about people groups, by which we most typically mean ethnolinguistic groups (see, e.g., http://www.worldmap.org). In some contexts this is relatively simple to describe; in others it's far more difficult. For example, Ethnologue online (http://www.ethnologue.com/) identifies five living languages spoken in Swaziland but 719 living languages in Indonesia!

Evangelicals also categorize peoples by their religious adherence. We differentiate at the broadest level (e.g., Muslims from Buddhists), the middle level (e.g., Sunni from Shia Muslims), and the micro level (e.g., folk Muslim practices and beliefs associated with particular geographic locations or ethnolinguistic peoples). Evangelicals write articles (Gray and Gray 2009a; 2009b) and books (e.g., Moon 2009) discussing results of methods among differing ethnolinguistic, religious, and philosophical settings around the world.

Another way evangelicals separate contexts is by socio-economic and stability indicators. We differentiate wealthy locations from poor ones. We recognize that we need entirely different strategies in war-torn and unstable settings than in relatively stable and peaceful settings. As with ethnolinguistic and religious addressees, each of these contexts can lead to different contextual methodologies.

From the dataset, however, five other clusters help us distinguish the *contexts* from each other. The first two (Table 7.4) are 1) the *scope of the contextual effort* and 2) the *stage of the contextual life cycle of a local body of believers*.

TABLE 7.4: THE SCOPE AND LIFE-CYCLE STAGE OF THE CHURCH IN EVANGELICAL CONTEXTUALIZATION							
What is the scope of the contextual effort?	Exclusive	Named	Totals	What stage of the contextual church life cycle is included?	Exclusive	Named	Totals
Spiritual Outreach	33%	16%	49%	Initiation stage	28%	14%	42%
Social Outreach	3%	10%	12%	Gathering Stage	4%	14%	18%
Body life	18%	16%	33%	Development Stage	40%	16%	56%
Theological Development	18%	14%	32%	Expansion Stage	2%	11%	12%
Equipping for Service	4%	10%	14%	Frontiering Stage	5%	6%	12%

By *scope* I mean the focus of the example. Some examples focus exclusively on evangelism, others on social development or action, others on worship or spiritual life within the local body, others on theological development, and still others on equipping people within the body for service. In every example, it was easy to determine at least one appropriate focus, though many examples had more than one. In some cases, as many as five categories were indicated.

By *stage* I recognize that every church has a life cycle, ranging from a) initiation and b) gathering people together to c) developing them as a body to d) expanding that body and finally to e) moving across frontiers by engaging new peoples or areas. Once a church has reached this stage, the cycle starts over in the new areas. Every example had at least one stage in view.

Some of the examples, such as Communicating the Gospel in Terms of Shame (Boyle 1984; Francis 1992; Blincoe 2001), focus on a scope of spiritual outreach and are limited to the initiation in the church life-cycle. However, at the other end of the spectrum, the Pauline Church Planting Model (Hesselgrave 2000b) includes every scope as well as all five stages in the life-cycle of the church.

For each stage in both clusters I indicate what percentage of the 249 examples are exclusive in scope and stage as well as what percentage non-exclusively include the scopes and stages. The "Exclusive" column indicates the percentage of examples limited to that particular scope or stage. The "Named" column indicates examples that include more than one answer for the scope or stage. None of the columns adds up to 100 percent since the "Exclusive" column excludes examples in the "Named" column, but the "Named" and "Total" columns count every example at least twice. Since the scopes and stages are non-exclusive, the percentages do not add up to 100 percent, though each indicates the accurate percentage of the 249 examples.

For example, spiritual outreach was the exclusive scope in 33 percent of the examples, and another 16 percent of the examples included it as one area. Altogether, spiritual outreach was part of the scope in 49 percent of the examples. For the stages of the contextual life-cycle of a church, 56 percent of the examples included the development stage—40 percent exclusively and 16 percent as one of the stages.

Category 3: What the Examples Indicate Is Being Addressed

In developing the dataset it became clear that the initiators (and those who wrote about the examples) did not confine themselves to theology; they addressed almost everything the church does. Two clusters capture this. I developed one inductively from the information in the examples (location of spiritual change) and the other deductively from my own approach to contextualization (dimensions of religion; Moreau 2006a). The majority of the examples addressed more than one area of spiritual change or dimension of religion. As in Table 7.4, in Table 7.5 I list the percentage of the 249 examples that focused exclusively on one area of spiritual change or dimensions of religion (the "Exclusive" column) as well as the percentage of examples that named two or more spiritual changes or religious dimensions (the "Named" column). The total column sums these. I order the listing of the individual elements in each cluster by total frequency of occurrence within the examples.

TABLE 7.5: LOCATION OF SPIRITUAL CHANGE AND DIMENSIONS OF RELIGION							
Location of Spiritual Change	Exclusive	Named	Total	Dimension(s) of Religion	Exclusive	Named	Total
Evangelism	9%	27%	37%	Social: Learning	1%	57%	58%
Theology	12%	18%	31%	Propagation	0%	45%	45%
Spiritual Formation/ Spirituality	4%	22%	26%	Doctrinal	5%	32%	37%
Church Planting	3%	21%	24%	Social: Association	0%	34%	34%
Church Development/ Growth	1%	19%	20%	Social: Exchange	0%	29%	29%
Training/ Teaching/ Preaching	2%	18%	20%	Social: Regulating	1%	27%	28%

Worship/ Expressing Faith	3%	16%	19%	Ritual	0%	27%	27%
Leadership Development	1%	14%	14%	Social: Structure of local Christian body	0%	24%	24%
Development	4%	6%	10%	Ethical	0%	13%	13%
Pre-evangelism	0%	9%	9%	Artistic (Material)	0%	13%	13%
Translation/ Bible	2%	2%	4%	(Supernatural) Experience	0%	9%	10%
				Mythic	0%	5%	5%
				Social: Kinship	0%	2%	2%

Inductively, many of the examples specified a particular ministry or other area addressed in a contextual fashion. As I worked through the examples, I identified eleven distinct fields in all. Given the evangelical emphases on conversion and activism, it is not surprising that so many of the examples had some type of evangelistic component (37 percent). The emphasis on biblicism is reflected in the 31 percent of the examples with a theological component and confirmed in the highest number of examples with an exclusive focus on theology (12 percent). Some might be surprised to see that some form of spiritual formation or spirituality is present in 26 percent of the examples, but this is a reflection of the anticipation of personal transformation evangelicals have as a result of conversion.

Deductively, I used the dimensions of religion I originally adapted from Ninian Smart (1996) to explore contextualization (e.g., Moreau 2005; 2006a; 2007; 2008a). However, in working through the examples,

I came to realize that I needed to add two additional categories. The first relates to the structure of a local body of Christ. While it best fits the social dimension, the fact that I saw I needed to specify it indicated that my previous understanding of the social dimension needed modification. I also added "propagation" to the list, another dimension not included prior to developing the dataset.

That the social component of "learning" (not limited to formal education) was top of the list should not be surprising, given the central role learning plays in life. As with the spiritual change categories, and given the evangelical emphases on conversion and activism, it is not surprising that so many of the examples had propagation (45 percent) as a component. The emphasis on biblicism is indicated in that 37 percent of the examples fit in the doctrinal dimension, as well as having the more examples exclusively focused on doctrine (5 percent) than any other dimension.

Category 4: What the Examples Indicate about the *Methods of Contextualization*

In chapter 5 I discussed the ways evangelicals (and particularly American evangelicals) differed over how to understand mission, especially the relationship between evangelism and social responsibility. There were fewer disagreements over whether both are necessary components of *church ministry* than over whether both are necessary components of *mission*. While this difference has the potential to help us distinguish categories, the perspective in the examples was seldom clear. Further, in practice the boundaries are not always clear—nor should they be (e.g., Myers 1999; Corbett and Fikkert 2009). Evangelicals who viewed mission holistically (more than twenty years ago) are comfortable using a larger variety of contextual models than those who maintain that mission is limited to evangelism and church planting; but they are also comfortable with the same models as the latter. For example, all types of evangelical initiators are comfortable with critical contextualization approaches. Thus, while it does help us distinguish among evangelical views on mission, it does not help in categorizing the examples in the dataset.

However, two clusters do provide help in categorizing the methods evangelicals use in contextualization (Table 7.6), namely, 1) the philosophical orientation of the example, and 2) the methodological flow of the example.

TABLE 7.6: THE METHODS OF EVANGELICAL CONTEXTUALIZATION				
Philosophical Orientation			**Flow**	
Naïve Realism	10%		Linear	35%
Correspondence Critical Realism	56%		Dialogue	32%
Dynamic Critical Realism	27%		Cyclical	7%
Philosophy Unclear	7%		Organic	18%
			Unclear	8%

Regarding the philosophical or epistemological orientation, non-evangelicals often believe that evangelicals are uniform. However, apart from the distinguishing factors that define us (Table 2.1), that is not true. In relation to philosophical orientation, a large majority of evangelicals involved in contextualization would identify themselves as critical realists. The rest would identify themselves as realists or modernists, since instrumentalism falls outside the definition of evangelical. However, the vigor of debates over contextual methods, what boundary markers are appropriate for contextualization, and what demonstrates syncretism indicates major differences in perspectives.

In section 1 I referred several times to a divide among evangelicals that has potential as a categorization method, namely, the two approaches to critical realism (introduced in chapter 3; see especially Figure 3.1 and Table 3.1). Both perspectives are critical realist, yet representatives of both indicate separation from the other, and this sometimes generates heated discussion and debate. Most of the examples in the dataset did not indicate which perspective they drew from—in fact, it is clear that many did not have a particular perspective in view in relation to their efforts. The majority of the examples evidenced a correspondence critical realist orientation (56 percent), followed by those that evidenced dynamic critical realism (27 percent).

The second cluster of criteria that delineate categories is the direction or flow of the models (Table 7.6). From most of the examples in consideration, it is easy to discern how the method should proceed. Drawing on a more limited set of examples, elsewhere (Moreau 2008b; 2010), I described a map of evangelical models exclusively in light of their flow.

Linear Flow

Linear methods—seen in 37 percent of the examples—chart a single-direction mechanical path with a set number of steps as the process of contextualization. Proponents recognize that the task of contextualization is never-ending, though they usually do not expand on the recursive nature of the process. If they do, they envision each use of the process as discrete.

Evangelicals too frequently export linear methods that work in our home culture to a new location, expecting that they will work the same way there as they do here (e.g., see Gener 2005). Contextualized evangelism and discipleship models must take into account such issues as local understandings of sin (Priest 1994; Tsu-kung 1996; Strand 2000), repentance (Pesebre 2005), decision-making (Hesselgrave 1978; Gener 2005), and religious ritual (Zahniser 1997) lest we push people to convert to our culture rather than to come to faith in Christ. Note, for example, the three steps of Jason Borges method for contextualizing theology in a Muslim context:

> 1) investigating the apostles' contextualization of an event for a specific purpose, 2) realizing how cultural conditions of the West have shaped modern theology and 3) asking how biblical events can be interpreted to relevantly address the questions of the Muslim world. (Borges 2005, 463)

Dialogical Flow

Some 32 percent of the examples indicate a dialogical relationship between such things as text and context, or initiator and addressees. Advocates of dialogical approaches emphasize the nature of contextualization as a dialogue among culture, Bible, and contextualizer (see, e.g., Tano 1984, 94; Grenz 1993, 90; Whiteman 1997). Kim prefers "conversation" to dialogue because contextualization involves many partners from around the world, not just two (contextualizer and context) and because of the more technical meanings inherent in the term *dialogue* (Kim 2004, 48–49). The term *dialogue,* however, does not imply an equal partnership (nor a dialectical process). The Bible is the normative pole in this dialogue (Feinberg 1982, 7).

Cyclical Flow

The roughly 7 percent of the examples that are cyclical (or spiral) recognize that contextualization is not a one-time process and that it will never be complete. Building on insights of the hermeneutical circle (or spiral) developed by Juan Luis Segundo (1976) in his approach to liberation theology, these models envision an ever-tightening spiral that intertwines our experience of life, the text of Scripture, new ways to see Scripture in light of life experiences, and new approaches to experiencing life. More than the first two metacontextual models, these integrate action (whether socio-political or pastoral; Bautista, Garcia and Wan 1984, 177) and social analysis (Adeney 1995, 239) into the fabric of the contextualization process.

Organic Flow

The fourth type of flow blends all three of the previous categories without being constrained to any one of them. I call this an "organic" flow ("liquid" could also apply), and it is found in 18 percent of the examples. The flow for examples that build on a dynamic interplay among several systems or dimensions cannot be characterized as either one- or two-way, though some of the elements in the examples may incorporate one- or two-way flow within a single system or in the interplay of all of the systems. Organic models incorporate simultaneous flows in multiple directions. They may focus on orientations of contextualization rather than methods, such as the metaphoric pictures of contextualization as a living tree (Stephens 1999), a river we navigate (Nicholls 1995), or a drama in which we improvise (Gener 2004; Vanhoozer 2006).

Unclear Flow

With a more extensive set of examples to explore than in my prior map-making ventures, it became clear that I needed to add a designation for those examples in which the flow was unidentifiable or unclear. Several of these examples listed composite images (e.g., African Initiated Churches) that did not fit any single category. In sum, the examples with an unclear flow accounted for 8 percent of the total.

Category 5: What the Examples Indicate about the Initiators of Contextualization

Evangelicals also differentiate the initiators of contextualization in a variety of ways. In the literature, the divides include such things as how the initiators view the Bible, their understanding of truth, their theological orientation, church tradition, and their view of the context itself. While these are important and helpful, many of them do not show up clearly in the examples themselves or offer a helpful means of categorizing the examples.

However, drawing from the examples themselves, three clusters can be distinguished among the initiators: 1) whether the initiator is an insider or outsider; 2) any needs of the initiator specifically identified in the examples; and 3) the role the initiator took on in starting in the contextualization process. I list the specific criteria for each cluster in Table 7.7 in order of frequency.

In terms of the first cluster, identifying the initiator, and given the stereotypes of evangelical missionaries, it is somewhat surprising to see that 42 percent of the examples focused exclusively on initiators who are insiders in the local setting. When we add both insider and outsider initiators, we see that an insider takes an initiating role in 66 percent of the examples. This indicates that evangelicals want insiders to take a—if not *the*—primary role.

TABLE 7.7: THE INITIATORS OF CONTEXTUALIZATION					
Who is the initiator?		**What needs for the initiator are specified?**		**What is the initiator's role?**	
Emic	42%	Not Indicated	67%	Guide	36%
Etic	34%	Competencies	18%	Pathfinder	29%
Both	24%	Training	6%	Herald	13%

TABLE 7.7: THE INITIATORS OF CONTEXTUALIZATION				
Who is the initiator?	**What needs for the initiator are specified?**		**What is the initiator's role?**	
	Strategies	4%	Facilitator	10%
	Character	3%	Restorer	7%
	Orientation/Lean in	2%	Prophet	5%

The second distinguishing cluster is what authors of the examples identified as specific needs for the initiators. While the bulk of the examples did not indicate a specific need (67 percent), among those that did, the most frequently mentioned were particular competencies (e.g., orality, counseling, developmental skills, and so on) (18 percent), followed by specific training (6 percent). This cluster is not as helpful in developing our map, but it does show some of the priorities for initiators.

The third cluster in this category distinguishes the type of role the initiator plays in the example. There can be little doubt that the role of the initiator (whether insider or outsider) is crucial in the contextual process, and I was surprised to discover six readily distinguishable roles in the dataset: 1) guide, 2) pathfinder, 3) herald, 4) facilitator, 5) restorer, and 6) prophet. Because I use these categories as the primary taxonomy for building my map of evangelical models, I briefly describe each here and reserve the bulk of the discussion for the remaining chapters in the book. Table 7.8 offers a synopsis of the core ideas of each type of initiator.

Guide

A *guide* is an initiator who has a reasonably clear idea of the direction to follow and who leads others along the same or a similar path. There is room for creativity and flexibility, but the guide knows at least the general direction and has an understanding of how to get there. The guide is the most common initiator role in the dataset; the 90 examples account for 36 percent of the total.

Pathfinder

In contrast to a guide, a *pathfinder* is less interested in following the trail of others than in discovering a path, blazing a trail, or otherwise experimenting with new ways of making faith come alive in the local setting. Pathfinders tend to be more entrepreneurial than guides and are also more likely to make others feel uncomfortable by moving too fast or too far. The 72 pathfinder examples are 29 percent of the dataset.

Herald

The *herald* announces God's good news to an unbelieving audience with a primary focus on proclamation. The herald serves as a type of ambassador, faithfully proclaiming the message as an envoy of the King of kings. The best heralds are careful to contextualize how they communicate, but all heralds are concerned with being faithful to the message of the gospel. The 32 examples in which the initiator role is a herald comprise 13 percent of the total.

Facilitator

The *facilitator* enables or empowers local Christians to make good decisions in light of the particular challenges they face. The facilitator is more concerned with equipping Christians to discover their own methods and means than identifying them or pointing them out. The 26 examples in which the initiator role is a facilitator make up 10 percent of the total.

Restorer

The *restorer* comes as a healer to bring peace or deliver people from some type of bondage, whether social, psychological, environmental, systemic, or spiritual. This initiator brings people to a state of health in which they can begin living as Jesus calls all of us to live. The 17 restorer examples are 7 percent of the total.

Prophet

The *prophet* feels compelled to speak God's truth into a local setting. This may include social or cultural issues in the setting, but it also includes issues within the local body of Christ. The 12 prophet examples make up 5 percent of the dataset.

TABLE 7.8: INITIATOR ROLES FURTHER DELINEATED						
	Facilitator	**Guide**	**Herald**	**Pathfinder**	**Prophet**	**Restorer**
Synonyms	Advocate, change agent, coordinator, and servant	Adviser, aide, associate, attendant, consultant, mentor and tutor	Ambassador, announcer, messenger, and teacher	Adventurer, experimenter, explorer, pioneer, trailblazer and vanguard	Commentator, gadfly, inspector, irritant, judge, monitor, and social critic	Counselor, deliverer, healer, reconciler, therapist, warrior
Agent's Role	Empower the local body of Christ—especially the marginalized or oppressed—to stand for Christ in appropriate ways in their context	Help people find and stay on the path of appropriate Christian response to faith challenges in local settings	Proclaim God's good news for all people in every context	Discover new ways of introducing Christ and enable the church to be a vibrant witness in its context	Declare God's truths into a local setting	Be used of God to deliver people from spiritual bondage
Primary Verb(s)	Enable, empower	Guide, lead, show	Proclaim, announce	Discover, explore	Declare, pronounce	Heal, deliver, restore

197

	Facilitator	Guide	Herald	Pathfinder	Prophet	Restorer
TABLE 7.8: INITIATOR ROLES FURTHER DELINEATED						
When Jesus took on the role . . .	Matthew 10:1–42; Luke 24:49; John 20:22; Acts 1:8; 2:1–4	Mattjew 6:5–15; 9:35–38; Mark 13; Luke 8:9–15	Matthew 4:17; Luke 8:1; John 4:1–42; Matthew 28:19–20; Mark 16:15; Luke 24:47; John 20:21; Acts 1:8	Matthew 5:17–48; 19:16–26 Mark 2:15–17; Luke 10:25–37; John 4:27	Matthew 23; Mark 11:12-17; Luke 4:18–19; John 4: 1–24; Revelation 2–3	Matthew 9:18–38; Matthew 11:28–30; Mark 5:1–20; Luke 4:18–19
Biblical Examples	Ananias (Acts 9:10–19); Priscilla and Aquila (Acts 18:24–29); Barnabas (Acts 11:22–27)	Paul, Peter, Barnabas, and James (Acts 15:5–21); James (1:19–27)	Philip (Acts 8:12); Paul (Acts 14:7, 21, 25; 17:13; 18:5; 20:25; 28:31; and Rom. 10:14–15)	John the Baptist (Matt. 3:1–6); Philip (Acts 8:26–40); Peter (Acts 10:1– 11:18); Paul (1 Cor. 9:19–23)	John the Baptist (Matt. 3:7–12); Paul (Gal. 2:11–21); Peter (2 Peter 2); James (James 2:1–26)	Elisha (2 Kings 5:1–1); Isaiah (38:1–8); Disciples (Luke 10:17– 20); Peter (Acts 9:32–42); Paul (Acts 14:8–10; 16:16– 18)

Categories for the Map Delineated: Initiator Roles and Flow of the Method

I use the six initiator roles in the dataset for the primary categories in my map. I was able to derive the categories directly from the examples, so they provide a classification system that coheres with what evangelicals are actually doing. Additionally, and building on previous work (Moreau 2008b; 2010), within each initiator role I delineate the examples by the type of flow. Table 7.9 indicates the number of examples for each initiator role and flow of approach, showing the overall distribution of the examples within the map. In Appendix F, I list all 249 examples by flow within the respective categories.

TABLE 7.9: INITIATOR ROLE AND METHOD FLOW IN EXAMPLES							
	Guide	**Pathfinder**	**Herald**	**Facilitator**	**Restorer**	**Prophet**	**Totals**
Linear	31	18	20	6	9	4	88 (35%)
Dialogue	36	22	6	9	5	2	80 (32%)
Cyclical	10	3	2	1	0	2	18 (7%)
Organic	10	22	1	7	1	3	44 (18%)
Not Clear	3	7	3	3	2	1	19 (8%)
Totals	90 (36%)	72 (29%)	31 (13%)	26 (10%)	17 (7%)	12 (5%)	

Conclusion

I now have a data-derived set of categories to map evangelical contextualization. Using this rubric, I start our tour of the map by exploring each initiator role in turn.

KEYWORDS FOR REVIEW

Cyclical flow: envision an ever-tightening spiral that intertwines our experience of life, the text of Scripture, new ways to see Scripture in light of life experiences, and new approaches to experiencing life

Development stage of church life-cycle: having been gathered, the process of maturing and developing the new body for service

Dialogue flow: emphasize the nature of contextualization as a back-and-forth dialogue among culture, Bible, and contextualizer.

Expansion stage of church life-cycle: the process in which the maturing local body of believers is growing, whether by adding more to their group or by splitting off new groups that are also growing

Facilitator: initiator role of one who enables or empowers local Christians to make good decisions in light of the particular challenges they face

Flow of contextualization: course or direction of a contextual process; ranges from linear to dialogical to cyclical to organic

Frontiering stage of church life-cycle: when the more matured local body of believers begins sending people from their group to cross frontiers (cultural, linguistic, economic) to initiate outreach among people in the "frontier" setting

Gathering stage of church life-cycle: the process of bringing together those among whom outreach was successful into what they perceive to be a fellowship or body of believers

Guide: initiator role of one who has a reasonably clear idea of the direction to follow in contextualizing and who leads others along the same or a similar path

Herald: initiator role of one who announces God's good news to an unbelieving audience with a primary focus on proclamation.

Initiation stage of church life-cycle: the initial work of outreach, whether overtly evangelistic or not, that starts the process of planting a church

Initiator of contextualization: person or persons who instigate a contextual effort; may be insiders, outsiders or both.

Life-cycle stage of the church: all churches go through roughly five
  stages ranging from a) initial outreach efforts and b) gathering
  people together in a local body to c) developing those gathered
  as a body to d) that body expanding and e) moving across frontiers by engaging new peoples or areas

Linear flow: chart a single-direction mechanical path with a set
  number of steps as the process of contextualization

Organic flow: build on a dynamic interplay among several systems
  or dimensions that cannot be characterized as either one- or
  two-way, though some of the elements in the examples may
  incorporate one- or two-way flow with a single system or in the
  interplay of all of the systems

Pathfinder: initiator role of one who prefers to discover a path,
  blazing a trail, or otherwise experiment with new ways of
  making faith come alive in the local setting

Prophet: initiator role of one who is compelled to speak God's truth
  into a local setting

Restorer: initiator role of one who comes as a healer to bring peace
  or deliver people from some type of bondage, whether social,
  psychological, environmental, systemic, or spiritual

QUESTIONS FOR REFLECTION

1. What initiator role most appeals to you? Why?

2. What initiator role makes you most uncomfortable? Why?

3. The most common initiator role among the examples is the *guide*. What characteristics of evangelicals (Table 2.1) might help explain why this is so?

4. The least common initiator role among the examples is the *prophet*. What characteristics of evangelicals (Table 2.1) might help explain why this is so?

Initiator as Facilitator

CHAPTER OVERVIEW

In this chapter, I explain the initiator role of *facilitator*. I begin with a description of what a facilitator role includes. I then indicate people I see as exemplars of the role from the Bible as well as church life.

The best way to understand the role is to see it in some of the examples, so I describe in greater depth selected examples from the dataset—arranged by the flow of the method.

I conclude the chapter with a short summary of some of the major strengths and weaknesses of examples in which the initiator takes the role of a facilitator.

CHAPTER OUTLINE

1. What Is a Facilitator?
2. Facilitator Perspectives
3. Exemplar Facilitators
4. Facilitator Examples
   a. Facilitator Linear: Community Health Evangelism (Rowland 1985; 2001)
   b. Facilitator Dialogue: Middle East Theology (Meral 2005)
   c. Facilitator Cyclical: Church as Hermeneutical Community (Arrastia 1982)
   d. Facilitator Organic: Church Planting Movements (Garrison 2004a; 2004b; 2004c)
5. Evaluation of Initiators as Facilitators

A facilitator concentrates on enabling or empowering local Christians to make good decisions in light of the particular contextual issues they face. Synonymous terms for this role include advocate, change agent, coordinator, or servant. In 26 (or 10 percent) of the 249 examples, the initiator took the role of a facilitator.

What Is a Facilitator?

The facilitator's primary job is to *enable* others. Often the facilitator acts on the side of the marginalized or the oppressed in a setting, enabling them to bring Christ's truths to bear and break the holds their societies have over them. Facilitators focus their energy and efforts on equipping other Christians. One component of this is equipping them to discover methods that work for them in the local setting. Another is equipping them to put those methods into practice. There is joy in sustainability for the equipper, especially for those who are outsiders to the local setting.

Facilitator Perspectives

As noted in the introduction to this section, I identified certain statistical trends among the examples in which the initiators take on the role of a facilitator, which I enumerate in Table 8.1.

These trends help us understand patterns that we are likely to see in evangelical contextual efforts when the initiators act as facilitators. Being more organic in their approaches, facilitators may draw from their own faith traditions for answers to local questions and challenges but are not bound by them. Because they focus on the marginalized, they are aware of the brokenness of societies but also have hope that transformation is possible. Typically, facilitators engage in developmental types of ministry, but they are not limited to them.

The historical means by which facilitators enable people to overcome their circumstances can be helpful for facilitators, though they may not always take the time to be aware of them. They focus not only on enabling local Christians to overcome marginalization but also on equipping local people for service who can, in turn, facilitate important change.

TABLE 8.1: STATISTICAL TRENDS OF FACILITATOR EXAMPLES	
Examples with facilitators as initiators are disproportionately *more* likely to:	**Examples with facilitators as initiators are disproportionately *less* likely to:**
Flow organically. Base their approaches on correspondence critical realism. Have both emic and etic initiators in view. Include social outreach and equipping for service in the scope of their contextual efforts.	Base their approaches on naïve realism. Include the gathering stage of the contextual church life cycle.

Exemplar Facilitators

Keeping in mind that initiators can take on any of the roles in our map, we can expect to find biblical examples who served as facilitators.

Jesus played the role of facilitator in the lives of his disciples. For example, he gave them authority over demons, sent them out to minister (Matt. 10:1–42), and, ultimately, empowered them with the Holy Spirit (Luke 24:49; John 20:22; Acts 2:1–4) to be his witnesses (Acts 1:8).

Ananias equipped Paul for ministry shortly after Paul's conversion (Acts 9:10–19).

Priscilla and Aquilla are exemplar facilitators, as indicated when they quietly took Apollos aside to teach him more about Jesus so that he could minister more effectively (Acts 18:24–28).

Barnabas was a facilitator for the believers at Antioch, teaching them together with Paul for a year (Acts 11:22–27).

In our contemporary world, people such as Mulugeta Abebe (1996), Duane Elmer (2006), Ziya Meral (2005), Bryant Myers (1999), Rene Padilla (1982), and Stan Rowland (1985; 2001) have either promoted facilitator roles for contextualizers or sought themselves to facilitate better contextual praxis and thought.

Facilitator Examples

Table 8.2 lists the 26 examples in which the initiator plays a facilitator role arranged by the flow of contextualization in the example. In this section, I use four examples to illustrate the role of initiator as facilitator, selecting one from each type of flow.

TABLE 8.2: EXAMPLES OF INITIATOR AS FACILITATOR	
Linear: 6 (23%) examples	Community Health Evangelism (Rowland 1985; 2001) Contextualization as a Developmental Method (Musasiwa 1996; Abebe 1996; McCarty 1996; Tyler 1996) Contextualizing Development (Bradshaw 1993) Tentmaking (Blair 1983; Anonymous 1992; Parshall 1998b) Touching the Mystical Heart Evangelism (Peters 1989) Urban Leadership Contextual Development (Garriot 1996)
Dialogue: 9 (35%) examples	Contextual Doctoral Programs (Starcher 2006) Contextualized Mission Training Model (Lewis 1993) Indigenization as Incarnation (Gaqurae 1996) Middle East Theology (romantic, not linear; Meral 2005) Missiological Principles as Necessary Foundations for the Contextualization of Theology (Harling 2005) Patron-Client Indigenous Leadership (Chinchen 1995) Traditional Arts to Implement Theology (Kafton 1987) Vernacular Treasure (Hill 2006) Wider-Sense Biblical Theology (Padilla 1982)
Cyclical: 1 (7%) example	Church as Hermeneutical Community (Arrastia 1982)
Organic: 7 (27%) examples	Church Planting Movements (Garrison 2004a; 2004b; 2004c) Contextual "Church" Development (Richard 2003; 2004; 2007) Contextualizing Christian Leadership Development (Elliston, Hoke, and Voorhies 1989) Cross-cultural Servanthood (Elmer 2006) Social Development Transformation (Bradshaw 1993; 2002) Transformational Development (Myers 1999) Urban Church in Its Community (Algera 1994)
Not Clear: 3 (12%) examples	Case Studies in Holistic Ministry (Myers 1995; 1996) Cases in Holistic Mission (McAlpine 1995) Contextual Evangelism (Tooke 1993)

Facilitator Linear: **Community Health Evangelism (Rowland 1985; 2001)**

Stan Rowland began Community Health Evangelism (CHE) in the 1980s while on staff for Campus Crusade for Christ (CCC; now Cru) in Uganda. Coming from a health background, Rowland wanted to improve the integration of the evangelistic orientation of CCC with his passion for enabling communities to meet their own health needs through primary health care training.

Since that time CHE has been implemented on every continent of the world, keeping the enabling of worldview change as a central focus among those who volunteer and participate. The purpose of CHE is

> to transform individual lives physically, emotionally, socially and spiritually in local communities by meeting people at their point of need. These transformed individuals are then involved in transforming their neighbors, thereby transforming the community from the inside out. This is multiplied to other areas with the goal of assisting in the transformation of the country for Jesus Christ. (Rowland 2001)

The CHE website offers a cogent summary of the program and flow:

> CHE is initiated in a community by a two- or three-person CHE training team—dedicated Christians who speak the language of the community and live close enough to visit frequently. CHE trainers are generally supervised by a local organization—whether a church, an association, a denomination, a mission agency, or an NGO.
>
> As they start out in the community, they raise awareness of need and opportunity, and facilitate a process by which the community itself identifies solutions and begins to work together in an organized way. The community gains hope and vision, and a development process is catalyzed.
>
> The trainers assure that community leaders understand CHE as a way they can address their physical, social and spiritual needs themselves, not a program that offers them money. The key to CHE is the community's willingness to take responsibility for addressing its own problems.

Through a series of open meetings, the community decides whether or not to do CHE as a community. If the training team has done its initial work well, most communities decide to do CHE.

The community then selects people to serve as their local leadership committee, which is prepared for its work by the training team. Then the CHE program is officially launched by the community.

The leadership committee selects other community members to be trained as volunteer CHEs (chays)—community health educators/evangelists. The work of these dedicated volunteers is crucial to achieving results.

Through frequent trainings, the CHEs are equipped to implement health-improving steps in their own homes, and they learn how to pass along what they are learning in home visits with other families. The CHEs become health educators and personal evangelists to their community.

The combined influence of the training team, the leadership committee, and the volunteer CHEs creates a dynamic process of learning and change in the community. Physical and social health improves, projects are accomplished, and spiritual growth occurs as people come to faith in Christ. The community changes from the inside-out. (http://www.chenetwork.org/whatische.php)

CHE programs integrate health training (disease prevention, hygienic practices such as pit latrines, dietary development, agricultural practices), spiritual outreach training (evangelism and discipleship) and, when appropriate, literacy training. There are two levels of training. The first is training of trainers (TOT), which incorporates extensive material in organizing and promoting CHE at a variety of levels. The training for the workers is extensive, and it is built on lesson plans contextualized with oral populations in mind.

CHE focuses on enabling local people to 1) decide whether they want CHE, and 2) utilize local resources in a sustainable ways. While the initial trainers are outsiders, the local community chooses a committee to oversee the training of local workers and the workers themselves. CHE is outspoken in identifying initiators as facilitators, and the linear nature of the contextual process is seen in training methodologies that are at the heart.

Facilitator Dialogue: Middle East Theology (Meral 2005)

Ziya Meral (from Turkey) came to Christ from a Muslim background. In his 2005 *Evangelical Missions Quarterly* article, he intended to provide a signpost to point Middle East Christians in a new direction for developing theology. With all of the tumultuous changes taking place in the Middle East, Meral notes:

> The church in the Middle East will survive this new era only by developing a relevant theology which is capable of delivering the life changing power of the gospel. And if the gospel is to take root in the Middle East, it will only do so through a theology which speaks to the peoples of the region. (2005, 210)

Even though the Middle East is not a coherent whole without differentiations, Meral identifies six characteristics that he believes are of central concern in developing an appropriate Middle Eastern theology (212–14):

1. The greatest difference between a Middle Eastern theology and a Western theology will be its theologians.

2. A Middle Eastern theology will provide a comprehensive understanding of life.

3. Middle Eastern Christians will do theology in a manner very different from their counterparts in the West.

4. A Middle Eastern theology will seek to find and teach the implications of the cross for its own context.

5. A theology for the Middle East will be focused on the community of faith.

6. An adequate theology for the Middle East has to be concrete.

The first characteristic indicates Meral's desire that Middle Easterners are the ones theologizing for their own settings. Characteristics 2, 4,

5, and 6 focus on scope, content, and implications, or theology, that fits Middle Eastern sensibilities. Characteristic 3 attends to theological methodology, and Meral posits reasons Middle Easterners should do their theology differently than Westerners do:

> The Middle Eastern mind is not exclusively linear like the Western or cyclical like the Indian. Though it certainly includes aspects from both, the Middle Eastern mind is mainly romantic. Knowledge is not processed at the practical level but at the ideological or heart level. . . . Thus a Middle Eastern theology will be directed primarily at the heart. It will use poetry, heart-felt stories and spiritual reflections. Instead of being systematic, it will be a romantic theology written in the tradition of Confessions of St. Augustine. (2005, 213)

In Middle East Theology, Meral envisions the initiator as facilitator and anticipates that theology will flow from a dialogical interplay of heart and mind rather than a linear set of thought processes.

Facilitator Cyclical: Church as Hermeneutical Community (Arrastia 1982)

The driving thesis behind Cecilio Arrastía's experiment was that "A representative group in each local church should become a hermeneutical community, which participates in the work of reflection which should precede the pastor's weekly sermon" (Arrastia 1982). In light of this thesis, Arrastía used his Advanced Homiletics course at Puerto Rican Evangelical Seminary to experiment with a more contextual preaching methodology. In his own words,

> The experiment consisted in simply converting a whole class into a community of biblical reflection—a 'hermeneutical community'—in order to involve it in a process of reflection as an introduction to the preparation of sermons by each group member. The same biblical passage was assigned to several small groups, and the members of the groups were asked to "take on" the passages, noting any homiletic possibilities. This was the raw material—a "homiletical dough"— which once baked, would produce a sermon. Each pupil had to keep

in mind his own context, against the background of his own culture and dedication to his studies. (1982, 18)

To do this he intended to combine the content and the process of developing a sermon into a single unit. Noting that the church already had various groups to plan Christian education, evangelism, stewardship, and so on, he wondered, "Why not think of the possibility of people who—embodying the anxieties and aspirations of distinct ages, sexes, cultural formation and secular work—might help the pastor in his work of planning and producing Sunday sermons?" (19)

The core idea involved three phases. In the first, the pastor develops a group comprised of church people who will "meet with the pastor and, reading together from various versions of the Bible passages which would serve as a base for future sermons, react, reflect and discuss the implications of the Word for their own particular contexts" (21).

In the second phase, the pastor studies the text with all the biblical tools available, develops a sermon, and then delivers it in light of the interaction with the group.

For the third phase the group recycles to the sermon, meeting with the pastor and explaining what they thought they heard and what it meant to them. As Arrastía explains it,

> The cold corpse of the homiletical piece is laid on the dissecting table and the pastor will listen to the group as they discern the divisions of his sermon, "reading" what the pastor has said. It will be like a measuring instrument that prepares God's prophet to evaluate his capacity to communicate—not only with charity but with clarity—the message of reconciliation that he has received from God for the people. (22)

There are several immediate contextual issues in the Hispanic setting that Arrastía hopes this method will overcome, especially an unprepared, extemporaneous approach to preaching that is not necessarily in tune with the congregation's needs. Further, the sermon becomes a joint product rather than simply the pastor's job, and those who are part of the "hermeneutical group" see the sermon in a completely new light, finding their thinking and lives reflected in the message. Ultimately, they are empowered to think more biblically in their own lives by hearing their thoughts filtered through the Bible in the sermon. The pastor, then, is the facilitator, and the means of his empowerment is a cyclical interaction of text and context every week from the pulpit.

Facilitator Organic: Church Planting Movements (Garrison 2004a; 2004b; 2004c)

Initially, cross-cultural workers *discovered* church planting movements rather than intentionally developed them (Garrison 1999). David Garrison has been a strong advocate for church planting movements, which he defines as, "rapid multiplication of indigenous churches planting churches that sweeps through a people group or population segment" (Garrison 2004a, 21).

Church planting movements are typically comprised of house or cell churches that grow along natural social webs. To qualify for the label, the growth of the movement has to be so rapid that there is not enough time for building church structures. This ensures that the movements are decentralized, requires the rapid development of local leadership, and—in sensitive locations—makes it easier to stay under the public radar when having a public presence would result in persecution.

Since the discovery of such movements in multiple locations around the world, practitioners have strategized how to develop such movements (Register 2000; Payne 2003; Ponraj and Sah 2003; D. Brown 2004; Garrison 2004b; 2004c; Lewis 2004; Zdero 2004; 2005; Cantrell 2006; Jamison 2007; Naja 2007)—as well as how not to hinder them (Garrison 2004d). The role of the outsiders, in particular, is to facilitate and nurture such movements by ensuring the development of indigenous leadership—and propagation styles—from the earliest stages.

Evaluation of Initiators as Facilitators

Evangelical examples that envision the contextualizers as facilitators offer helpful ways to encourage not only contextual thinking and action but also empowerment in ways that enable their continuation after the facilitators move on.

In the initiator role the focus is not on the facilitator but on the development of indigenous resources and empowerment of people—especially those in need. Facilitators view the addressees not as empty slates or as passive recipients, but as people who bring energy and commitment to their God-given tasks. They anticipate that local leaders will want to lead, and they find helpful ways to ensure that this happens.

At the same time, however, we note potential *weaknesses* when initiators take a facilitative role. First, the facilitator may be tempted to *determine* what the insider needs, rather than learn from the insiders themselves. Facilitators may also use manipulative techniques to ensure their own ideology is facilitated (essentially serving as spiritual puppet-masters), especially when the addressees do not grow or develop in ways the facilitator envisions they should. Finally, facilitators may also be tempted to empower people in ways that require external resources or support, which can result in dependence if not handled appropriately.

KEYWORDS FOR REVIEW

Community Health Evangelism: contextual example integrating evangelism with primary health care training that enables communities to meet their own health needs

Middle East theology: theology that flows from a dialogical interplay of heart and mind rather than a linear set of thought processes

Church as hermeneutical community: Proposal that a representative group in each local church should become a hermeneutical community participating in reflection which precedes and grounds the pastor's weekly sermon. *Church planting movements*: a "rapid multiplication of indigenous churches planting churches that sweeps through a people group or population segment" (Garrison 2004a, 21)

QUESTIONS FOR REFLECTION

1. What characteristics of the *facilitating* initiator are most attractive to you personally?

2. What characteristics of the *facilitating* initiator are least attractive to you personally?

3. What would characterize the types of settings in which the *facilitator* may be the best approach for an initiator?

4. What would characterize the settings in which the *facilitator* may not be a good approach for an initiator?

FOR FURTHER STUDY

Arrastia, Cecilio. 1982. "The Church: A Hermeneutical Community." *Occasional Essays* 9.2 (December): 18–25.

Garrison, David. 2004a. *Church Planting Movements: How God Is Redeeming a Lost World*. Bangalore, India: WIGTake.

_____. 2004b. "Church Planting Movements vs. Insider Movements: Missiological Realities vs Mythological Speculations." *International Journal of Frontier Missions* 21.4 (October–December): 151–54.

_____. 2004c. Church Planting Movements: The Next Wave?" *International Journal of Frontier Missions* 21.3 (July–September): 118–21.

Meral, Ziya. 2005. "Toward a Relevant Theology for the Middle East." *Evangelical Missions Quarterly* 41.2 (April): 210–15.

Rowland, Stan. 1985. "Training Local Villagers to Provide Health Care." *Evangelical Missions Quarterly* 21.1 (January): 44–50.

———. 2001. "What Is Community Health Evangelism?" *Medical Ambassadors International* Online: http://www.strategicnetwork. org/index.php?loc=kb&view=v&id=4179, accessed 3 November 2009.

Initiator as Guide

CHAPTER OVERVIEW

In this chapter I explain the initiator role of *guide*. I begin with a description of what a guide role includes before describing tendencies seen in analysis of guides compared with the other initiator roles. I then indicate people I see as exemplars of the guide role from the Bible as well as church life.

The best way to understand the role is to see it in some of the examples. I describe in greater depth selected examples in which the initiator is a guide—arranged by the flow of the method. Finally, I conclude the chapter with a short summary of the major strengths and weaknesses of models in which the initiator takes the role of a guide.

CHAPTER OUTLINE

1. What Is a Guide?
2. Guide Perspectives
3. Exemplar Guides
4. Guide Examples
   a. Guide Linear: Critical Contextualization (Hiebert 1984; 1987)
   b. Guide Dialogue: Contextualized Hymnody (Molyneux 1990; Krabill 1990)
   c. Guide Cyclical: Metaphoric: Theodrama (Vanhoozer 2006)
   d. Guide Organic: Comprehensive Critical (Moreau 2005; 2006a; 2007; 2008a)
5. Evaluation of Initiators as Guides

What Is a Guide?

A guide is an initiator who has a clear sense of direction in contextualization and perceives his or her function as guiding, directing, or leading others in that direction. At times guides may need to show those they guide just where the path is or what direction they need to go, but more often their task is to guide with creativity and flexibility. Alternate terms that describe this type of initiator include adviser, aide, associate, attendant, consultant, mentor, and tutor. In sum, the primary job of the guide is to steer or direct people along a path known to the guide. The most common initiator role is the guide, found in 90 (or 36 percent) of the 249 examples.

Guide Perspectives

Per the discussion in the introduction to this section, I derived characteristics for the examples from the database in which the initiators take on the role of a guide (Table 9.1) from statistical comparisons among the examples.

TABLE 9.1: STATISTICAL TRENDS OF GUIDE EXAMPLES	
Examples with guides as initiators are disproportionately *more* likely to:	**Examples with guides as initiators are disproportionately *less* likely to:**
Flow dialogically or cyclically.	Flow organically.
Be a proposal for a contextual method (rather than an existing method).	Be a case study of a contextual method (rather than a proposal).
Attend to the activity in and of itself.	Include spiritual outreach or social outreach in the scope of their efforts.
Include theological development in their scope and anticipate it will be the area of spiritual change.	Include evangelism as the location of spiritual change.
Focus on the development and equipping for service stages in the church life cycle.	Include the initiation or gathering stages of the church life cycle.
Base their approaches on correspondence critical realism.	Base their approaches on naïve realism.
	Focus on non-Christian addressees in the local setting.

These trends help us understand patterns that we are likely to see in evangelical contextual efforts when the initiators act as guides. The metaphor of an initiator as a "guide" assumes that the guide knows the path or direction to follow, so it makes sense that the examples are proportionately less disposed toward an organic flow (for which guiding is considerably more difficult) and more toward dialogue or cyclical flows. Similarly, it makes sense that the examples with initiators as guides are disproportionately disposed to correspondence critical realism; guides operate on the assumption that there are appropriate paths, even if the guides do not yet know them in their entirety.

It also is logical that those with stronger theological constraints are more likely to serve as guides than as pathfinders; that guides disproportionately focus on theological development fits this pattern. While guides may be *open* to theological change, they likely consider such changes only after careful study and reflection. After all, the paths they know have worked well for them and for the generations that preceded them. Thus, they are more likely to resist change to the established pathways for contextual identity and framing.

Exemplar Guides

Paul took on a guide role in leading Gentiles to recognize they were full participants in the body of Christ (Gal. 2). He—together with Peter, Barnabas, and James—convinced the rest of the apostles that this was God's plan (Acts 15:5–21). Jesus played the role of guide to his followers many times in his ministry. He taught them how to pray (Matt. 6:5–15) and what to pray for (Matt. 9:35–38), explained the parables more clearly to them than to the crowds (Luke 8:9–15), and told them how to react in the trials to come (Mark 13).

In our contemporary world people such as Paul Hiebert (1994; 2008), Emilio Antonio Nuñez (1985), Kwame Bediako (1998a; 2004), Hwa Yung (1997; 2004a), and Ziya Meral (2006) have operated as guides to help the church more clearly think and act contextually.

Guide Examples

Table 9.2 shows a sample of the ninety examples in which the initiator was a guide arranged by the flow of contextualization. In this section, I illustrate the role of initiator as guide using four examples, selecting one from each type of flow.

TABLE 9.2: EXAMPLES WITH INITIATORS AS GUIDES	
Linear: 31 examples (34% of total)	Contextual Ethical Guidelines for Church Planters (Payne 2010) Contextualized Youth Ministry (Livermore 2001) Contextualizing Theological Curriculum (Imasogie 1983) Critical contextualization (Hiebert 1984) Culture and Biblical Hermeneutics (Larkin 1988) Eight Phase Church Planting (Scoggins; http://www.dickscoggins.com) Indigenous Art (Jordan and Tucker 2002) Meditation Center (Bali Dhyana Pura) (Mastra 1978) Nehemiah Model of Cultural Revitalization (Tollefson 1987) Rite of Passage Discipling (Courson 1998) Theological Workshops (Gration 1984)

Dialogue: 36 examples (40% of total)	Aspects of Iman Theology for Islamic Settings (Marantika 1995) Community Life Evangelism (Vincent 1992) Contextual Christology (Padilla 1986) Contextual Discipling through Symbols and Ceremonies (Rituals) (Zahniser 1991; 1997) Contextualized Hymnody (Molyneux 1990; Krabill 1990) Dream Interpretation Evangelism (Musk 1988; Scott 2008) Holistic Discipleship (Meral 2006) Local Village Theology (Hoefer 1981) May Puritix: Praying into Smoke (Brooks 2000) Open Field Contextual Theology (Athyal 1980; 1995) Parabolic Preaching (Goldsmith 1980) Relational Centers (Nicholls 1979a; 1984, 256–61) ROPES (Karianjahi—Tanari Trust) Spiritual Journey Evangelism (W. T. Kim 2005; Richardson 2006)
Cyclical: 10 examples (11% of total)	Contextualizing to an Urban Cultural System (Hall 1983) Hermeneutical Circle (Padilla 1979b; 1981; Bautista, Garcia and Wan 1984, 177) Metaphoric: Theo-drama (Vanhoozer 2006) New Song Fellowships (King 2006) Theological Advisory Groups (Gehman 1983; 1987; 1996)
Organic: 10 examples (11% of total)	Comprehensive Critical (Moreau 2005; 2006a; 2007; 2008a) Finding Jesus in Dharma (Bharati 2001) Javanese Church Model (Dixon 2002) Jesus Hall (Reitz 2006) Metaphoric: Tree (Stephens 1999) Scripture-Infused Arts (Schrag 2007)
Not Clear: 3 examples (3% of total)	Contextualization of Urban Theological Education (Jackson 1993) House Church as Missiological Model (Birkey 1991)

Guide Linear: Critical Contextualization (Hiebert 1984; 1987)

Paul Hiebert's *critical contextualization* is perhaps the most widely used evangelical model for contextualization in academic settings (Whiteman 2006, 57; see also Chang et al. 2009). Critical contextualization involves a four-step linear process.

The first step is the *exegesis of the culture* (or particular presenting issue). This may come through a crisis in the church over a particular practice or belief in the culture or as a question addressed to or by the local church. It is important that analysis of the cultural issue or question be done phenomenologically. The central ideology of a phenomenological approach is the suspending of any evaluation (whether the issue is right or wrong or the belief is true or false) until the issue or belief is truly understood on its own terms. It involves gathering and analyzing all the traditional beliefs and customs associated with the question at hand without making prior judgments about their truth or their value. Hiebert offers an example:

> [I]n asking how Christians should bury their dead, the people begin by analyzing their traditional rites: first by describing each song, dance, recitation, and rite that makes up their old ceremony; and then by discussing its meaning and function within the overall ritual. The purpose here is to understand the old ways, not to judge them. (1987, 109)

In the second step, a leader or group of leaders guides the community in *exegesis of the Scriptures* related to the issue being examined. These leaders—whether indigenous or expatriate—must have a "metacultural framework that enables him or her to translate the biblical message into the cognitive, affective, and evaluative dimensions of another culture" (Hiebert 1987, 109). At times the Scriptures are quite clear even on particular practices found in other cultures (e.g., infanticide). More often, various types of scriptural evidence will be needed since the question at hand is not directly addressed in the Bible or not addressed as clearly as some would prefer (e.g., what should a polygamous convert do?). The goal in this step is not to find a single passage or teaching as a type of "magic bullet" that completely answers the question, though that may occur. Rather, it is to look at the whole of biblical evidence to uncover God's attitude toward the practice or question at hand. Hiebert notes:

> This step is crucial, for if the people do not clearly grasp the biblical message as originally intended, they will have a distorted view of the gospel. This is where the pastor or missionary, along with theology, anthropology, and linguistics, has the most to offer in an understanding of biblical truth and in making it known in other cultures. While the people must be involved in the study of Scripture so that they grow in their own abilities to discern truth, the leader must have the metacultural grids that enable him or her to move between

cultures. Without this, biblical meanings will often be forced to fit the local cultural categories. (1987, 109–10)

The third step is a *community-wide critical evaluation of cultural practice in light of Scripture* together with a decision on how to respond. It is crucial that the people themselves are engaged in the decision-making process:

> Moreover, it is not enough that the leaders be convinced about changes that may be needed. Leaders may share their personal convictions and point out the consequences of various decisions, but they must allow the people to make the final decision in evaluating their past customs. If the leaders make the decisions, they must enforce these decisions. In the end, the people themselves will enforce decisions arrived at corporately, and there will be little likelihood that the customs they reject will go underground.
>
> To involve the people in evaluating their own culture in the light of new truth draws upon their strength. They know their old culture better than the missionary, and are in a better position to critique it, once they have biblical instruction. Moreover, to involve them is to help them to grow spiritually by teaching them discernment and by helping them to learn to apply scriptural teachings to their own lives. It also puts into practice the priesthood of believers within a hermeneutical community. (1987, 110)

In this step, Hiebert identifies three possible responses: the community may 1) keep old ways which are not unbiblical, 2) reject old ways which are unbiblical, or 3) modify the old ways to make them biblically acceptable. There are four options to modify the old ways: 1) Keep the form of the old ways but give new meanings to them (e.g., the Christmas tree), 2) Substitute new symbols/rites to replace old ones (e.g., building a church where an idol was worshipped), 3) Adopt new rites drawn from Christian heritage (e.g., worshipping together on Sundays), or 4) Develop new symbols or rituals—whether from their own culture or another—that feel and look indigenous to them (e.g., a Christian ashram [Ralston 1987] or a messianic synagogue [Goble 1974; Spielberg and Daurmann 1997]).

The fourth and final step is for *the community to arrange any new practices into a contextualized ritual* that expresses the Christian meaning of the event. This (when appropriate) enables a transformation through attaching new meanings to indigenous forms:

> Having led the people to analyze their old customs in the light of biblical teaching, the pastor or missionary must help them to arrange the practices they have chosen into a new ritual that expresses the Christian meaning of the event. Such a ritual will be Christian, for it explicitly seeks to express biblical teaching. It will also be contextual, for the church has created it, using forms the people understand within their own culture. (Hiebert 1987, 110)

While the overall process is linear, some of the individual steps are dialogic. Additionally, Hiebert notes that critical contextualization is "an ongoing process in which the church must constantly engage itself" (1987, 111), indicating that these four steps are to be repeated as necessary.

Guide Dialogue: Contextualized Hymnody (Molyneux 1990; Krabill 1990)

> "The vast majority of Christians actually put their faith into words when they sing hymns."
>
> —(Felde 1989, 18)

Music plays an integral role in every worship function of churches around the world. In some cases, contextual hymnody has developed in ways that were unattached to Western initiators. The *Eglise de Jésus-Christ sur terre par le Prophète Simon Kimbangu* [Church of Jesus Christ on Earth through the Prophet Simon Kimbangu; EJCSK], the largest of the African Initiated Churches, grew from only five months of ministry by Simon Kimbangu in 1921.[1]

---

1. Interested readers can find details of the fascinating story of the EJCSK in numerous places (e.g., Bertsche 1966; Martin 1976; 1978; Ndofunso 1978; Nguapitshi 2005; Thomas 1977).

While most do not consider the EJCSK to be evangelical (see, e.g., Nguapitshi 2005), the ways contextual hymnody was developed and integrated into the life of the church have been examined by evangelical missiologists as a means of better understanding the contextual process in Africa as a whole.

Over the course of almost four decades of underground operation, indigenously composed hymns nurtured and sustained the Kimbanguist movement. After gaining legal status in Zaire in 1960, the EJCSK developed a committee whose responsibility was to evaluate every new hymn and determine whether to incorporate it into the official EJCSK corpus.

At the time Gordon Molyneux studied their contextual methodology, 565 hymns had been recognized (Molyneux 1990; 1993). Typical characteristics of Kimbanguist hymns include repetition, antiphony, allusive rather than direct lyrics, an inspirational focus rather than a rational one, and usability by the community rather than solos.

The evaluators of the hymns serve as guides in the contextual process. The composer performs the hymn in front of them, and they use three criteria in a dialogical evaluative process to make their decision. First, the evaluators must be convinced that the hymn was given by God through revelation. Further, it must be pleasing to their sense of musical taste. Finally, it must be honoring to God. As an overarching consideration, the evaluators look for signs of pride or an improper sense of accomplishment in the person to whom God revealed the hymn. Impropriety in this regard can lead to the rejection of a hymn.

Guide Cyclical: Metaphoric: Theodrama (Vanhoozer 2006)

Theologizing may be called "theodramatic" in that it concerns both God and his relation to the world as well as God's speech and action, especially as they culminate in the person and work of Jesus.

It involves what Kevin Vanhoozer calls the "canon principle," namely, "the Spirit speaking in Scripture about what God was/is doing is the supreme rule for Christian faith, life and understanding" (Vanhoozer 2006, 109). The canon principle has three subprinciples: 1) the *contextual* principle (the people of God engage Scripture in and from their particular locations); 2) the *critical* principle (the Bible can be interpreted in ways that address situational injustice); and 3) the *cultural* principle (we can forge theology out of indigenous materials).

God is a missionary God. The history of humanity is essentially a drama in which God engages in his missionary purposes among humankind. This is not a "religious" drama per se, but a drama in which God pursues relationships with humanity in spite of our brokenness out of his compassion for us—a *theo*drama because it is God who shapes the narrative in his missionary pursuit. Therefore, "the whole theodrama is essentially missional, consisting in a series of historical entrances and exoduses (e.g., incarnation, crucifixion, resurrection, ascension, Pentecost)" (110). Following this reasoning, we can describe theology as "faith seeking theodramatic understanding" (109), and "All other truths must be engrafted into and encompassed by the drama of Jesus Christ" (110).

Guide Organic: Comprehensive Critical (Moreau 2005; 2006a; 2007; 2008a)

Over the decades, many have noted that contextualization is more than theology—it involves everything the church does. At the 1928 Jerusalem meeting of the International Missionary Council, *indigenization* (the precursor to contextualization) involved not only theology but also worship, service, art, and architecture (see Robert 2002, 58). Rolv Olsen, for example, defines contextualization as "A way of Christian theological thinking and practice, where the gospel, its message and spirit, the church, its tradition and life, and the people, its culture and living conditions, are examined and reinterpreted" (2002, 104).

Contextualization must incorporate such things as preaching, music, discipleship, leadership selection and development, architecture, educational processes, conflict resolution, economic activities, sources of authority and maintaining discipline and order, rituals, ethical obligations, poetry, symbols, art, witness, and so on (see, e.g., Smalley 1958, 55; Kraft 1973b, 117; Taber 1979a, 144; Yego 1980; 154; Ro 1984, 67; Tano 1984, 94; Sumithra 1984, 225; Hesselgrave 1995a, 115; Tiénou 1992, 262; Escobar 2002, 19-20; Talman 2004, 11). I have explored this approach more systematically (Moreau 2005; 2006a) using Ninian Smart's seven dimensions of religion (1996), namely, the 1) social, 2) mythical, 3) ethical, 4) artistic (or material), 5) ritual, 6) experiential, and 7) doctrinal (or theological). In organic fashion, comprehensive contextualization poses the types of questions for each of the seven dimensions listed in Table 9.3.

TABLE 9.3 QUESTIONS TO ASK OF THE SCRIPTURES AND THE SETTING(SOURCE: MOREAU 2006A, 329)		
Questions for the Scriptures	**Questions for the Setting**	
	Cultural Bridges	**Social Change**
Starting Questions What has God revealed about the Christian faith that is essential to be incarnated or indigenized in each religious dimension of this culture? What does the Bible affirm in each religious dimension, and what does it condemn?	How has God already been revealing himself in and through the various religious dimensions of the setting? What bridges for contextualization are present in each dimension? How can they be best used to make the whole of our faith indigenous in the setting?	What areas within the religious dimensions of the setting are in need of social change? Who and where are the oppressed and marginalized? How might the gospel enable them to live Kingdom-centered lives in each of the religious dimensions in the midst of oppression?

Evaluation of Initiators as Guides

Evangelical models that envision the contextualizers acting as guides frame their role as steering people along a path. They do not force people to take a path but come alongside them and either help them find it or help them stay on it once they start out. Given that orientation, what are strengths and weaknesses of contextual models in which the initiators have a primary role of guiding?

An important strength of this initiator role is that the initiator does not force the contextual action. Rather, she or he is available to assist those following the path. Further, the guide is free to give his or her energy only to that part of the path on which the addressee currently travels rather than the entire path. This enables other guides to assist on parts of the path where their strengths can be helpful.

A weakness of the initiator as guide, perhaps more than the facilitator, is that they may succumb to the temptation to determine not only the path but also the *only* way to travel the path. They may also use manipulative techniques to ensure that those on the path see it as the best or true path. When they do this, they operate as enforcers rather than guides. This is more likely to happen when the addressees do not grow or develop in ways the guide envisions they should.

KEYWORDS FOR REVIEW

Comprehensive critical contextualization: using the critical contextualization process and organically working through seven dimensions of faith, namely, the 1) social, 2) mythical, 3) ethical, 4) artistic (or material), 5) ritual, 6) experiential, and 7) doctrinal (or theological)

Contextualized hymnody: composing and performing hymns and songs to inculcate the Christian faith into the life of a community

Critical contextualization: framed in correspondence critical realism, a four-step contextualization process involving 1) phenomenological exegesis of culture, 2) exegesis of relevant Scripture, 3) community-wide critical evaluation of cultural practice in light of Scripture, and 4) arranging any new practices into a contextualized ritual response

Theodrama: history as a God-directed and God-constrained drama in which God engages in the missional pursuit of all humanity; those who follow Christ improvise as we act out his love for others

QUESTIONS FOR REFLECTION

1. What characteristics of the *guiding* initiator are most attractive to you personally?

2. What characteristics of the *guiding* initiator are least attractive to you personally?

3. What would characterize the types of settings in which the *guide* may be the best approach for an initiator?

4. What would characterize the types of settings in which the *guide* may not be a good approach for an initiator?

FOR FURTHER STUDY

Hiebert, Paul. 1987. "Critical Contextualization." *International Bulletin of Missionary Research* 11: 104–11.

Krabill, James R. 1990. "Dida Harrist Hymnody (1913–1990)." *Journal of Religion in Africa* 20.2 (June): 118–52.

Molyneux, K. Gordon, 1990. "The Place and Function of Hymns in the EJCSK" (*Eglise de Jésus-Christ sur terre par le Prophète Simon Kimbangu*). *Journal of Religion in Africa* 20.2 (June): 153–87.

_____. 1993. *African Christian Theology: The Quest for Selfhood.* San Francisco: Mellen Research University Press.

Moreau, A. Scott. 2006. "Contextualization That Is Comprehensive." *Missiology* 34.3 (July): 325–35.

Vanhoozer, Kevin J. 2006. "'One Rule to Rule Them All?' Theological Method in an Era of World Christianity." In *Globalizing Theology: Belief and Practice in an Era of World Christianity*, ed. Craig Ott and Harold Netland, 85–126. Grand Rapids: Baker.

Initiator as Herald

Chapter Overview

In this chapter I explain the initiator role of *herald*. I begin with a description of what a herald role includes before describing tendencies seen in analysis of heralds compared with the other initiator roles. I then indicate people I see as exemplars of the herald role from the Bible as well as church life.

The best way to understand the role is to see it in some of the examples. I describe in greater depth selected examples in which the initiator is a herald—arranged by the flow of the method. I conclude the chapter with a short summary of the major strengths and weaknesses of models in which the initiator takes the role of a herald.

CHAPTER OUTLINE

1. Initiator as Herald
2. What Is a Herald?
3. Herald Perspectives
4. Exemplar Heralds
5. Herald Examples
    a. Herald Linear: Caudillo-Type Pastors (Thornton 1984)
    b. Herald Dialogical: Spirit-First Approach to Muslim Evangelism (Steinhaus 2000)
    c. Herald Cyclical: Pauline Church Planting Model (Hesselgrave 2000b)
    d. Herald Organic: Cultural Chameleon (Poston 2000; Hale 2007)
6. Evaluation of Initiators as Heralds

What Is a Herald?

A herald proclaims or announces the good news to an unbeliev-ing audience. Heralds serve as ambassadors of Christ; they focus on faithfully proclaiming the gospel message as envoys of the King of kings. The best heralds are careful to contextualize the way they com-municate. Alternate terms for this initiator role include ambassador, announcer, messenger, and teacher. In sum, the primary job of the herald is to announce the good news to people in spiritual need. In 32 (or 13 percent) of the 249 examples, the initiator took on the role of a herald.

Herald Perspectives

As previously noted, I identified certain statistical trends among the examples in which the initiators take on the role of a herald, listed in Table 10.1. Such characteristics help us understand patterns that we are likely to see in evangelical contextual efforts in which the initiator is a herald.

TABLE 10.1: STATISTICAL TRENDS OF HERALD EXAMPLES	
Examples with heralds as initiators are disproportionately *more* likely to:	**Examples with heralds as initiators are disproportionately *less* likely to:**
Flow linearly.	Flow organically.
Engage in evangelism and spiritual outreach and attend to non-Christian addressees.	Focus on emic initiators.
Attend to the stage of initiation in the church life cycle.	Base their approaches on dynamic critical realism.
Base their approaches on naïve real-ism.	Attend to the developmental stage in the church life cycle.
	Include either theological develop-ment or social outreach in their scope.

It is no surprise that heralds tend to be linear, for heralds most typically communicate the gospel message as a linear message. Likewise, this fits with their tendency toward a philosophy of naïve realism and relative aversion to dynamic critical realism. It is also makes sense that they tend to focus their ministry efforts on propagation and less on theological development or social outreach. Together, these tendencies indicate two of the herald's assumptions: 1) a "pure gospel" that is propositional in nature and 2) a view of local contexts as fallen and generally irredeemable.

Exemplar Heralds

Many biblical examples fit the herald role. Jesus exemplified this role after his baptism when he began to proclaim the good news (Matt. 4:17), when he traveled with his disciples preaching (Luke 8:1), and, perhaps most poignantly, in preaching to the Samaritan woman and the people from her town (John 4:1–42). The various versions of his postresurrection commission to the disciples to go and proclaim repentance and forgiveness of sins to the ends of the earth (Matt. 28:19–20; Mark 16:15; Luke 24:47; John 20:21; Acts 1:8) have motivated Christians over the centuries.

When Philip preached the gospel in Samaria (Acts 8:12), and when Paul proclaimed Christ to the Gentiles on Mars Hill (Acts 17:18–31) they did so as heralds. Throughout Paul's missionary journeys, Luke notes his preaching ministry (e.g., Acts 14:7, 21, 25; 17:13; 18:5; 20:25; 28:31). Paul's oft-quoted statement in Romans indicates the motivation behind heralds:

> How, then, can they call on the one they have not believed in? And how can they believe in the one of whom they have not heard? And how can they hear without someone preaching to them? And how can they preach unless they are sent? As it is written, "How beautiful are the feet of those who bring good news!" (Rom. 10:14–15)

Contemporaries such as Billy Graham (Turpie and Graham 2000), John Sung (Moreau 1995d), Festo Kivengere (1977), Luis Palau (1994), and Ajith Fernando (2002) have clearly and consistently proclaimed Christ in locations around the globe—though using different means and working to fit the message to the needs of the audience.

Herald Examples

Table 10.2 lists the 32 examples in which the initiator plays a herald role arranged by the flow of contextualization in the example. In this section, I illustrate the role of initiator as herald using four examples, selecting one from each type of flow.

TABLE 10.2: EXAMPLES WITH INITIATOR AS HERALD	
Linear: *20 (63%)* *examples*	Apostolic Accommodation (Hesselgrave 1979; Hesselgrave and Rommen 1989) Back to Jerusalem (Hattaway 2003) Become Like Muslims to Present the Gospel (Terry 1996) Case Studies as a Means of Contextualizing the Message (Fritz 1995) Caudillo-Type Pastors (Thornton 1984) Christian Folk Songs (Baskaran 1989) Chronological Bible Storying (McIlwain 1987; Steffen 1995; Terry 1997; Lovejoy *et al* 2001) Communicating the Gospel in Terms of Shame (Boyle 1984; Francis 1992; Blincoe 2001) Contextual Christian Worship (Tarus 1996) Contextual Ethics (Eitel 1987) Contextual Preaching (Flemming 2002; Fukuda 2001) Contextualized Apologetics (Netland 1988) Evangicube (E3 Resources, www.e3resources.org.) Four Laws for Chinese (Francis 1992) Jesus Film (Eshleman 1985; 2002; Steffen 1993) P.E.A.C.E. Plan (www.thepeaceplan.com) Picture Four Spiritual Laws (Africa; Campus Crusade for Christ) Possessio (Beyerhaus 1975) Public Debate Evangelism (Smith 1998)
Dialogue: *6 (19%) examples*	Biblically oriented Theology Relevant to Asian Needs (Ro 1978) Bruchko (Olson 1978) Dialogue with Bible as Normal Pole (Feinberg 1982) New Christian Apologetic (Larson 1996) Soularium Cards (Young 2008) Spirit-First Approach to Muslim Evangelism (Steinhaus 2000)

Cyclical: *2 (6%) examples*	Disciple a Whole Nation (Montgomery and McGavran 1980; Montgomery 1984; DAWN Ministries) Pauline Church Planting Model (Hesselgrave 2000b)
Organic: *1 (3%) example*	Cultural Chameleon (Poston 2000; Hale 2007)
Not Clear: *3 (9%) examples*	Blended Muslim Evangelism Model (Terry 1996; 1998) Christian Bhajans (Minz 1996; Hale 2001) Contextualization in the Local Church (Ramirez 1978)

Herald Linear: Caudillo-Type Pastors (Thornton 1984)

Based on observations and research among pastoral types in Bogota and Medellin (Colombia), Philip Thornton recognized a type of pastoral role in the local setting that attended to needs in ways that fit cultural expectations. Thornton observed that growing churches in these two cities

> were being led by what I have come to call a "spiritual *caudillo*" (*caudillo* being the word used to describe a very strong leader). As I studied these men, who represented various theological persuasions ranging from Pentecostalism to Calvinism, I noted that all of them seemed particularly effective in their pulpit ministries. (1984, 235)

Thornton noted that one of the reasons the caudillo pastors are successful is the development of a core group of congregants who anchored their ministry, and, "While not neglecting the ministry to the larger group, the more successful pastors demanded, and indeed received, a great deal of loyalty from this select group" (236).

Outsiders may see this type of leader as a dictator, but it fits an accepted cultural pattern of the socio-economic class among which most Protestants minister. Especially important from Thornton's perspective is that the congregations under these caudillo-type leaders *wanted* them to be strong leaders (236–37).

Given the strong leadership types found in the society, Thornton differentiates between closed and open systems (238). In the former, the positions of power are few, and rising to the top of the hierarchy is impossible for people who are not connected or skilled politically. As a result, younger natural leaders have to go outside the system to advance (238–39).

An advantage within Protestantism as opposed to Catholicism is that Protestants have more options in terms of planting churches or starting new ministries. This allows strong leaders to grow and find a place within the culture. Congregants serving under such leaders consider their strong leadership to be healthy.

One consequence is that new organizations constantly split off from established ones. On one hand, such splitting opens doors to new, younger leaders who need to get out from under those who stifle their initiative. On the other hand, this churning can be detrimental to Christian witness.

Thornton advises missionaries and agencies to plant churches that harmonize with local leadership norms and values:

> While not automatically setting aside doctrinal heritage with regard to church structure, missionaries need to be open to adaptation when it comes to structure, so that the church they plant is in harmony as much as possible with other cultural institutions. This is a must for obtaining and keeping good leaders. (241)

His final conclusions aptly summarize his perspective on *caudillo*-type pastors:

> I would suggest that some of our present problems in finding and keeping good leaders in our churches in urban Latin America might be lessened, if not eliminated, if we kept in mind the following:
> 1. Leadership, including church leadership, must be culturally appropriate in style and characteristics.
> 2. Any strategy that places missionaries in key positions of leadership and later seeks to transfer that leadership to national hands is not one that will attract strong, natural leaders—at least not in present-day, urban Latin America.
> 3. Leadership must be in line with the target audience at the point of social status.

4. It is possible to structure against church growth by structuring against the attraction of and multiplication of natural leaders. In other words, if the ecclesiastical structure in question does not offer a sufficient number of culturally appropriate leadership positions, those potential leaders in that structure will simply find another group that affords them greater freedom. (241)

Herald Dialogical: Spirit-First Approach to Muslim Evangelism (Steinhaus 2000)

A concern that has been part of evangelism among Muslim populations is initial resistance to starting discussion regarding the Trinity, the deity of Christ, or Christ's work on the cross; healthy discussion is cut off before it can even begin. S. P. Steinhaus, who at the time of the article had been ministering among Muslims in Southeast Asia for a decade, framed an approach that starts with discussion of the Holy Spirit instead:

Simply put, my approach is to focus initial discussion on the Holy Spirit thereby initially postponing discussion of the person of Jesus. By first discussing the Holy Spirit, I am able to get a hearing for the gospel and to reveal the source for meeting personal needs without being immediately rebuffed by standard Muslim objections. Many times Muslims ask us, "What is your religion?" When we simply answer "Christian," often the conversation is over. Instead of directly answering that question, I now tell them that what matters most is if we have the Spirit of God living in us, and he is the power source for us to live a life that is pleasing to God. (23)

This low-key dialogical evangelistic approach enables the initiator to avoid ending conversations prematurely.

As I begin to discuss the Spirit, often interlaced with stories from my own walk with God and appropriate scriptures, Muslims become interested. Since I am not immediately discussing Jesus, they seem to be caught off-guard and don't feel that I am promoting "another god". I believe this approach works because Muslims have very little knowledge about the third person of the Trinity and therefore have not yet developed a standard polemic against this teaching. While we certainly cannot avoid the stumbling block of the cross, by focusing discussion on the other members of the Trinity (the Holy Spirit and the Father) we can help Muslims see the benefits of the Cross before we ever discuss it. (23)

Steinhaus indicates that initially focusing on the Spirit meets several needs among Muslims. First, Muslims (as with all people) have a strong felt need for peace that the Spirit grants. Second, the Spirit provides power to deal with the spirit realm, another strongly felt need for many Muslims. He also empowers people to live holy lives that are pleasing to God. He notes,

Several times while talking about the Spirit with a Muslim I've been interrupted with this wonderful question, "Yes, but how does a person receive the Spirit".

Depending on the person and the circumstances, I may or may not immediately answer the question. But if I decide to go on, it is time to mention the fact that the Holy Spirit of God is just that—holy—and therefore he will never enter an unclean vessel. Usually Muslims are quick to admit that they are far from perfect and that they, and all men everywhere, are unclean and therefore distanced from God. (24)

Once a person makes an initial decision to accept God's Spirit, the period of testing and trials begins. Stein is careful to note that the particular battles going on behind the scenes in the person's life may be opaque to the evangelist, but the evangelist's role is to continue the conversation and nurture faith. In his conclusion, he notes:

Rather than comparing religions, we are interested in discussing the question whether a person can be acceptable to God if he doesn't have God's Spirit? This is the foundation on which we help people to begin thinking "outside the box" of religions and by so doing be open to the need of meeting and knowing Jesus. In other words, this is a way to move people towards Jesus, rather than trying to totally describe the work of Christ on the cross at the initial stages of discussion. (28)

Herald Cyclical: Pauline Church Planting Model (Hesselgrave 2000b)

David Hesselgrave identified ten steps in Paul's church planting cycle as seen in Acts. As shown in Figure 10.1 and summarized in Table 10.3, the Pauline Church Planting Model starts by commissioning missionaries, cycles through the ten steps, and then restarts with the commissioning of new missionaries from the churches that had been planted in the first cycle.

According to Hesselgrave, while this church planting method has a beginning and an end, it is cyclical and continues until the Lord returns. It is a process in which the planter can proceed step by step as well as work on all steps simultaneously. This can apply to a church in any stage of existence as well as to pioneer situations (2000b, 49–51).

TABLE 10.3: OBJECTIVES FOR EACH PHASE IN THE PAULINE CHURCH PLANTING CYCLE	
Phase	**Basic Intention of the Phase**
1: Missionaries Commissioned	Having fostered the kind of missionary spirit that encourages all in the church to participate in the God-given task of planting churches in adjacent and more distant unreached communities, believers are mobilized and sent.
2: Audience Contacted	The missionaries gain the understanding and good will of the local citizens in order to reach them and invite them into the church fellowship.
3: Gospel Communicated	Missionaries mobilize, train, and deploy local believers in appropriate methods of evangelism in the target area that are clear, convincing, and compelling.

4: Hearers Converted	People come to Christ out of true understanding and in ways that take into account culturally appropriate patterns of decision making to ensure that their response to the gospel will be genuine and lasting and result in spiritual fruitfulness.
5: Believers Congregated	Missionaries and local believers establish times and places for the assembling of believers into local fellowships that will be in line with Christian practice and local customs in ways that are spiritually meaningful and helpful.
6: Faith Confirmed	Believers in local congregations worship in ways that are uplifting and God honoring. They are discipled so they know what they believe and how they should live, learn to live as citizens of God's kingdom, learn how to communicate their faith to others, and practice faithful stewardship in accordance with the resources God has given them.
7: Leadership Consecrated	Local leaders emerge who are gifted and spiritually qualified for leadership in the local church. They will eventually establish a permanent organization of the church that is scriptural, functional, effective, and expandable.
8: Believers Commended	Pioneer(s) work through the process of withdrawing from the established congregation at the best possible time (as soon as practicable) in an orderly fashion.
9: Relationships Continued	Missionaries continue a relationship with the planted church which is spiritually stimulating and mutually rewarding. They also help to ensure that local churches are linked to each other and to the larger body of Christ.
10: Sending Churches Convened	The churches, now established in their own right, gather with other churches and begin developing and implementing means by which they themselves engage in missionary efforts across cultural and other boundaries.

A great strength of this approach is that it comes from biblical sources. However, since it is a composite drawn from all of Paul's church planting efforts, it should not be mistaken for an actual strategy that Paul had in mind as he traveled on his missionary journeys. This method has been taught to and used by numerous church planting missionaries since the first edition of the book was published in 1980.

Herald Organic: Cultural Chameleon (Poston 2000; Hale 2007)

Larry Poston, professor of religion at Nyack College, observes that Paul's remarks to Corinthians believers about becoming all things to all people (1 Cor. 9) have formed the foundation for many contemporary missionaries and missiologists as they develop contextual approaches. However, a crucial distinction in Poston's model is the view that Paul focuses on contextualizing himself as a messenger rather than contextualizing "a message, a theology, an ethical system, or a church structure" (463), and adds:

> He appears never to have engaged people in a discussion of an abstract system of ideas, a set of theological constructs, a moral standard, or a series of religious rituals. He sought instead to attract others to a personal model; a living example that could be observed and copied at street level. (463)

Poston points out three primary components of Paul's contextual practice: 1) adapting to a specific cultural context by immersion; 2) adapting one's manner of thinking, speaking, and acting to a specific context; and 3) demonstrating to one's audience what a Christ-centered life would look like in their cultural context. Ultimately,

> In Paul's form of contextualization, a fully immersed person will himself be contextualized, and thus his thoughts, speech, and actions will automatically be contextualized. Just as when someone learns a new language he eventually finds himself choosing the right word or phrase automatically, when someone has immersed himself into and adapted his lifestyle to a specific cultural context, he will begin

to know what the appropriate thought, word, or action will be for a Christian in any specific situation. (464)

Poston argues that, in the New Covenant era, God's people do not have a specific cultural or social model for understanding or attempting to develop the kingdom of God. This, he rightly notes, gives us freedom. At the same time, it also constrains us to focus on transforming individuals rather than social structures, and we do this best by following Paul in contextualizing ourselves as messengers. In his own words:

> Members of the church who are reaching across cultural barriers must accommodate themselves to the political, economic, judicial, linguistic, and social structures of the people around them. This is not to say that they will necessarily approve of these structures. They may seek to introduce change at individual and local levels, although they should never succumb to the belief that they are in some physical sense "building the kingdom of heaven." Christians must seek to enter society at the "basic level of humanity"—the level of family, neighbor, work, marketplace, and local community relationships. (468)

However, Poston argues forcefully that our accommodation in new cultural and social settings is not infinitely flexible, noting restrictions on religious accommodation:

> But they may not accommodate themselves to competing religious structures, and they may not adopt general cultural practices either absolutely (in accordance with the Bible) or relatively (in accordance with a specific culture) immoral.

Having taken on the lifestyle, traits, and manner of life of those around them, contextual missionaries are free within those constraints to focus on basic issues and dialogue over other issues:

> The gospel may then be preached in its simplest form ("Christ crucified and resurrected"), and issues of theology, ethics, and the like may be worked out in a cooperative effort of dialogue. (468)

Poston's focus on a contextualized messenger, based on his observations of Paul's approaches, enables the herald to clearly communicate a basic message in no small measure by adapting to a lifestyle fully commensurate to the political, economic, judicial, linguistic, and social structures of the people where he or she ministers. Thus, this is an organic approach, with multiple linear, dialogical, and cyclical components anchored to a core message.

Evaluation of Initiators as Heralds

Evangelical models that envision the contextualizers acting as heralds proclaiming the good news among those who are not believers focus on keeping the primary concerns of the Christian faith in the center of their ministries.

A strength of this initiator role is that heralds can communicate fearlessly in settings where such proclamation can be dangerous. They also work to ensure that the message itself remains constant, including the brokenness of all people, their need for redemption, and the universal relevance of the death of Christ as the only way to meet this need.

At the same time, however, it is important to note potential *weaknesses* seen when initiators are heralds. The greatest danger is that the herald can be so focused on the content of the message that issues of contextualization may be cast aside as irrelevant. After all, the herald may reason, the *message* never changes, so apart from translating it properly, there is no real need to contextualize. As a result, outsider heralds may impose a type of standardization on local heralds to enforce conformity to the message as initially delivered, ignoring issues such as how thought processes and cultural values affect the reception of messages and their meanings.

KEYWORDS FOR REVIEW

Caudillo-type pastors: very strong leadership style of pastoral role that fits idealizations of what a local leader should be in some cultural settings

Cultural chameleon: contextualizing ourselves using principles from Paul's practices, including 1) adapting to a specific cultural context by immersion; 2) adapting one's manner of thinking, speaking, and acting to a specific context; and 3) demonstrating to one's audience what a Christ-centered life would look like in their cultural context

Pauline Church Planting Model: Ten-step cyclical model of church planting derived from Paul's methodology as seen in Acts

Spirit-first approach to Muslim evangelism: in Muslim evangelism, focusing initial discussion on the need for having the Spirit of God living in us as the power source to live a life that is pleasing to God rather than discussing the person of Jesus

QUESTIONS FOR REFLECTION

1. What characteristics of the *heralding* initiator are most attractive to you personally?

2. What characteristics of the *heralding* initiator are least attractive to you personally?

3. What would characterize the types of settings in which the *herald* may be the best approach for an initiator?

4. What would characterize the types of settings in which the *herald* may not be a good initiator?

FOR FURTHER STUDY

Hale, Chris. 2007. "Aradhna: From Comfort to Discomfort, from Church to Temple." *International Journal of Frontier Missions* 24.3 (Fall): 147–50.

Hesselgrave, David J. 2000. *Planting Churches Cross-Culturally: North America and Beyond.* 2nd ed. Grand Rapids: Baker.

Poston, Larry. 2000. "Cultural Chameleon: Contextualization from a Pauline Perspective." *Evangelical Missions Quarterly* 36.4 (October): 460–69.

Steinhaus, S. P. 2000. "The Spirit-First Approach to Muslim Evangelism." *International Journal of Frontier Missions* 17.4 (October): 23–30.

Thornton, W. Philip. 1984. "The Cultural Key to Developing Strong Leaders." *Evangelical Missions Quarterly* 20.3 (July): 234–41.

Initiator as Pathfinder

CHAPTER OVERVIEW

In this chapter I explain the initiator role of *pathfinder*. I begin with a description of what a pathfinder role includes before describing tendencies seen in analysis of pathfinders compared with the other initiator roles. I then indicate people I see as exemplars of the pathfinder role from the Bible as well as church life.

The best way to understand the role is to see it in some of the examples. I describe in greater depth selected examples in which the initiator is a pathfinder—arranged by the flow of the method. Finally, I conclude the chapter with a short summary of the major strengths and weaknesses of models in which the initiator takes the role of a pathfinder.

CHAPTER OUTLINE

1. Initiator as Pathfinder
2. What Is a Pathfinder?
3. Pathfinder Perspectives
4. Exemplar Pathfinders
5. Pathfinder Examples
   a. Pathfinder Linear: Camel Evangelism Method (Greeson 2004)
   b. Pathfinder Dialogue: Alternative Participation in a Parallel Cultural Event (Ritual) (Perry 1990)
   c. Pathfinder Cyclical: Dynamic-equivalence "Churchness" (Kraft 1979c; 1980; 2005c)
   d. Pathfinder Organic: Locally Initiated Churches (Aikman 2003; Anderson 2000; Pew Forum 2006; Zdero 2004)
6. Evaluation of Initiators as Pathfinders

What Is a Pathfinder?

A pathfinder draws energy from discovering a new path or blazing a trail. An entrepreneurial bent undergirds the desire to experiment with new ways of introducing Christ or enabling the church to be a vibrant witness in the local setting. Alternate terms for this initiator role include adventurer, experimenter, explorer, pioneer, trailblazer, and vanguard. In sum, the primary job of the pathfinder is to discover new methods that more effectively communicate the gospel than current methods. The pathfinder is the second most common initiator role among the 249 examples, found in 72 (or 29 percent) of them.

Pathfinder Perspectives

In Table 11.1, I list characteristics of the examples in which the initiators take on the role of a pathfinder. These characteristics indicate perspectives that pathfinders bring to their contextual work.

TABLE 11.1: STATISTICAL TRENDS OF PATHFINDER EXAMPLES	
Examples with pathfinders as initiators are disproportionately *more* likely to:	**Examples with pathfinders as initiators are disproportionately *less* likely to:**
Flow organically.	Follow a cyclical flow.
Be a case study or example.	Attend to the contextual activity in and of itself.
Attend to the way the example "leans into" contextualization.	Have social outreach, theological development, or equipping for service as the scope of the contextual effort.
Have spiritual outreach or evangelism as the scope of the effort and gathering as the stage in the church life cycle.	Focus on theology as the location of spiritual change.
Base their approaches on dynamic critical realism.	Base their approaches on either correspondence critical realism or naïve realism.
Have an emic initiator.	Attend to the developmental stage in the church life cycle.

Pathfinders attend primarily to outreach and gathering people into local fellowships in ways that fit local sensibilities, and their entrepreneurial bent lends toward an organic flow. They hold their own faith traditions more lightly than other models and are willing to experiment in a variety of directions. They are less concerned about the actual methods than about the ways initiators are oriented toward (or lean into) contextualizing. Methods are largely neutral—generating new and better methods is a natural result of an orientation toward flexibility and experimentation.

The dynamic critical realist orientation of the pathfinder lends pathfinders to a more neutral view of the context. As a result, pathfinders are more likely than the other types of initiators to use local non-Christian religious forms in creative ways to enable greater impact for Christ. This is also reflected in pathfinders being less focused on theology than other types of initiators. Creative energy for spiritual outreach and less emphasis on theology can result in a corresponding lack of concern over avoiding heresy or syncretism. Pathfinders may be more willing to explore options skirting syncretism because they anticipate that certain methods have the potential to draw people to Christ more effectively.

Exemplar Pathfinders

At times Jesus took on the role of pathfinder. When he took old teachings and stretched them into new covenant ideals (Matt. 5:17–48) he shook the old order. He astonished his disciples by talking with the Samaritan woman (John 4:27) and told parables that were shocking to his audiences (the Good Samaritan, Luke 10:25–37). He ate with sinners (Mark 2:15–17) and denied the inherent blessings of the rich (Matt. 19:16–26).

John the Baptist played both pathfinder (Matt. 3:1–6) and prophet roles (Matt. 3:7–12). When Philip followed the leading of the Spirit to meet the Ethiopian eunuch (Acts 8:26–40) he acted as a pathfinder. Peter's willingness to obey God's vision and go to Cornelius's house (Acts 10:1–11:18) can be seen as a pathfinder type of role, though God was the one who directed Peter to go against Peter's instincts. In this case we also see the challenge given to Peter by the leaders in Jerusalem to defend his actions (Acts 11:1–18), an experience pathfinders go through more often than those who take on other initiator roles. The ultimate expression that resonates with pathfinders is Paul's willingness to become all things to all people in order to win some (1 Cor. 9:19–23).

Contemporary evangelicals such as Herbert Hoefer (2001a), Charles Kraft (1979e; 1995), Wayan Mastra (1978; 1984), Bruce Olson (1978), and Sundar Singh (Moreau 1995c) have lived out pathfinder roles. Over the past several decades pathfinders have commonly advocated new approaches to contextual faith (e.g., Kraft 2005a), and especially evangelism among Muslims (e.g., Parshall 1980; 2003; Woodberry 2008), Hindus (e.g., Hoefer 2001a; 2005), and Buddhists (Lim, Spaulding, and De Neui 2005; De Neui 2008).

Pathfinder Examples

Table 11.2 shows a selection of the 72 examples in which the initiator was a pathfinder. In this section, I illustrate the role of initiator as pathfinder using four examples, selecting one from each type of flow.

TABLE 11.2: EXAMPLES WITH INITIATOR AS PATHFINDER	
Linear: 18 (25%) examples	Camel Evangelism Method (Greeson 2004) Comprehensive (Talman 2004) Evangelistic Sacrifices (Nussbaum 1984) House Masjid for New Creation Muslims (Goble & Munayer 1989) Issaan Development Foundation (DeNeui 1993; Gustafson 1998) Theology of Power (Dye 1984a; 1984b) Underground Jamaats (Churches in Muslim Settings) (Massey 1996) Yoido Full Gospel Church Cell Groups (Cho 1984; Adams 1991; Hong 2000; Hwa 2004b)
Dialogue: 22 (31%) examples	Alternative Participation in a Parallel Cultural Event (Ritual) (Perry 1990) Best Practices Training for Contextual Church Planting (Downey 2008) Contextualized Christian Social Transformation (Elliston 1989) Contextualized Comics (Chen 1992) Hindu Satsang ("Gathering of Truth," Stevens 2007) Integrated Holistic Development (Gustafson 1991; 1998) Muslim-Culture Church Model (Brislin 1996) Re-Contextualization Church Renewal (Marchak 1989) Redeeming the Arts (Harbinson *et al* 2005) Sharia as a Contextual Bridge (Greer 2008) Using Case Studies to Understand/Evaluate Contextual Ministries (Travis 2000)
Cyclical: 3 (4%) examples	Dynamic-equivalence "Churchness" (Kraft 1979c; 1980; 2005c)
Organic: 22 (31%) examples	Christian Ashrams (Taylor 1979; Ralston 1987) Churchless Christianity (Hoefer 2001a; Richard 2002) Gatherings (Francis Chan's house-type churches; Brandon 2009) Grounded Contextualization (Vanden Berg 2009) Insider Movements (Garrison 2004b; Travis & Travis 2005b; Higgins 2006; Brown 2007a) Locally Initiated Churches (Aikman 2003; Anderson 2000; Pew Forum 2006; Zdero 2004) Movements to Christ within Natural Communities (2007a) New Friars (Bessenecker 2006) Theology in Song (Balisky 1997) Yeshu-Bhakta Movement (Stevens 2007; Hoefer 2007; Peterson 2007a)
Not Clear: 7 (10%) examples	Indian Instituted Churches (Hedlund 1999) Out-of-Step Evangelists (Conn 1990)

Pathfinder Linear: CAMEL Evangelism Method (Greeson 2004)[1]

Christians from Muslim backgrounds originally developed the CAMEL

---

1. Drawn from Moreau 2010 with minor editing modifications.

method to reach Muslims for Christ. It incorporates evangelism and church planting. The *evangelism* component of the CAMEL method uses three steps with a focus on finding a person of peace. The intention is to start with the Quran, which Muslims know, and then to the Bible, which they do not know. The first step is to arouse curiosity, perhaps through a comment such as "I have discovered an amazing truth in the Koran that gives hope of eternal life in heaven. Would you like to read Surah Al-Imram 3:42–55 so we can talk about it?" (Greeson 2004, 56–57). Another way to arouse curiosity is to introduce an old Muslim cultural tradition which maintains that there are 100 names of God rather than the 99 that all Muslims know. According to this tradition, only the camel knows the one hundredth name, and the camel is not talking! Thus, while the evangelist is free to choose among methods, arousing curiosity is the first step.

For those who want to learn about hope of eternal life or who are curious about the one hundredth name of God, the second step is to identify whether the listener is a "person of peace" who is interested in exploring the implications of the ideas presented. To do this, the initiator uses Surah Al-Imram 3:42–55 to demonstrate that Jesus is more than a "Prophet"—he is in reality 'Isa Masi (Jesus the Messiah). At this point CAMEL becomes an acronym for the key points from the passage:

- Mary was Chosen to give birth to 'Isa (Jesus);

- Angels announced the good news to her;

- 'Isa would do Miracles;

- He is the way to Eternal Life.

The primary focus in evangelism is to enable Muslims to see how the Koran teaches that 'Isa is holy, has power over death, and knows the way to heaven (Greeson 2004, 58–60).

If the reaction of the person demonstrates that he or she is a person of peace, the third step is to bridge to the Bible for an explanation of Christ and give the person of peace an opportunity to respond. Reaching this opportunity can take weeks, months, or even longer.

The initiator trains those who come to Christ in evangelism and sends them to witness to family members while also incorporating them into a fellowship of like-minded believers. In the original movement which developed the method, believers referred to themselves as Isahi Muslims ("followers of Jesus" Muslims), which was seen as appropriate within their culture and aroused further curiosity among their families, leading to opportunities for witness (Greeson 2004, 11).

As the new believers begin to look for other persons of peace (starting with their own family members) and the gospel spreads along extended family lines, a church planting movement develops. This movement stays separate from the known local "Christian" community—and from their stigma as "Christians" (in many Muslim settings, "Christians" are equivalent to "Westerners"—and viewed as immoral and secular). While almost all of the new believers initially experience persecution, the gospel spreads so fast in movements generated by the CAMEL method that persecution is not as severe (Greeson 2004, 15).

Pathfinder Dialogue: Alternative Participation in a Parallel Cultural Event (Ritual) (Perry 1990)

Cindy Perry, working in Nepal, explains ways Nepalese Christians came to grips with important festivals from their Hindu heritage. Initially the Nepali church rejected out of hand anything related to Hinduism. Over the past few decades, however, Nepali Christians have started to explore new options for participating in some of their rituals, especially ones that traditionally cemented families together. Perry identifies the driving questions behind this shift:

> The question is slowly taking form, "How can we retain our integrity as Nepalis and affirm the positive values in our culture, especially those consistent with biblical values?" Perhaps more importantly, "How can we see and portray Christ incarnate in the Nepali culture rather than as a foreign Christ?" (178)

From one of the rituals, Tij Braka (a festival for women), an alternate event emerged. The new festival uses forms compatible with the original festival though framed in biblical teaching. Perry offers a wonderful depiction of the means through which the alternative ritual was developed:

[I]n 1986 the first nationwide Christian Women's Conference was purposely scheduled to coincide with Tij. It was the first gathering of its kind, drawing together village and urban Christian women from east to west in a large three-day festive gathering. It was a natural time for them to be released from their normal duties, due to the national holiday, and also to travel, as married women often return to their *maita* (mother's home).

At one of the first meetings a Brahman Christian lady presented the cultural form of Tij, and two others responded with reflections as Christians. The following day there was voluntary fasting, biblical teaching on fasting and why we fast as Christians. This culminated in a festive meal and worship service. The following year the women were also encouraged to wear their traditional tribal/caste dress for each other.

There was teaching on family and relationship to husbands, the need to honor and pray for them, and a time of joint public prayer for blessing on the women's husbands. Throughout the conference there was emphasis on God's love for them as women (in contra-distinction to the Hindu low view of women), their high calling as women of God, and their active involvement in ministry. Thus, both compatible forms of Tij were utilized, and key themes (well known and ingrained in most all women in Nepal) were paralleled with corrective biblical teaching.

Although not envisioned by the planners, the conference ended on a high note of spontaneous singing and dance (a folk-style en-acting of indigenous Nepali Christian songs) which went on for al-most two hours following the final benediction. Rather than being "robbed" of participation in a traditional festival, for these Christian women Tij had been transformed and infused with a new spirit.

In this case, Nepali Christians, rather than seeking to contex-tualize Tij by participation of Christians alongside of their Hindu neighbors, developed a completely alternative festival for Christian women—at the same time, using some of the same forms (i.e., feasting, fasting, worship, prayer, celebration, fancy dress) and following some of the same themes.

It is in the latter regard that special care needs to be taken and the full inherent meanings of Tij investigated. Simplistic paralleling could result in syncretism and unconscious affirmation of non-Christian values. For instance,

1. It should be made clear, especially to new believers, concerning fasting—(a) that for Christians it is in no way a reenactment of Parvati's fast; (b) that the biblical basis of fasting and the reasons for doing it are neither means of manipulating God, nor ways of gaining merit; (c) that the source of our power is God and not the fast.

2. The good wishes for women's husbands can be affirmed and built upon, emphasizing the biblical teaching of honoring their husbands, and encouraging regular prayer for their husbands. But there should also be corrective teaching related to the belief that women are somehow responsible for their husbands' long lives, and the belief that sin is attached to widowhood. (179–80)

The pathfinders in this case were women in the Nepali church. In dialogue with each other, they developed an alternative that allows new as well as long-established Christians opportunity to connect in a ritual that is part of their heritage. The spontaneous dancing at the end of the conference indicates the joy the women experience through the alternate celebration. Perry's conclusion is apt, "Not only was the Nepali believers' sense of identity with their culture heightened through this process, but it brought renewed opportunities to witness to their faith" (183).

Pathfinder Cyclical: Dynamic-equivalence "Churchness" (Kraft 1979c; 1980; 2005c)

Charles Kraft developed one of the earliest contextual models. He argued that those working in other cultures should focus on planting dynamic-equivalent churches. As he explains it, "*A contemporary church, like a contemporary translation, should impress the uninitiated observer as an original production in the contemporary culture, not as a badly fitted import from somewhere else"* (2005c, 249; emphasis his). Kraft applies his understanding of dynamic equivalence to the church and proposes that this is "the kind of church that will take indigenous forms, capture them for Christ, adapt and employ them to serve Christian ends by fulfilling indigenous functions, and convey through them Christian meanings to the surrounding society" (2005c, 251). He illustrates the five-step process as in Figure 11.1, with the cyclical nature of the last three steps indicated by the arrows.

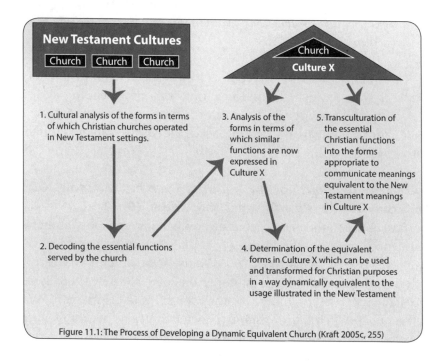

Figure 11.1: The Process of Developing a Dynamic Equivalent Church (Kraft 2005c, 255)

The first two steps involve analyzing the forms the New Testament church used in its cultural settings and then decoding from them the essential functions that lie behind them. This is the kernel-in-husk model (see discussion in chapters 1 and 2), and the kernel (the "essential functions served by the church"), once identified, is transplanted in the new cultural setting.

Steps three through five of the process are cyclical, for cultures are never static and thus dynamic equivalence churches should never be static. The underlying idea for the three steps is that the various characteristics of the receptor church should be evaluated to ascertain the appropriateness of the forms employed in conveying meanings and meeting needs in ways equivalent to the New Testament models. *The priority must be for conveying in the receptor society a content that is equivalent to that conveyed in the original society.* This may require that the cultural forms in terms of which that content is expressed differ widely in the receptor culture from those of either the New Testament or of the culture of the missionary. *As with translation, so with the transculturating of the church—the extent of the divergence of forms should depend upon the distance between the cultures in question.* (2005c, 255–56)

Pathfinders following this approach are not tied to previous church forms; they experiment to find new ones in a never-ending cycle of evaluating—and changing—their church forms so that the impact of those forms is equivalent to the impact of the New Testament churches in their various contexts.

Pathfinder Organic: Locally Initiated Churches (Aikman 2003; Anderson 2000b; Pew Forum 2006; Zdero 2004)

We find tens of thousands of indigenous congregations, churches, and denominations around the world that do not look and feel very "Western" (e.g., Jenkins 2002; 2006; Walls 1996; 2002). These include African Initiated Churches (e.g., Anderson 2000b; Barrett 1968; Barrett and Padwick 1989), Chinese House Churches (e.g., Aikman 2003; Hattaway 2003), Indian ashrams (Hoefer 2001a), the Non-Church movement in Japan (Nabetani 1983; see chapter 14), Latin American indigenous Pentecostal churches (Pew Forum 2006), and global experiments in house churches (e.g., Simson 1999; Zdero 2004).

For the most part, they are contextual not because a Western missionary founded them with contextual intent, but because they originated within local settings. Often the underlying reason behind the initial development is a reaction to elements ranging from missionary domination to religious or societal persecution. In Africa, access to a vernacular Bible fueled many. In Latin American settings the messages of Jesus empowering those who were once powerless was the impetus. In Asian locales the refuge Christ offers to those undergoing societal tidal waves, whether religious or economic, played a significant role. Many, though not all, of these locally initiated churches are more biblically literal and theologically conservative than their Western counterparts, and resonate with evangelicals.

It would be appropriate to consider every evangelical indigenous church an example of contextualization. The breadth of this phenomenon makes it impossible to categorize beyond saying that typically an insider charts a new path rather than mimicking outsider paths. Further, the insider typically follows a path that is circuitous at best and better described as organic.

Evaluation of Initiators as Pathfinders

Evangelical models in which the contextualizers are pathfinders—who experiment with or chart new ways to contextualize—focus on making the gospel come to life in creative ways in new cultural settings.

Pathfinding initiators are not confined to "business as usual" in approaching contextual opportunities. They energetically look for ways to make the new Christian faith at home in their cultural settings. They are less concerned with the reaction "back home" and more concerned with what is happening where they serve. If anything, their deep and passionate commitment to those who do not know Christ drives them to experiment and explore ways to break down or break through barriers to the gospel.

As with every initiator role, there are also potential weaknesses for initiators who serve as pathfinders. The entrepreneurial orientation of the pathfinder may result in a tendency to change too much too quickly—and perhaps even lose the message in the process. Alternately, pathfinders may be so committed to blazing new trails that they do so even when new trails are not necessary and may even be distracting to local fellowships. "New and improved"—when it becomes a philosophy of ministry—can lead to experiments that distort faith rather than enhance it. A frequent result is that pathfinders, more than any other type of initiator, face accusations of syncretism or heresy by fellow evangelicals.

KEYWORDS FOR REVIEW

Alternative participation in a parallel cultural event: Christians develop
an alternative event or festival for Christians, rather than participating alongside their non-Christian neighbors

CAMEL evangelism method: evangelistic and church-planting
method using the acronym CAMEL to find a "person of peace"
by building a bridge from teachings in the Quran to the Bible;
once a person follows Christ, he or she uses the same method
to reach relatives and friends

Dynamic-equivalence "Churchness": developing a church that uses
indigenous forms, capturing them for Christ, adapting and
employing them to serve Christian ends by fulfilling indigenous
functions; they use these forms to convey Christian meanings
to the surrounding society

Locally initiated churches: fellowships or congregations founded by
indigenous initiative and, for a variety of reasons, typically
independent from missionary or traditional existing Christian
groups

QUESTIONS FOR REFLECTION

1. What characteristics of the *pathfinding* initiator are most attractive to you personally?

2. What characteristics of the *pathfinding* initiator are least attractive to you personally?

3. What would characterize the types of settings in which the *pathfinder* may be the best approach for an initiator?

4. What would characterize the types of settings in which the *pathfinder* may not be a good approach for an initiator?

FOR FURTHER STUDY

Aikman, David. 2003. *Jesus in Beijing: How Christianity Is Transforming China and Changing the Global Balance of Power.* Washington, DC: Regnery Publishing.

Anderson, Allan H. 2000. *Zion and Pentecost: The Spirituality and Experience of Pentecostal and Zionist/Apostolic Churches in South Africa.* Pretoria: University of South Africa Press.

Greeson, Kevin. 2004. *Camel Training Manual.* Bangalore, India: WIGTake.

_____. 1980. "The Church in Culture: A Dynamic Equivalence Model." In *Down to Earth: Studies in Christianity and Culture,* ed. John R. W. Stott and Robert Coote, 211–30. Grand Rapids: Eerdmans.

Perry, Cindy. 1990. "Bhai-Tika and Tij Braka: A Case Study in the Contextualization of Two Nepali Festivals." *Missiology* 18.2 (April): 177–83.

Pew Forum on Religion and Public Life. 2006. *Spirit and Power: A 10 Country Survey of Pentecostals.* Online: http://pewforum.org/ newassets/surveys/pentecostal/pentecostals-08.pdf, accessed 9 December 2009.

Zdero, Rad. 2004. *The Global House Church Movement.* Pasadena: William Carey Library.

Initiator as Prophet

CHAPTER OVERVIEW

In this chapter I explain the initiator role of *prophet.* I begin with a description of what a prophet role includes before describing tendencies seen in analysis of prophets compared with the other initiator roles. I then indicate people I see as exemplars of the prophet role from the Bible as well as church life.

The best way to understand the role is to see it in some of the examples. I describe in greater depth selected examples in which the initiator is a prophet—arranged by the flow of the method. Finally, I conclude the chapter with a short summary of the major strengths and weaknesses of models in which the initiator takes the role of a prophet.

CHAPTER OUTLINE

1. Initiator as Prophet
2. What Is a Prophet?
3. Prophet Perspectives
4. Exemplar Prophets
5. Prophet Examples
   a. Prophet Linear: Theology of Vindication (Harootian 1987)
   b. Prophet Dialogue: Contextual Urban Theology (Monsma 1979; 1981)
   c. Prophet Cyclical: Critical and Constructive Theology (Escobar 1994; Padilla 1985b; Costas 1982; 1989)
   d. Prophet Organic: Non-Church (Japan) (Nabetani 1983; Howes 2007)
6. Evaluation of Initiators as Prophets

What Is a Prophet?

Initiators who take a prophetic role focus on speaking God's truth into local settings. In using "prophet" as the designation for this role, I intend the forth-telling function of the prophet rather than the foretelling function. Thus, the primary action of this type of initiator is to "declare." Parallel terms include commentator, gadfly, inspector, irritant, judge, monitor, and social critic.

The role of the prophetic initiator includes discerning social or spiritual bondages and bringing Christ's truths to bear on them. Prophets proclaim God's attitude toward social ills, especially when the body of Christ is lagging in or even going against biblical priorities or responsibilities. This includes such things as ignoring or overlooking the needs of the marginalized, failing to speak out against injustice or victimization, or ignoring spiritual responsibilities such as evangelism or discipleship. The prophet is the least common initiator role of the 249 examples, found in only 12 (or 5 percent) of them.

Prophet Perspectives

In Table 12.1 I list statistical trends among initiators who take on the role of a prophet. These trends help us understand patterns that we are likely to see in evangelical contextual efforts when the initiators act as prophets.

TABLE 12.1: STATISTICAL TRENDS OF PROPHET EXAMPLES	
Examples with prophets as initiators are disproportionately *more* likely to:	**Examples with prophets as initiators are disproportionately *less* likely to:**
Follow a cyclical flow. Include in their scope the area of theological development. Have an emic initiator.	Attend to spiritual outreach or the initiation stage in the church life-cycle.

The congruence of examples with prophetic initiators being more likely to be emic initiators may result in part from the reality that contemporary missionaries—unlike their forebears—seem to have greater reticence to speak out against social ills while living as guests in new locales. It seems reasonable to suppose as well that insiders are more capable of speaking out against social ills because they know how to address them in ways that others in the setting will understand.

Examples with prophets as initiators were disproportionately likely to include theological development in their scope. This stems mostly from the number of the prophetic initiator examples in which evangelicals respond to or advocate some variant of liberation theology. Prophetic types more likely would view the context as fallen and in need of change that only God can provide. They are also more likely to be suspicious of the status quo in their own faith tradition, since they see where the tradition needs to change.

Exemplar Prophets

This statement made by Jesus concerning his own ministry is a prophetic declaration: "The Spirit of the Lord is on me, because he has anointed me to preach good news to the poor. He has sent me to proclaim freedom for the prisoners and recovery of sight for the blind, to release the oppressed, to proclaim the year of the Lord's favor" (Luke 4:18–19). He announced God's judgment on the religious leaders of his day (Matt. 23), threw the money changers out of the temple (Mark 11:12–17), and exposed the truth of the Samaritan woman's life (John 4: 1–24). Most of his pronouncements to the seven churches in Revelation are prophetic in nature (Rev. 2–3).

The Old Testament prophets—such as Isaiah, Jeremiah, and Amos—exemplify the role of the prophetic initiator. As noted in chapter 13, John the Baptist initiates repentance as a path-clearing measure in preparation for Jesus' coming (Matt. 3:7–12). The pronouncements James makes (James 2:1–26) against those who discriminate on the basis of wealth or other factors are prophetic, as are Paul's denunciations of Peter and Barnabas when they discriminated against Gentile believers (Gal. 2:11–21) and Peter's judgments against false teachers (2 Peter 2).

Christians such as Uchimura Kanzō (1861–1930), whose rejection of Western denominationalism led to the founding of the non-church movement in Japan (Moreau 1995e), are prophetic initiators, as are Samuel Escobar (1994), Rene Padilla (1985a; 2009), Timothy Monsma (1981), Ron Sider (1977; 2005), and Vinay Samuel (1987).

Prophet Examples

Table 12.2 shows the 12 examples in which the initiator was a prophet arranged by the flow of contextualization. In this section, I illustrate the role of initiator as prophet using four examples, selecting one from each type of flow.

TABLE 12.2: EXAMPLES WITH INITIATOR AS PROPHET	
Linear: 4 (38%) examples	Contextualizing Universal Values (Adeney 2007) Delighting in God's Law for Incarnational Witness (Massey 2004b; 2004c) Seeking the Peace of the City (Seeking 1989) Theology of Vindication (Harootian 1987)
Dialogue: 2 (17%) examples	Contextual Urban Theology (Monsma 1981) Word of Action Liberation (Costas 1991)
Cyclical: 2 (17%) examples	Second Generation Contextualization (Ortiz 1993) Critical and Constructive Theology (Escobar 1994; Padilla 1985b; Costas 1982; 1989)
Organic: 3 (25%) examples	Environmentalism (AICs; Daneel 1996) Messianic Movements (Fuchs 1976) Non-Church (Japan) (Nabetani 1983; Howes 2007)
Not Clear: 1 (8%) example	Contextualization of Theological Education (Kim 1974)

Prophet Linear: Theology of Vindication (Harootian 1987)

Abigail Harootian, a Filipino, began to explore God's vindication in response to working among Filipino peasants "oppressed both by the government in power and a group trying to overthrow that government" (1987, 81). As she listened to them and began to understand their plight—victimized by absentee landlords, promised free land by a revolutionary group, and threatened by the government—she grew to realize that

> Christian theology (at least, the kind of theology I have been exposed to as a middle-class Asian Christian) has treated very lightly the fact that God vindicates (cf. Isaiah 34:8; Nahum 1:2; Romans 12:9). Many theologians treat the vindication of God against injustice in a soft and lenient way, failing to explore many of the related issues. For example, how is God's vindication fulfilled? Is it through violent means or "accidental" and natural calamities? Cannot the oppressed, as they follow Christ and become His instruments, do anything concrete to bring about God's vindication for themselves? (84)

She went back to the Bible to wrestle with God's perspective and saw that God was sympathetic toward the plight of the poor and marginalized and that Jesus lived out God's concern in all that he did. She came to the conclusion that

> A theology among Filipino peasants should affirm that God vindicates the oppressed. Thus, the peasants can pray (with hope) to God for His vindication to come quickly, just as He promised to His followers who cry out to Him. The peasants can have faith in God based on what Jesus has said-that God will vindicate them. It is God's prerogative, and not man's, to determine how and when the vindication will take place. (84–85)

However, this prophetic theology of vindication is not isolated from other scriptural truths. It comes in the context of the biblical picture of salvation, which, in addition to exposing the genuine reality of sin among the peasants themselves,

> should also include deliverance from subserviently fulfilling their oppressive landlords' unjust whims and demands. There has to be an alternative whereby peasants can collectively and creatively refuse injustice toward them (being sinned-against) through nonviolent means. Unconditional obedience to the oppressive landlords' demands, which are clearly against God's ideals, makes the peasants

participants in their oppressors' sin. This refusal of injustice must be accompanied by a faith that is ready to suffer the consequences. (86)

The goal of God's vindication cannot be overlooked either—God does not vindicate for the destruction of the oppressors. Rather, his vindication is framed in forgiveness with hope for reconciliation:

> A theology of forgiveness should aim to restore relationships *among the peasants* and *between the peasants and their landlords*. Jesus said that one cannot worship God without being reconciled to his brother (Matthew 5:23–25). Christianity is not only reconciliation between God and man, but also reconciliation between man and man.

Harootian's prophetic word for the Filipino peasants is that God regards them as people he loves, and he will vindicate their injustices. However, he will not do so without calling them into account for their own sin or simply for the sake of revenge. Rather, he vindicates in order to accomplish his purposes, namely, the reconciliation of God to people and people to each other.

Prophet Dialogue: Contextual Urban Theology (Monsma 1979; 1981)

Timothy Monsma, noted urban missiologist, frames his concerns for a contextual urban theology in light of contextual realities, which requires that we "put our message and ministry in context with our present world and people's life situation" (1981, 11).

Monsma's urban theology has three core components: 1) concern for structural change, 2) concern for urban community, and 3) concern for the laity. The prophetic component is concentrated in the first component, of which Monsma relates

> The teaching and preaching ministry of the organized church must point out the need for changing structures that are evil. Slavery was abolished in the world partly because the church came to see the evils of slavery and preached against it. The church today must see the evil of racial or tribal discrimination as well as economic exploitation,

and sensitize Christians to these evils. Once Christians are sensitized they will begin to act. (11)

Prophet Cyclical: *Critical and Constructive Theology (Escobar 1994; Padilla 1985b; Costas 1982; 1989)*

Samuel Escobar, widely regarded theologian from Peru, noted that Latin American evangelicals were searching for the answers to multiple questions in their own context but found that neither ecumenical dialogue nor Catholic liberation theology were adequate to the task as evangelicals saw it. He aptly summarizes the generative forces and the resulting issues for evangelicals in Latin America:

> A fresh reading of the Bible within the social crisis of the sixties in Latin America caused theologians of every tradition to rediscover some aspects of the biblical message that had remained obscure, unknown or even purposefully forgotten. It became necessary to acknowledge that themes such as *justice, poverty, oppression,* and *liberation* are not accidental departures here and there from the great lines of biblical teaching. They are teachings which cannot be separated from the core of God's self-revelation through Jesus Christ. They are intrinsic to other themes such as revelation, relationship with God, repentance, and the nature of Christian life. The understanding of every point of biblical teaching requires adequate regard to the wholeness of the message. (207)

Escobar delineates Latin American evangelical efforts in struggling for a contextual theology as a two-pronged, interweaving, and ongoing dialogue in relation to five themes. The first prong is the critical (or prophetic) task. This critical task has taken on at least two fronts. The first is that of the ongoing debate with Liberation theologians over biblical, hermeneutic, and socio-political issues. In this critical task, as Escobar notes, "What is distinctive of the evangelical stance is an emphasis on the primacy of biblical authority in their theological method and the insistence on keeping evangelistic activity at the center of the mission of the church" (1994, 204).

The second front of the critical prong was challenging the theological and ideological framing of the church growth movement, especially in its "overwhelming institutional and propagandistic weight" (204).

The second prong is what Escobar calls "the *constructive* task of developing a theology of mission that would express the dynamic reality and the missionary thrust of their churches in Latin America" (204). This task involves developing biblical bases for "new patterns of evangelism and discipleship, in continuity with their heritage of a Bible-centered form of presence and mission committed to spiritual and social transformation" (Ibid). For Latin American evangelicals,

> a fresh exploration is required into the depths of the biblical text, with the questions raised by the Latin American context. Moreover, commitment to biblical authority should not be limited to certain beliefs in the area of soteriology, but also to fresh explorations into a biblically-based social ethics. (Ibid)

This constructive task, Escobar notes, dealt with five themes that were of immediate concern to evangelicals (205–6), namely:

- The search for a pneumatic and contextual hermeneutics

- The development of a missiological Christology

- A holistic missiology with contributions in the areas of soteriology, anthropology, and historical theology

- A grassroots and postwestern ecclesiology

- A missiological pneumatology and a self-critical Pentecostal ecclesiology

Escobar describes as exemplars of this two-pronged approach C. Rene Padilla (1985b) and Orlando Costas (1982; 1989). This ongoing cyclical dialogue of critique and construction continues to shape evangelical theological reflection in Latin America today, and Escobar's own contribution in this two-pronged discussion is his reflections on the shaping of missiological Christology in light of Latin American issues.

Prophet Organic: Non-Church (Japan) (Nabetani 1983; Howes 2007)

Many recognize the Japanese social and church critic Kanzo Uchimura as the founder of the non-church movement in Japan. This movement predates the coining of contextualization but demonstrates a profound attempt to embody the gospel in the Japanese setting. His choice to follow the Samurai tradition of choosing the harder but more honorable path of life (Sasaki 2009) ultimately resulted in his rejection not only of Japanese imperial orthodoxy but of the institutional Christian church as well.

Uchimura argued from biblical expositions, and his primary influence was among the intelligentsia rather than the common person (Nabetani 1983, 78). As I noted elsewhere:

> He was a passionate advocate of democracy, pacifism and personal independence, though he frequently declared that he loved only two J's: Japan and Jesus. His most significant contribution to an indigenous Japanese Christianity was the founding the Mukyokai movement, a Bible study movement not affiliated with an institutional church. (Moreau 1995e)

Uchimura argued that what we see today in our denominational organizations are not representative of the early church. Churches today organize to meet the needs of religious sentiment, but in the time of the early church they banded together as societies to build the type of kingdom on earth that Christ declared to be true of heaven. Once the papacy was established, he noted, the church devolved into less than Christ called it to be. Even Protestants, seen in the bitter disputes between Calvin and Luther, were no better (Miura 1996, 88).

He prophetically condemned the contemporary churches in Japan as little more than branches of the churches in Europe and the United States. In 1911, he described his understanding of the true church:

> There is a true church. It is Mukyokai (Non-church). It is not a church where a man rules over the others under the system. It is a church where people love, encourage, and help each other through the spirit. Their union and harmony are invisible. There, there is no danger at all of them becoming corrupted. This is the true Holy Catholic Church. (Cited in Miura 1996, 98)

He was fully committed to Bible study, writing study materials in great volume through his life. He was fully committed to Jesus, never wavering in his personal faith. Over several decades Uchimura struggled to reform the church as it existed in Japan but finally gave that up and turned his back on the church—but not on his faith. For him, to stay in church was to lose faith, because church was not what Christ desired it to be. In turning his back on the church, he anticipated being able to have better relationships with non-Christians and bring them the gospel, just as Paul turned his back on the Jews to reach out to Gentiles (Miura 1996, 102–3).

Uchimura poses a significant contextual challenge to evangelicals. He prophetically discerned significant issues with the church—and the church's understanding of itself. Ultimately turning his back on it, he still centered his life and thought on Bible study and growing in his understanding of Jesus—but in a way that made sense to him as a Japanese lover of Jesus, not as a Westerner.

Evaluation of Initiators as Prophets

Evangelical approaches in which initiators act as prophets focus on discerning and announcing God's life-inviting judgment in new cultural settings. A great strength of initiators as prophets is that they are not constrained by contemporary opinion or the need to be politically or socially correct. They discern God's perspective—whether through scriptural immersion or divine-given insights—and deliver it to those who need to understand it. Though often less welcome than other initiator models, evangelicals need prophetic voices to provoke us to more godly action and reflection.

As with every initiator role, there are potential weaknesses for initiators who serve as prophets. Prophets can be tempted to limit their prophetic role to judgment without offering encouragement. They are more dangerous, however, when they are not careful to ensure that they are following God's leading and simply follow their own inclinations. This can result in pronouncements that are more harmful than helpful for the people they exhort.

Keywords for Review

Theology of vindication: theological affirmation that God vindicates the oppressed in ways that offer forgiveness for the oppressors with hope for reconciliation

Contextual urban theology: urban theology that has three core components: 1) concern for structural change, 2) concern for urban community, and 3) concern for the laity

Critical and constructive theology: a two-pronged (critical *and* constructive), interweaving, and ongoing dialogue in relation to five themes: critical (or prophetic) challenges to 1) Liberation theologians and 2) the ideological framing of the church growth movement and constructive It looks like text is missing here.

Non-Church (Japan): the Mukyokai movement consists of Bible study groups not attached to existing denominational organizations; people gather to love, encourage, and help each other through the Spirit to build the type of kingdom on earth that Christ declared to be true of heaven

QUESTIONS FOR REFLECTION

1. What characteristics of the *prophetic* initiator are most attractive to you personally?

2. What characteristics of the *prophetic* initiator are least attractive to you personally?

3. What would characterize the types of settings in which the *prophet* may be the best approach for an initiator?

4. What would characterize the types of settings in which the *prophet* may not be a good approach for an initiator?

FOR FURTHER STUDY

Costas, Orlando. 1982. *Christ outside the Gate*. Maryknoll: Orbis.

_____. 1989. *Liberating News*. Grand Rapids: Eerdmans.

Escobar, Samuel. 1994. "The Search for a Missiological Christology for Latin America." In *Emerging Voices in Global Christian Theology*, ed. William A Dyrness, 199–228. Grand Rapids: Zondervan.

Harootian, Abigail F. Ramientos. 1987. "Doing Theology among Filipino Peasant-Farmers." *International Journal of Frontier Missions* 4: 81–90.

Howes, John F. 2007. "Christian Prophecy in Japan: Uchimura Kanzō." *Japanese Journal of Religious Studies* 34.1: 127–50.

Monsma, Timothy M. 1979. *An Urban Strategy for Africa*. Pasadena: William Carey.

_____. 1981. "Urban Explosion and Missions Strategy." *Evangelical Missions Quarterly* 17.1 (January): 5–12.

Nabetani, Gyoji. 1983. "An Asian Critique of Church Movements in Japan." *Evangelical Review of Theology* 7.1 (April): 73–78.

Padilla, C. René. 1985. *Mission between the Times: Essays on the Kingdom*. Grand Rapids: Eerdmans.

Initiator as Restorer

CHAPTER OVERVIEW

In this chapter I explain the initiator role of *restorer*. I begin with a description of what a restorer role includes before describing tendencies seen in analysis of restorers compared with the other initiator roles. I then indicate people I see as exemplars of the restorer role from the Bible as well as church life.

The best way to understand the role is to see it in some of the examples. I describe in greater depth selected examples in which the initiator is a restorer—arranged by the flow of the method. Finally, I conclude the chapter with a short summary of the major strengths and weaknesses of models in which the initiator takes the role of a restorer.

CHAPTER OUTLINE

1. What Is a Restorer?
2. Restorer Perspectives
3. Exemplar Restorers
4. Restorer Examples
   a. Restorer Linear: Contextualized Deliverance Ministry (Cordillera Rehabilitation Center; Cole 2003)
   b. Restorer Dialogue: Allegiance, Truth, and Power Encounters (Kraft 1991c; 2002a; 2005g)
   c. Restorer Organic: Power Evangelism (Wimber and Springer 1986; Wagner and Pennoyer 1990; Wimber 1990; Wagner 1991a)
5. Evaluation of Initiators as Restorers

What Is a Restorer?

The restorer comes to heal or deliver people from bondage of any type. For an individual, this may involve psychological, physical, or spiritual healing. On behalf of a group, it may involve social, systemic, or environmental restoration. Whereas the prophet denounces or discerns what is under the surface and exposes it, the restorer attends to the needed healing or restoration. The restorer uses appropriate means to bring or return people to a state of health so they can live the way Jesus calls us all to live. Alternate terms for this initiator role include counselor, deliverer, healer, reconciler, therapist, and—in some cases—warrior.

In 17 (or 7 percent) of the 249 examples in the database, the initiator took on the role of a restorer. Restorers may concentrate on physical, psychological, spiritual, or socio-economic restoration—or any combination of them. The majority of the examples in our list attend to spiritual issues—especially deliverance or spiritual warfare. Strong controversy among evangelicals exists in this area (e.g., Rommen and Netland 1995; Moreau et al. 2002). I focus on them in this chapter to help us better understand evangelical perspectives and contextual practices in this regard.

Restorers can act as pathfinders when they explore new restorative techniques (see, e.g., Kraft 1995), but most often they focus on delivering people from oppression as an aspect of restoring them to spiritual health. Practitioners may distinguish different types of demons (e.g., Wagner 1996; 1998; Kraft 2002a) and the perspectives of the people who need deliverance (e.g., M. Kraft 1995). However, I am unaware of discussion that consciously attends to whether *spirits themselves* are affected by human culture or have any type of variation in their worldviews. This is evidence that evangelicals consider demons *qua* demons somehow immune to contextual or worldview considerations.

Restorer Perspectives

In Table 13.1, I list statistical trends among the initiators who take on the role of a restorer. These trends offer insights on patterns that we are likely to see in evangelical contextual efforts when the initiators act as restorers.

TABLE 13.1: STATISTICAL TRENDS OF RESTORER EXAMPLES	
Examples with restorers as initiators are disproportionately *more* likely to:	**Examples with restorers as initiators are disproportionately *less* likely to:**
Be unclear in their flow. Focus on the contextual activity in- and-of itself.	Flow cyclically. Include in their scope theological development.

It is not surprising that restorers would attend to the activity more frequently than other initiators. After all, their greatest concern is the activity itself. It also makes sense that restorer initiators are less likely to include theological development in the scope of their contextual methods; theology may come after restoration, but it is only part of it when it helps in the restorative process.

Exemplar Restorers

It is difficult to find a more concentrated focus on the restoring work of Jesus than in Matthew 9:18–38. In this short passage, we read that he healed a dead girl (18–19, 23–26), cured a woman who had bled for twelve years (20–22), restored sight to two blind men (27–31), and delivered a mute demoniac so that he could speak (32–34). As a synopsis, Matthew notes that Jesus went through the villages and towns teaching, preaching, and healing people from "every disease and sickness." Jesus had compassion on the harassed and helpless crowds, and he called on his disciples to pray for laborers. His declaration of prophetic ministry (Luke 4:18–19) includes restorative work: proclaiming freedom for prisoners, recovery of sight for the blind, releasing the oppressed. He delivered people from demons (Mark 5:1–20) and offered a light yoke of forgiveness (Matt. 11:28–30).

Occasionally the Old Testament prophets acted as restorers. Elijah healed Naaman (2 Kings 5:1–14). Isaiah declared Hezekiah's healing

(Isa. 38:1–8). In the New Testament, under Jesus' authority, the disciples cast out demons (Luke 10:17–20). Peter healed Aeneas (Acts 9:32–35) and raised Dorcas from the dead (36–42). Paul healed (Acts 14:8–10, though with some unexpected results) and cast out demons (16:16–18).

Contemporary evangelicals who take on spiritual restorer roles in contextualization include Carlos Annacondia (Wagner 1991b), Amsalu Tadesse Geleta (2002); Hwa Yung (2002), Charles Kraft (2002), Meg Kraft (1995), Juliet Thomas (2002), and C. Peter Wagner (1992; 1996).

Restorer Examples

Table 13.2 shows the 17 examples in which the initiator is a restorer, arranged by the flow of contextualization. In this section, I illustrate the role of initiator as restorer using three examples, each with a different flow. Note that none of the restorer examples follows a cyclical flow.

Restorer Linear: Contextualized Deliverance Ministry (Cordillera Rehabilitation Center; Cole 2003)

Harold Cole, American Pentecostal missionary in the Philippines, partnered with Rev. Antonio Caput Sr. (Tito) in evangelistic crusades and church planting over a multiyear span. During that time, Tito brought people with him to various events and introduced them to Cole as his "patients." Over time, Cole's curiosity led him to try to understand Tito's ministry better. Out of this came Cole's reflections on the Cordillera Rehabilitation Center (CRC).

Tito and his wife started the CRC in their home as a means of delivering demonized people from neighboring villages. During the eighteen years the ministry had operated at the time of Cole's reflection (1985–2003), 83 people had gone through CRC, and Tito delivered all of them from the demons that plagued them. Cole outlines the steps Tito uses as follows.

First, Tito meets with the family of a prospective patient so that they can explain to him the problem and the solutions they have already attempted. As part of his willingness to accept someone for treatment, Tito requires that the entire family receive Christ and begin attending a Bible-believing church. They also have to bring the magical protective items they use to Tito's house so that Tito and the family can together burn them. During the recovery phase, he also requires them to bring food and other essentials for their family member, though they make no monetary payments for Tito's ministry.

TABLE 13.2: EXAMPLES WITH INITIATOR AS RESTORER	
Linear: **9 (53%)** **examples**	Conflict Management (Palmer 1990) Contextualized Deliverance Ministry (Cordillera Rehabilitation Center; Cole 2003) Contextualizing Missionary Medicine (M. C. Kim 2005) Deep-level Healing (Kraft 1993; 2002; Travis and Travis 2008) Power Encounter (Tippett 1971) Social Services Centers (Hwang and Ng 1990) Spiritual Mapping (Caballeros 1993; Otis 1993; Wagner 1993a; 1993b) Strategic Level Spiritual Warfare (Wagner 1991a; 1991c; 1992; 1996; 1998) Truth Encounter (Anderson 1990)
Dialogue: **5 (29%)** **examples**	Allegiance, Truth, and Power Encounters (Kraft 1991c; 2002a) Authentic Vernacular Understanding of Christ (or Bridging Contextual Theology) (Bediako 1993) Contextualized Medical Clinics (Parshall 1985b) Ritual Analysis as an Aid to Contextualization (Conkey 1992) Theophostic Ministry (Smith 2004)
Cyclical: **0 (0%)** **examples**	
Organic: **1 (6%)** **examples**	Power Evangelism (Wimber and Springer 1986; Wagner and Pennoyer 1990; Wimber 1990; Wagner 1991a)
Not Clear: **2 (12%)** **examples**	Kingdom of God as Organizing and Integrating Theological Paradigm for Contextualization (Love 1994) Power of the Extended Family (Peters 1987)

Tito handles the deliverance component of the ministry with only one person at a time. Once Tito accepts a person for care, he puts the person on a waiting list. As they await their turn, he works with both the families and their village pastors to ensure that the family is being discipled. When the time arrives for that person's deliverance,

Tito always takes five days to prepare for a patient's arrival. He takes three days to pray and fast, and then he rests the two days before the patient comes. Patients are required to bring their own guard to feed, wash and care for them and keep them from running away. They are usually family members. The cell or room that the patient first stays in has a bunk bed in it for the guard to stay with patient. For the first two days, the guard is the only one who has contact with the patient. During these first two days, Tito and other prayer warriors from the church do all their praying outside of the room.

On the third day, Tito talks to the guard and explains to him how he will go about the deliverance. He tells the guard that he will be speaking very strongly to the demons. He does not want the guard to think he is yelling at the patient but rather the demons that are controlling the patient.

When Tito begins to cast out the demons, they usually try to show their strength by causing the patient to start kicking, boxing, screaming or spitting. Tito never touches the patient during this time. He pleads the blood of Jesus over the patient and commands the demons to go to hell. He does not carry on any conversations with the lying spirits even though they make many appeals to Tito. He feels that they have no rights, and he speaks the word of God to them.

Once delivered, the patient usually eats and rests. The immediate postdeliverance recovery takes approximately one week. The person assigned by the family as a guard stays until this phase is completed, after which the patient's guard returns home and the patient moves into a room set aside for the next phase. These rooms are located on the second floor of the church, which is on the same compound as Tito's home.

The patient now starts taking steps to assimilate into normal life, which may take several months. During this time, patients attend all church meetings and Bible studies. They also work around the compound (cooking, cleaning, landscaping), eating all of their meals with

Tito and his wife. The patient's family is required to come twice each month for reconciliation and to ensure that the family is continuing in discipleship in their home village.

After the patient fully recovers, the church has a celebration service for the person, including coming forward for prayer by the congregation. Patients then return home to their village, restored to normal life and ready for further discipleship with the family in their home village.

Tito's contextual approach as a whole is linear, though components within the larger program range from linear (e.g., the deliverance) to organic (e.g., the cycle of life in the compound).

Restorer Dialogue: Allegiance, Truth, and Power Encounters (Kraft 1991c; 2002a; 2005g)

Charles Kraft argues that, while power encounters have become part of evangelical missiological discussion, power encounter is not the only type of encounter needed in Christian witness. It is a critical component of appropriate missional engagement, but not the only one. In 1991, Kraft posited an important cyclical model of three types of encounters seen universally by Christians, involving encounters of truth, commitment, and power. He notes:

> Jesus battled Satan on a broader front than simply power encounters. If we are to be biblically fair and balanced, we must give two other encounters equal attention—commitment encounters and truth encounters. We need to focus on the close relationship in the New Testament between these three encounters.

> 1. Concerning power. This results in power encounters to release people from satanic captivity and bring them into freedom in Jesus Christ.

> 2. Concerning commitment. This results in commitment encounters to rescue people from wrong commitments and bring them into relationship to Jesus Christ.

> 3. Concerning truth. This results in truth encounters to counter error and to bring people to correct understandings about Jesus Christ. (1991c, 259)

Much more can be said about each of these types of encounters, and a significant portion of Kraft's writing has focused on one area or another (see, especially, 2002b; 2005a; 2005b; 2005c; 2005g; and 2008).

Kraft's approach calls for cycling among the three types of commitment as necessary. The initiator may focus on one at a time or in any combination of two or even all three together. As people experience healing in one area, initiators shift focus to another. Kraft notes:

> So, our Christian experience and our efforts at contextualisation are to be concerned with three crucial dimensions. The most important of these is our relationship to Christ, with all the love and obedience that entails. Built on this, then, are the understanding that comes from continually experiencing his truth and the spiritual power Jesus gives us to use as he used it to express his love to others. Any approach to Christianity that neglects or ignores any of these three dimensions is an incomplete and unbalanced Christianity. (2002a, 294)

Restorer Organic: Power Evangelism (Wimber and Springer 1986; Wagner and Pennoyer 1990; Wagner 1991a)

Power evangelism involves consciously incorporating God's power into the evangelistic process, not trying to shape how that will happen but inviting God to engage people and trusting him to respond as he sees fit.

John Wimber, coming from a dispensationalist background, would not seem a likely candidate to initiate the type of ministry he did. He began to re-examine his theological foundations as a result of interacting with fellow students at Fuller Theological Seminary who came from around the world and had seen God use them in evangelism through encounters that were inexplicable from a human perspective.

He wrestled with three questions: "First, how did Jesus evangelize? Second, how did Jesus commission the disciples? Third, in light of their commissioning, how did the disciples evangelize?" (1991, 16). Among many other things, he noted the numerous times in the life of the early church that God's power was coupled with evangelistic outreach (e.g., Acts 3:1–4:22; 8:6–8; 14:8–18; 19:11–12; 28:1–10).

Because of what he learned, he began to pray for God to heal people, and he integrated prayer for healing into the small church he and his wife were starting. He saw that "as people were healed and as I encouraged members of my congregation to pray for the sick (and open themselves up to other works of power), evangelism took off. Put simply: the church exploded" (27). Eventually he coined the term "power evangelism" to describe what he practiced.

Wimber is careful to note that power does not *replace* communication in evangelism. Rather, it *reinforces* it. Responding to critics who accused him of adding to the gospel, he notes:

> In power evangelism we don't add to the gospel, or even seek to add power to the gospel. But we do turn to the third Person of the Triune God in our evangelistic efforts, *consciously* cooperating with His anointing, gifting and leading. Preaching and demonstrating the gospel are not mutually exclusive activities; they work together, reinforcing each other. (1991, 28; emphasis in original)

Power evangelism is not a method but an attitude coupled with trust that God will be in the process:

> I define power evangelism as a *presentation of the gospel that is rational but also transcends the rational.* The explanation of the kingdom of God comes with a demonstration of God's power through works of power. It is a spontaneous, Spirit-inspired, empowered presentation of the gospel. It is usually preceded and undergirded by demonstrations of God's presence. (29)

Power evangelism includes such things as power encounters, supernatural insights, and divine appointments. However, Wimber maintains that "power evangelism cannot be reduced to a technique or method" (29). Because this organic approach depends on God's leading and engagement, the initiator is not in control of the methods, the timing, or the procedures.

Evaluation of Initiators as Restorers

Evangelical contextualizers who act as restorers focus their energies on discerning what is broken or damaged and finding appropriate ways to restore the broken to health. They may attend to physical, psycho-logical, or spiritual issues. Because I limited my discussion to examples of restorers who attend to spiritual issues, I limit my evaluative com-ments to that slice of initiators who are restorers.

Initiators who focus on spiritual restoration recognize that God alone equips and enables them to deliver people from evil powers. We welcome this constant refrain from those who engage the demonic in their restorative work.

A criticism of initiators as restorers is that practitioners rarely dis-cuss their methods as explicitly contextual. Charles Kraft argues that while power encounter has become part of evangelical missiological discussion, evangelicals reflect very little on contextualizing this area. His challenge is one that evangelicals need to consider:

> Where are the discussions concerning biblically legitimate and cul-turally appropriate approaches to such areas of Christian experience as warfare prayer, deliverance from demons, healing, blessing and cursing, dedications, visions, dreams, concepts of the territoriality of spirits, angels, demons and the like? Shouldn't we be discussing the contextualising of spiritual warfare? What are the scriptural prin-ciples applicable to every cultural situation and what are the cultural variables in this important area? (2002a, 290–91)

Exceptions such as Cole's presentation of the Cordillera Rehabilitation Center are uncommon. The general—and largely un-questioned—assumption is that when God steps in, culture will somehow lose all significance in ministry. Kraft's challenge seems to be right on target.

KEYWORDS FOR REVIEW

Allegiance encounter: bringing God's power to bear so as to rescue people from wrong commitments and bring them into relationship to Jesus Christ

Deliverance ministry: bringing God's power into the lives of people to release them from bondage of any kind

Power encounter: bringing God's power to bear so as to release people from satanic captivity and bring them into freedom in Jesus Christ

Power evangelism: bringing God's power into the evangelistic process, not trying to shape how that will happen but inviting God to engage people and trusting him to respond as he sees fit.

Truth Encounter: bringing God's power to bear so as to counter error and to bring people to correct understandings of Jesus Christ

QUESTIONS FOR REFLECTION

1. What characteristics of the *restoring* initiator are most attractive to you personally?

2. What characteristics of the *restoring* initiator are least attractive to you personally?

3. What would characterize the types of settings in which the *restorer* may be the best approach for an initiator?

4. What would characterize the types of settings in which the *restorer* may not be a good approach for an initiator?

For Further Study

Cole, Harold L. 2003. "A Model of Contextualized Deliverance Ministry: A Case Study: The Cordillera Rehabilitation Center." *Journal of Asian Mission* 5.2: 259–73.

Kraft, Charles. 1991. "What Kind of Encounters Do We Need in Our Christian Witness?" *Evangelical Missions Quarterly* 27.3 (July): 258–65.

_____. 2002. "Contextualisation and Spiritual Power." In *Deliver Us from Evil: An Uneasy Frontier in Christian Mission*, ed. A. Scott Moreau, Tokunboh Adeyemo, David G. Burnett, Bryant L. Myers, and Hwa Yung, 290–308. Monrovia: MARC/World Vision.

_____. 2005. "Contextualization in Three Crucial Dimensions." In *Appropriate Christianity*, ed. Charles Kraft, 99–115. Pasadena: William Carey Library.

Wagner, C. Peter. ed. 1991. *Engaging the Enemy: How to Fight and Defeat Territorial Spirits*. Ventura: Regal.

Wagner, C. Peter, and F. Douglas Pennoyer, eds. 1990. *Wrestling with Dark Angels: Toward a Deeper Understanding of the Supernatural Forces in Spiritual Warfare*. Ventura: Regal.

Wimber, John, and Kevin Springer. 1986. *Power Evangelism*. London: Hodder and Stoughton.

Future Trajectories

CHAPTER OVERVIEW

Trying to peer into the future is always risky business. In 2003, it would have been impossible to imagine that Websites like YouTube or Facebook would so dramatically affect culture. With that in mind, I offer in this chapter what I think are things that will continue to influence evangelical contextualization in the immediate future. If I'm honest with myself, the areas I've chosen meld together some of the things that concern me, some of the things that give me hope, and some of the things that I wish would happen. It is, then, a personal list—but one based on a significant amount of interaction, pondering, questioning, and praying.

I start by touching on arguments and debates that have the potential to split evangelicals into ever smaller and isolated camps—from our epistemology to our image of holism to our understanding of culture to battles over syncretism.

Then I shift toward things I anticipate are coming "around the next bend"—from a better understanding and recognition of social power to a willingness to see contextualization as more local than global. It will happen everywhere on the planet, but we will not be as tempted as we are today to think that what works well in one place must be exported everywhere. I anticipate that we will see much greater engagement from Pentecostal circles in intentional contextualization.

In the final section, I anticipate the day of the domination of Western evangelicals coming to a close—if it has not already happened. My prayer is that this will happen not because of Western evangelical decline, but because the exponential growth in vibrancy and contextual energy of our Majority World sisters and brothers simply—and wonderfully—eclipses ours.

CHAPTER OUTLINE

1. The Evangelical Divide
2. Holism
3. Insider Movements
4. Syncretism
5. Social Power
6. Bite-sized Contextual Efforts
7. Pentecostal Engagement on All Levels
8. From the Rest to the West?

Evangelicals are passionate about contextualization, especially developing and implementing methods that make differences in the lives of others for the sake of the kingdom of God. Even though at times we are so taken with contextualization that we read it *into* biblical discussion (see Glasser 1995, 13), the richness of evangelical resources, together with the healthy diversity in approaches as seen in the initiator roles, bodes well for the ongoing development of evangelical efforts.

> The evangelical theology of the future will definitely have to be *biblical* in its foundations, *ecclesiastical* in its close relationship to the community of faith, *pastoral* in its attempt to be an orientating voice for the people of God, *contextualized* with regard to that which is social and cultural, and *missionary* in its purpose to reach with the gospel those who are not Christians.
>
> —Emilio Antonio Nuñez (1985, 280)

It is always risky to try to project into the future. I have the privilege of accessing several communities that afford me a cloudy glimpse of potentials to come. These include too much literature to even read in my lifetime (let alone absorb), interaction with friends and colleagues of all ages and geographic locales as well as a variety of settings within the evangelical missions community, and the sheer delight of learning as I pour into members of the next generation of global Christians.

I would be surprised if the literature on evangelical efforts represents more than a small fraction of what evangelicals from all over the world are doing as I write this. I am fortunate to be in a position to hear regular reports from a variety of perspectives about contextual experiments, struggles, breakthroughs, and setbacks. But I also realize that I do not know even a small fraction of the ways God is using evangelicals around the world today.

With that caveat, I offer the following tentative considerations in light of two certainties: 1) God's reign over creation will continue unimpeded whatever may transpire, and 2) God will empower and inspire those who love Christ to facilitate, guide, announce, experiment, pronounce, and restore—all to God's glory.

The Evangelical Divide

Perhaps the area of greatest contention among evangelicals is over something that few can clearly define. As I see it, the bulk of evangelicals involved in contextualization and who are familiar with the term would self-identify as critical realists. However, as discussed in chapter 3, there is no single, unified understanding of critical realism. Drawing from previous discussion, I indicate in Table 14.1 a few of the more critical differences in the correspondence and dynamic approaches to critical realism. I purposefully articulate the more radical ways to express the two orientations so that the differences are even clearer.

TABLE 14.1: THE EVANGELICAL CONTEXTUALIZATION DIVIDE		
Dynamic Equivalence Critical Realism	*Area of Consideration*	**Correspondence Critical Realism**
Impact (with truth): generate the same *impact* on receptors today as biblical writers did on their receptors.	*Central Task*	Truth (with impact): convey the same *concepts* to receptors today as biblical writers conveyed to their receptors.
Since content is constructed by receptor, freedom to try new ways to enable the generation of content that parallels biblical content.	*Experimentation*	Content is conveyed in the message; freedom allowed only as long as content is not threatened.
Content-focus *to the exclusion* of process-focus and resulting impact.	*Concerned to avoid*	Syncretism in false understanding, false living, or false teaching.

Develop means to transform indigenous interpretation of social/religious structures to create proper allegiance.	*Energy directed toward*	Develop the means to "package" messages so that local people correctly understand the content of the message.
Structures and allegiances: structures largely neutral; can be separated from allegiances.	*Religion*	Structures and allegiances: not always neutral; not always separable from allegiances.
Structures and forms that generate false allegiances or false meanings.	*What is syncretism?*	Structures and forms that convey false content and actions that convey false allegiances.

Advocates on either side may not be as far apart as I indicate here. More importantly, they may not always (or even often) be aware of the presuppositional issues driving their methodologies. For example, of the 249 examples in the database, only 15 specifically noted a particular epistemological position. For the most part, evangelicals know that they prefer certain methods or models that fit one end of the spectrum or the other without necessarily being able to articulate the underlying philosophical orientation.

Those whose orientation aligns with dynamic equivalence critical realism are more likely to criticize methods aligned with correspondence critical realism for being too static and focusing on content while ignoring process. Alternately, those whose orientation aligns with correspondence critical realism are more likely to criticize methods aligned with dynamic equivalence critical realism for methodological or theological syncretism or lacking biblical support.

What will the future bring? Generational differences may end up being the most important factor in the answer. Given what I see among younger practitioners and students, I suspect that ever more evangelical contextual efforts will be oriented in dynamic equivalence ways as time goes by. I do not think this will result from conscious decisions but from the pragmatic tendencies that characterize evangelicals in contextualization.

Holism

It seems clear that the next generation of evangelical missionaries—and perhaps missiologists—will *assume* holism as the appropriate biblical picture rather than explore the text to discover whether it is. If that is accurate, it represents a significant shift. One likely result is that we would expect an increase in the percentage of new contextual practices that are consciously holistic. However, it may well turn out that self-identifying a method as holistic may become less important over time simply because evangelicals will more likely *assume* that contextualization is holistic rather than not.

I see two potential directions that evangelicals may shift in the next few decades. First, can evangelicals avoid the drift toward a social gospel—at the expense of evangelism—seen in the late nineteenth century? Second, in the next few decades will evangelicals revisit in a newer form the fundamentalist-modernist controversy fought in the twentieth century among American Christians? I suspect that neither will happen as I describe them here, but I'm convinced that the question of the scope of the ministry of the church among evangelicals is not yet fully settled.

Insider Movements

A flash-point among evangelicals is that of insider movements. I believe that this will continue to generate considerable reflection (and debate) in the coming decades. The resulting tensions increase the potential for splitting among missionaries and organizations for the immediate future.

This may be an evangelical equivalent of the Chinese Rites Controversy among Catholics. However, evangelicals have no equivalent to a pope to adjudicate the various positions. Ultimately, the debates among missionaries from the United States might fade away in light of the vigor and vitality of Global South Christians—for whom many of today's questions and debates are less relevant than they are to American evangelicals.

Syncretism

Attempts to clarify the distinction between contextualization and syncretism will be an ongoing concern for evangelicals. That this question stretches back to the Old Testament points to the unlikelihood that someone will articulate a consensus decision.

The greatest danger to core evangelical convictions in the immediate future may be the shift in conciliar circles toward seeing syncretism as both inevitable and positive (e.g., Schreiter 1993). This shift has not yet surfaced among many evangelicals. However, over the past thirty years, many evangelicals have moved toward positions closer to conciliar thinking than earlier evangelicals would have dreamed, even if such shifts occur several decades after conciliar wrestling began (e.g., concerns for justice; recognizing mission as being to/from all continents; *missio Dei* as a grounding point for missiology). If recent history is a reliable indicator, this will become a debate among evangelicals.

Social Power

For far too long a vacuum of understanding the role social "capital" and power has characterized contextualization. Recent attempts to redress this (Howell and Zehner 2009) have opened a door for ongoing reflection. Brian Howell points out one of the issues that we can identify with the idea of a "context":

> However, the central notion of contextualization, i.e. "context;" maybe more problematic than it seems. In common U.S. English, to speak of the context is generally to refer to a social or even physical location; a "class context" would mean everyone identified with the particular socioeconomic class in question; a "local context" would mean people who live in a given area. . . . [H]owever, context is adapting and adaptable, rather than a "place" in an unchanging or discrete sense. As such, *identifying a context is not simply naming a place, group or identity, but is an activity laden with power and purpose that has theological and social dimensions.* (2009, 5; emphasis mine)

In numerous places throughout the book, I have touched on areas of contention or controversy among evangelicals, including the nature of revelation, form and meaning, critical realist epistemology, dynamic equivalence contextualization, hermeneutics, syncretism, insider movements, praxis, power encounters, and so on. Each of these areas of tension has opponents engaged in ongoing power struggles over who is right, who is wrong, and who is "really" evangelical. I do not anticipate these will lessen in the future. However, I expect that the insights from areas like anthropology and sociology will offer helpful insights—and critique—on the more hidden agendas that frequently undergird our debates.

Bite-sized Contextual Efforts

Solutions to some of the thornier problems may come in the form of localizations ("bite-size theologies," which parallel the "little theologies" of Sedmak 2002) rather than universals. One advantage is that there is less at stake if we do not try to see every contextualized effort as universally applicable. This may open the door for more on-the-ground creativity. However, when contextual answers to problems in one location *contradict* contextual answers to parallel problems in another location, potential declarations of "local truth" that ultimately threaten universal concepts of truth—and core evangelical identity—will arise and generate intense scrutiny.

Pentecostal Engagement on All Levels

Given the size of Pentecostalism around the world, I would be astonished if we do not see a significant multiplication of the number of significant Pentecostal contributions to all of these issues as well as the new ones they will raise. There have been Pentecostal contributions to date (e.g., Lord 2001; Clark 2001; Anderson 2003; also the January 2007 issue of *Missiology* is focused on Pentecostalism), but this stream should become a flood in the next decade or so.

From the Rest to the West?

Attentive readers may wonder why I leave this to the last, noting that I articulate each of the above issues as though the entire locus is among Western missions and missiology. It is possible that the Western voice in the global church will become increasingly muted—and even insignificant—in the decades to come (e.g., Escobar 2003). This could be a cause for rejoicing—if it indicates the growth and strength of the world church. However, if this happens because the church in Western settings ceases to have any relevance or voice in world Christianity, it will be a cause for sorrow for all Christians.

Should the latter be the case, my prayer is that our sisters and brothers in vibrant Christian communities around the world will re-double their engagement in the task of contextualizing the gospel—but now to reach the nations that once were the source of missional energy and efforts. If that should happen, the descendents of to-day's initiators may very well be the addressees of tomorrow's global initiators.

One potential as the "rest" continues to come to the "West" is the proliferation of entrepreneurial (and contextual) ways to fund and organize mission. Western missionaries, especially evangelical ones, have relied primarily on mission *agencies* (whether denominational or other) as the primary vehicle for organizing and funding contextual efforts for the past two hundred years. In contrast, Majority World Christians are generating and developing strength in economies that do not enable the development of agencies seen in the West. They exist, and in large numbers. However, they do not necessarily resemble their Western counterparts. The standard faith agency model does not work as well, and the inherent Western organizational framing of agencies can hinder the organic efforts Majority World Christians use. The en-tire Back to Jerusalem movement was not birthed by or organized by any Chinese agency (Hattaway 2003). Agencies like University Bible Fellowship (from Korea) do not look or operate like Western agen-cies even though they borrow from them (Schafer, Yoon and Moreau 2009). I anticipate that as the "rest" continues to bring contextual faith to the "West," we will see this happen in ever changing forms that have little or no parallels to the agency model that has so domi-nated Western mission history.

As Tim Tennent wisely notes, "It takes a whole world to under-stand a whole Christ" (Tennent 2005, 176). It is my hope and prayer that tomorrow's evangelicals from every part of the world will con-tinue to play a vital role in that process.

KEYWORDS FOR REVIEW

Evangelical divide: division among evangelical missiologists and
  missionaries over how to understand and apply critical realism
  Dynamic equivalence critical realists criticize *correspondence*
  critical realist methods as static and content-focused; *correspondence* critical realists criticize *dynamic equivalence* critical realist
  methods as syncretistic or non-biblical

Syncretism: inappropriate blending of non-Christian religious ideas
  or practices with Christian faith

Holism: on an individual level, ministry attending to the whole
  person (body and soul); on the societal level, ministry attending
  to all areas of society (religion, politics, economics, education,
  and so on)

Insider movements: movements to obedient faith in Christ that remain integrated with or inside their natural community

Bite-sized contextual efforts: contextual efforts focused on particular
  issues or questions in a setting

From the rest to the West: the growth and strength of the world
  church outside of Western contexts has resulted in the Majority
  World church now reaching Western secularized or post-Christian populations

QUESTIONS FOR REFLECTION

1. Given the tensions that have developed, and based on your own experience, do you anticipate that the evangelical divide over critical realism will narrow or widen in the future?

2. Is there a possibility that evangelicals will adopt a social gospel position that demeans evangelism? What evidence do you have for your answer?

3. Evangelicals in the United States have dramatically shifted positions on engagement in politics over the past few decades. What role might contextualization play in helping shape political engagement choices that churches make?

4. More than any other theological orientation, Pentecostals expect and engage in the miraculous. What might it mean to "contextualize" miracles?

FOR FURTHER STUDY

Adeney, Miriam. 2009. *Kingdom without Borders: The Untold Story of Christianity*. Downers Grove: InterVarsity.

Hattaway, Paul. 2003. *Back to Jerusalem: Three Chinese House Church Leaders Share Their Vision to Complete the Great Commission*. Waynesboro, GA: Gabriel Resources.

Howell, Brian M., and Edwin Zehner, eds. 2009. *Power and Identity in the Global Church: Six Contemporary Cases*. Pasadena: William Carey Library.

Ott, Craig, and Stephen Strauss, with Timothy C. Tennent. 2010. *Encountering Theology of Mission: Biblical Foundations, Historical Developments and Contemporary Issues*. Encountering Missions Series, edited by A. Scott Moreau. Grand Rapids: Baker.

Plueddemann, James E. 2010. *Leading Across Cultures: Effective Ministry and Mission in the Global Church*. Downers Grove: InterVarsity.

Schafer, Joseph L., Mark Yoon, and A. Scott Moreau. 2009. "University Bible Fellowship: What Happens When Missionaries from Korea Descend on North American College Campuses?" In *Missions from the Majority World: Progress, Challenges, and Case Studies.*,121–49. EMS 17. Edited by Michael Pocock and Enoch Wan, Pasadena: William Carey Library.

Dean Gilliland's Map

In this appendix I explain the map of contextualization developed by Dean Gilliland. Gilliland does not indicate the rubric he uses to classify his models, though he clearly draws nomenclature and definitions from Bevans and Schreiter. He has produced three versions of his approach over the years (1989, 2000, and 2005). I evaluate his most recent effort (2005).

In his first two publications (1989 and 2000), he included all the models of Bevans and Schreiter's maps but noted that the assumptions and methodology of some of the models makes them inappropriate for an evangelical approach (1989, 313; 2000, 226). In his most recent map (2005), he lists six models in alphabetical order: 1) adaptation, 2) anthropological, 3) critical, 4) praxis, 5) synthetic, and 6) translation. Though his diagram (Figure A) includes the synthetic model, he does not discuss it in the essay (2005, 514) Altogether the models

> . . . are a kind of toolbox for communicating and applying the message in diversified situations. The particular task in this or that context must be carefully thought out, the end product kept in mind and the right tool (model) selected. Doing this work will usually require a combination of these tools and often a new tool must be fabricated to match the particularities of a given task. (2005, 497)

Gilliland builds his map on his positing that the incarnation is God's contextualization model, the matrix in which we are to see and evaluate all other models. He indicates this by placing it as the circle in which all other models are located, as indicated in his visual map (Figure A). He discusses each model in how it reflects one or more facets of the incarnation, looking for insights and application from each that accord with God's intention in the incarnation.

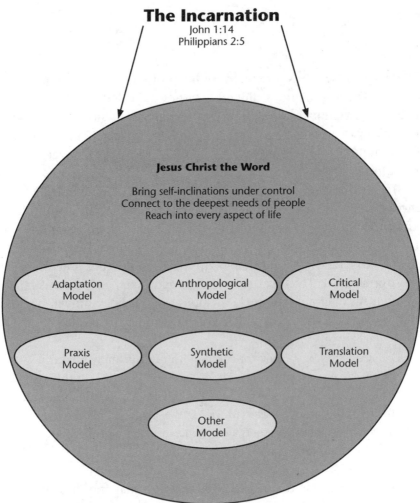

The Incarnation
John 1:14
Philippians 2:5

Jesus Christ the Word

Bring self-inclinations under control
Connect to the deepest needs of people
Reach into every aspect of life

Adaptation Model

Anthropological Model

Critical Model

Praxis Model

Synthetic Model

Translation Model

Other Model

Figure A: Relationship of Human Contextualization Models to the Divine Model
(Source: Gilliland 2005, 514)

Adaptation

Adaptation essentially refers to the process of changing to meet the needs of an environment that has changed. In relation to the Christian faith, "Adaptation refers to finding ways to express the Gospel in forms and ideas that are familiar to the culture so that they will "fit" within it" (Pocock, Van Rheenen and McConnell 2005, 325). Evangelicals pointed to an important nuance: it is not the gospel itself that needs to change, but how we express (or incarnate) the gospel in the new setting. Historically evangelicals pointed to John taking the Greek philosophical term *"logos"* (word) and investing it with new meaning in the Greek environment so that people could connect to the gospel more easily.

Gilliland indicates that adaptation as a contextual model is inadequate in that it focuses on terms and external forms rather than deeper levels of culture (2005, 507). Thus evangelicals recognize the inadequacies of adaptation. Even so,

> There is something incarnational about the struggle with foreignness that began with these *adaptation* ideas. They represent the first serious attempts by 'outsiders' to understand a particular people in their milieu with the objective of setting aside or modifying irrelevant dogma and forms. This led to a new kind of humility and introspection in mission that was not known before. Here was a search to understand what expressing Jesus Christ should mean for every person, regardless of religion or culture. (2005, 507)

Anthropological

Gilliland argues that the anthropological method parallels the incarnation in that Jesus came as a human being revealing God to us while being grounded within a particular society. He notes that evangelicals tend to view a method that looks for truth within a culture with suspicion (2005, 507). In the case of some evangelicals, the publication of Charles Kraft's *Christianity in Culture* allayed those suspicions. For others, however, Kraft's approaches provoked controversy. In any event, in Gilliland's understanding the anthropological model

> . . . seeks to identify symbols and ideas that are precious to people and can serve to articulate and confirm God's truth. . . . If evangelists take the time to listen and learn from culture they will find confirmation of the biblical message, much as did Paul when he declared in Lystra that, "(God) has not left himself without a witness (Acts 14:17)." (508)

It seems clear from this definition that Gilliland's understanding of the anthropological model is closer to Don Richardson's redemptive analogies than Steven Bevans's anthropological model. As I noted in chapter 1, Bevans's focus was that practitioners examine the local society for what it has to offer as a result of God's revelatory work within them, and not so that they can learn how to bring an external message. Bevans's model includes Gilliland's understanding but is more radical than simply finding confirmation of the biblical message in the culture. In fact, Bevans's model views Scripture as culturally conditioned and incomplete (2002, 141).

Critical

By critical, Gilliland refers to Paul Hiebert's critical contextualization method rather than a class of models. The goal of the method is to arrive at biblically faithful beliefs and culturally authentic practices which have the consensus of the redeemed community (Gilliland 1989b, 317). Though not a model in the same way the others are, it merits separate mention because of its unique and careful handling of both Scripture and culture. Gilliland notes, "The human and divine aspects are also engaged in doing critical contextualization as cultural forms and meanings, precious to Christian believers of every culture, are placed along-side serious interaction with the Bible" (508).

It addresses the risk that of uncritical acceptance of cultural forms as well as the risk of uncritical rejection of them by mediating the importance of exegeting *both* culture and Scripture.

> Critical contextualization calls us to take seriously these deep level beliefs and practices and to understand the meanings they convey. The idea then, is to apply these familiar or modified forms to Christian living, worship and theology. When engaging the critical process, modifications of old forms are found and, hopefully, new forms will result. Appropriate Christianity is the expression of this critical process. (509)

The critical approach reflects the incarnation in that Jesus, as an insider to his own culture, was able to reject some of the religious forms, accept some of them, and modify others—all with a focus on both culture and Scripture (see chapter nine for a more detailed presentation).

Praxis

Western evangelicals have largely rejected praxis contextualization because of their identification of praxis-focused models with liberation theologies. Evangelical characterizations of liberation theologies include inappropriate hermeneutical approaches, a denigrating of human sin, a focus on salvation as humanization, and an uncritical use of Marxism for social analysis. However, Gilliland, while agreeing with these criticisms, also notes

> A more recent understanding of praxis has to do with corporate reflection on issues followed by action. Praxis is best understood in the reciprocity between thinking critically about real problems and making decisions to bring about constructive change. (510)

Evangelicals have more recently come to appreciate praxis models over the past two decades, primarily because evangelical sisters and brothers from Majority World settings cleared up some of the misconceptions and cast some of the praxis concerns in ways that were more biblically grounded (e.g., Nuñez 1985). This recasting of praxis models focused on the need for "social change on behalf of (or in cooperation with) marginalized populations" (Moreau 2006a, 328), something that evangelicals could recognize as an important part of the whole ministry of the church.

Gilliland connects praxis to the incarnation by noting that the "Incarnation of Jesus Christ is the divine praxis of God, the final answer to the human dilemma of sin and the need for peace and salvation" (Gilliland 2005, 510). We see the connection in the need for problems to be thoroughly understood in their own context. However, we must follow understanding with deciding how to act and then acting. Finally, this action is ongoing, and reflection on the action is part of that process. Finally, we must note that what Gilliland means by praxis is not an exact match with what Bevans means. As I noted in chapter 1, practitioners of praxis have tended to follow a Marxist approach to understanding local settings as giving them a frame of reference for their praxis. As with the anthropological model, Bevans's praxis includes Gilliland's understanding but is more radical than simply struggling against injustice. In fact, Bevans's praxis model views Scripture as culturally conditioned and incomplete (2002, 141).

Synthetic

By synthetic Gilliland does not mean artificial. Rather, by synthesis he means "that components of the totality of life are brought together into wholeness and ways are found so that these values and insights from one place can be shared with believers in other contexts" (2005, 511). We see this synthesis in two dimensions.

First, the particular circumstances of any place or people communicate truth about them in ways that help us understand them and their particular needs from all aspects of life. This includes the orientations of both the anthropological (cultural) and praxis (life circumstances) models.

The second dimension is the fact that Christians in every time and place connect to the Christians in every other time and place. Each can learn to see their own peculiar circumstances in light of the circumstances of the various other parts of the larger body of Christ around the world and over the millennia.

The synthetic model attends to both dimensions, and "In this, we are very close to one meaning of the Incarnation, that is, through the Incarnation, the way is open for diverse nations to share in the one body of Christ" (2005, 511). As with the anthropological and praxis models, however, Gilliland's synthetic is not the same as Bevans's synthetic model. Like Bevans's anthropological and praxis models, his synthetic model views Scripture as culturally conditioned and incomplete (2002, 142).

Translation

The translation model is the best known and most widely used contextualization model. Gilliland's understanding of this model is essentially the same as I discussed in chapter 1. He notes that this model attends to two primary questions (2005, 512).

The first question is "What is the message?" Central to this model is the belief that there is a universal message that we are tasked to translate into every human setting. The first question focuses on the content of that message and can lead to the kernel and husk approach.

However, as I noted in chapter 2, this does not accurately characterize evangelical consensus today.

The second question, then, follows from the implications of the first: "How should we present the message?" Gilliland's answer to this question is Charles Kraft's dynamic equivalence, namely, "the appropriate use of local forms in order to convey the intended meanings" (513). He then indicates the connection of the translation model to the incarnation:

> . . . it demonstrates God's self expression in ways that are accessible and understandable to people. God is pure and infinite Spirit. The Word who became flesh, is God "speaking" his loving desire for relationship with, finite and temporal human beings. Through the Incarnation there is a form we can grasp; it is the humanization of Spirit. (513)

Evaluation

Dean Gilliland's map has the advantage of using standard nomenclature that missiologists who focus on contextualization will all recognize. He also demonstrates that putting all evangelical models under the translation label does not do justice to the variety of ways we engage contextualization. Perhaps the greatest strength is how he frames his entire map in the incarnation as God's ultimate model of contextualization. This provides an overarching orientation and has the potential to guide our evaluations of each model. His characterization of each model by how it characterizes one or more facets of the incarnation illustrates its richness, and he builds into his map room for additional models.

There are also disadvantages of Gilliland's map. While there are advantages of using standard nomenclature, the models he works with as portrayed by Bevans and others do not adhere to the characteristics of evangelicals. To make them less opposed to evangelical convictions, Gilliland must redefine some of them in significant ways. For example, his *synthetic* model is so different from Bevans's *synthetic* model that in using the same label he confuses rather than helps. Gilliland's *anthropological* model, as noted above, is more congenial to evangelical convictions than is Bevans's *anthropological* model. By recasting them so significantly, Gilliland is proposing different models than Bevans. In fact, careful inspection of them can lead to the conclusion that they are in reality little more than facets of the incarnational model rather than truly separate models.

Ultimately the overarching orientation to the incarnation is not only a great strength of his map; it is also a limitation that weakens it too much for our intentions. The weakness is that the incarnation is so fluid that we can link virtually any model to some facet of it. If this is true, then the incarnation has power as an overall orientation but lacks power as a means of distinguishing (and discarding) approaches since theoretically anything is possible (and that is certainly not Gilliland's intention). We can also add to this the concern of some evangelicals (mentioned in chapter 5) that the very uniqueness of the incarnation should give us pause in using it as a matrix under which we place all of our contextual models.

Marc Cortez's Map

In this appendix, I explain the map of contextualization developed by Marc Cortez, who constructs the categories for his map on the basis to their correspondence to three levels of biblical discourse (2005a).

Cortez expresses appreciation for the map of Bruce Nicholls (chapter 3) but insists that his bipolar approach is too dichotomistic. Cortez proposes inserting an extra category that mediates the extremes, yielding a map with three categories: 1) translation, 2) synthetic, and 3) praxis.

Layers of Discourse

Cortez agrees with Bevans's important insight that different situations call for the use of different contextual approaches. Bevans advocates using the best model for each situation. Cortez, however, notes that all three models in his map have utility in every situation. To enable that, he offers criteria for determining how to use a particular model in a given situation from the nature of biblical and theological discourse (2005a, 89).

In an argument far more nuanced than space allows here, Cortez outlines three layers of perspective and three corresponding layers of biblical discourse (Table B.1). At the primary layer are *paradigms* and the corresponding biblical *assertions*. At the secondary layer are *models* and the corresponding biblical *inferences*. Finally, at the tertiary layer are *theories* and the corresponding biblical *speculations*. Cortez does not define biblical *speculations* as wild guesses but as "ways of making a particular theological model *vital* and *coherent* in a given situation" (2005a, 100).

Layer of Perspective	Explanation	Layer of Biblical Discourse
TABLE B.1: LAYERS OF PERSPECTIVE AND BIBLICAL DISCOURSE IN CORTEZ'S MAP		
Paradigm	conceptual structure through which *some particular portion* of reality is perceived. A paradigm thus serves to order sensory experiences according to some pre-determined interpretive pattern (2005a, 90 n. 38)	**Assertion**
	comprises all the particular statements of the Bible and thus includes not only its various propositions but also its narrative and symbolic elements (2005a, 94)	
Model	a relatively simple, artificially constructed case which is found to be useful and illuminating for dealing with realities that are more complex and differentiated (2005a, 91)	**Inference**
	those ideas which may be reasonably drawn from the affirmations of the biblical text (2005a, 95)	
Theory	any concept that seeks to elucidate more or less precisely the content of some model (2005a, 93)	**Speculation**
	a thoughtful deduction from or extension of those assertions and inferences. Particular speculations should thus be understood as contextually defensible theological formulations (2005a, 05)	

I illustrate the correspondence of perspectives with biblical discourse (Table B.1) by lining the definitions directly above each other but leaving the end of the center definition box open in the direction that corresponds to the term defined. In sum, Cortez uses two discourse types (biblical and conceptual) for each contextualization model, and each model is best suited to a particular layer of applicability. In Table

B.1, I illustrate the layer of each contextual model with the corresponding types of discourse.

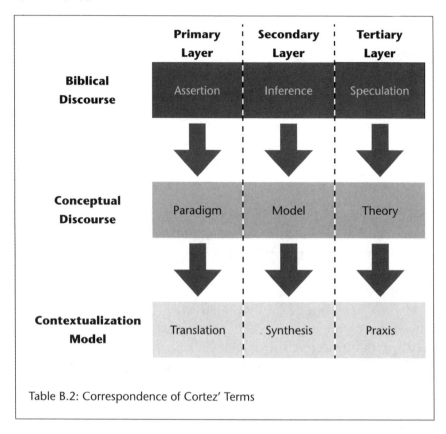

Table B.2: Correspondence of Cortez' Terms

In every setting, we may use all three contextual methods. However, each method corresponds to the layer of discourse it represents. For each layer of *biblical* discourse, we should use only contextual models at the same layer or lower. From Table B.2, we use only the contextual models directly underneath or to the right of the layer of biblical discourse. For example, at the inference layer of biblical discourse, we may appropriately use synthetic and praxis contextualization but not translation contextualization.

Translation contextualization focuses on the biblical pole: "The key idea of this model is therefore the existence of supracultural biblical truths that can be both distinguished and separated from their cultural form and articulated in an alternate cultural guise" (Cortez 2005a, 87).

Synthetic contextualization is the same as Bevans's synthetic model, bringing together translation and praxis ideals so that "culture and world events become the very sources of the theological enterprise, along with and equal to scripture and tradition" (Cortez 2005a, 88; citing Bevans).

The *praxis* model is the same as Bevans's praxis model and focuses on the contextual pole. "This model argues that contextualization must unite knowledge as content with knowledge as action in order to properly engage the situation" (Cortez 2005a, 87).

Cortez notes the difficulties of sorting within our theological constructions the levels of each type of statement we make. However, he freely borrows from models that do not see Scripture as the ultimate authority by confining their use to layers of discourse below the paradigmatic. This approach allows "for the imaginative creativity and theological flexibility necessary for engaging a world in constant flux" (2005a, 102) without jeopardizing our commitment to biblical absolutes.

Evaluation

The greatest strength of Cortez's map is that he offers a clear rubric in demarcating among the models. He also shows how each type of model draws from biblical framing—and limits the potential for the synthetic and praxis models to challenge biblical authority by confining them to particular discourse levels.

However, ultimately Cortez uses the same term ("model") in two different ways: 1) "models" of contextualization *and* 2) the "model" layer of conceptual discourse (see Table B.3). The two are not conceptually identical; his use of the same term for both illustrates the conundrum. A consistent use of terminology requires the renaming of his contextual "models" as contextual "discourses." Mapping layers of contextual *discourse*, however, is not the same as mapping contextual *models*, since every contextual model can have all three layers of contextual discourse associated with it. In fact, Cortez anchors his approach in this point.

That Cortez is not discussing contextual "models" is even clearer in his applications of the discourse approach to each "model," in which he has to treat the "models" *not as* models but as *layers of discourse*. However, it is impossible to apply his definitions of the synthetic and praxis models to their respective layers of discourse without contradicting the definitions he uses. As I already noted, he defines the synthetic model as an orientation that "culture and world events become the very sources of the theological enterprise, *along with and equal to scripture and tradition*" (88; emphasis mine). However, by relegating synthetic "models" to the *model* layer of discourse (which is below the assertion/paradigm layer and illustrates the two ways he uses "model"), Cortez must void the idea that culture is equal to Scripture in his own definition. The same logic applies to the praxis model, which is at the *speculative* layer of biblical discourse. In terms of providing a map of contextualization, then, Cortez does not help.

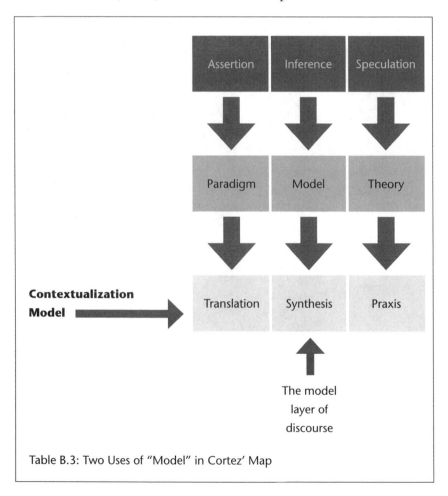

Table B.3: Two Uses of "Model" in Cortez' Map

Even so, his use of layers of discourse is a helpful analytic tool. For example, agents of Paul Hiebert's critical contextualization could profitably use all three layers of discourse identified by Cortez (translation, synthetic, and praxis) while operating within Hiebert's method. However, others already used these same labels, and it would be better to change them. It seems preferable to and easiest to use the labels Cortez gives to the layers of biblical discourse: assertion, inference, and speculation.

Charles Van Engen's Map

In this appendix, I explain the map of contextualization developed by Charles Van Engen. Van Engen describes the models in his map in chronological development, though he classifies them by directional flow, as either flowing in one direction (one-way models) or in two (two-way models) (2005a).

Van Engen presents five perspectives of contextualization developed over the past few centuries.[1] It is clear that he uses "perspectives" as essentially the same thing that the other maps call "models." He intends his map to serve as a type of guide for the chronological development of appropriate contextualization perspectives over those centuries. Appropriate contextualization, therefore, will draw on all five perspectives. Using them all, in a follow-up essay he constructs his own model for a "contextually appropriate methodology for mission theology" (2005b). Table C.1 summarizes his map of five models split into two major categories (his visual map is in Figure C below).

TABLE C.1: VAN ENGEN'S LIST OF APPROPRIATE MODELS	
Models of Contextualization	
One-Way	Indigenization
	Communication
	Translatability
Two-Way	Epistemological
	Local Theologizing

One-Way Models

Van Engen notes a major divide among the five perspectives. The first three—communication, indigenization, and translatability—"deal

---

1. Even though the title of Van Engen's chapter is "Five Perspectives of Contextually Confirmed Appropriate Missional Theology," in personal communication (2009) he indicated that his focus is on five approaches to contextualization rather than missional theology.

generally with a one-way movement of gospel proclamation in word and deed: a movement from those who know God and believe they understand the gospel to those who do not know, have never heard, or no longer can hear of God's love for them" (2005a, 192).

Communication

The first perspective Van Engen labels *communication* (or adaptation or accommodation) which he equates with Bevans's (and therefore Gilliland's) *translation* model. Van Engen prefers communication since 1) this model focuses on appropriate means to communicate the gospel and 2) the new label prevents confusion with *translatability*, which he reserves for the third model in his map (2005a, 183–85). Historically, however, Schreiter (1985) and Bevans (1985) follow Haleblian in using "translation" as the label to employ for these models, and until Van Engen's proposal, it is the only designation found in the literature.

As Van Engen sees it, the communication perspective is an integrative one in which people in the new setting come to understand the gospel (2005b, 203). Using Charles Kraft's dynamic equivalence as a guiding idea, Van Engen indicates that *understanding the gospel* has twin foci: 1) *understanding* comes from the contextualizer being receptor-oriented, and 2) *the gospel* requires of the contextualizer faithfulness to the message.

Indigenization

Once the people understand the gospel, local fellowships develop as indigenous churches. Thus the *indigenization* perspective of contextualization recognizes that the gospel must be localized so that there is a "fit between the forms and life of the church and its surrounding context" (2005a, 187). While all of the other maps exclude indigenization (largely because contextualization was coined to replace it), Van Engen notes that contextualization was intended to include indigenization and go beyond it. In the historical development of contextualized communities, it is a critical step that is still contained within the contextualization rubric (see discussion in chapter 5).

Translatability

Van Engen's third model is that of the "translatability" of the gospel, theologically seen in the incarnation. This perspective arose from the reflections of Andrew Walls (e.g., 1990, 24–39), Lamin Sanneh (e.g., 2003, 23–26), Kwame Bediako (e.g., 1995, 173), and others who noted that, as the gospel took root in new settings, the result was not necessarily what the original communicators had intended. Rather, as indigenous faith communities reflected on the Scriptures for themselves, members of those communities realized how Christ both fit and did not fit their own culture, and they shaped their faith using both the incarnated gospel and their own cultural milieu. The translatability perspective, then, is based on the "incarnational nature of the gospel as being infinitely translatable into any and all human cultures" (2005a 184). This is "broader, deeper and more pervasive than mere communication of a message" (2005a, 188), so must be distinguished from the translation model in the other maps.

As Christians plant the gospel in new soil, the gospel begins to take on characteristics of the soil in ways that allow it to flourish as an indigenous plant. This process can be started by a variety of methods such as Bible translation, evangelism, and church planting, but the reality is that over time the gospel and the church are translated in ways that develop "vernacular credibility" (Sanneh, cited in Van Engen 2005a). This "translatability" is God's agenda demonstrated in the incarnation; it is not under human control. As Sanneh notes, "Being the original Scripture of the Christian movement, the New Testament Gospels are a translated version of the message of Jesus, which means that Christianity is a translated religion without a revealed language" (2003, 97). The contextualizer participates in this process, never really controlling or directing it, especially once there is an appropriate and accessible translation of the Bible available. After that, translatability is essentially out of the hands of agents of contextualization. As a result, Bevans understands this idea as a metaphor of the seed already being in the ground, with only water needed for it to sprout, which describes his anthropological model (Bevans 2007).

Two-Way Models

The last two of Van Engen's models are the most recently developed. Unlike the first three models, the local theologizing and epistemological approaches "involve an intentional two-way conversation between church and Gospel, on the one hand, and the contextual reality, on the other" (2005a, 192).

Local Theologizing

Van Engen chooses *local theologizing* (Van Engen 2005a, 192–96) as a label "as a way to cut through today's confusion over contextualization" (192). He recognizes that the original effort for which contextualization was conceived is not the way evangelicals use the term today. Thus, to refer to the original more technical meaning, a new term must be coined. He opts for local theologizing based on the widely read books by Roman Catholics Robert Schreiter (*Constructing Local Theologies; 2005*) and Clemens Sedmak (*Doing Local Theology*; 2002). They envision a model that is in line with the technical origination of the term, so Van Engen uses their term as a label for what contextualization originally meant. The problem he hopes to avoid is clear: he cannot use the original label "contextualization" because it will be too confusing given the evolution of the term. Using "contextualization" as the name of a particular model in a map of all "contextualization models" is indeed confusing.

Local theologizing, Van Engen explains, is an approach that focuses on "the impact of socio-political, economic, cultural and other forces in a context on the task of doing theology in that context" (193), which (as noted in chapter 1) is the original technical intent of the term *contextualization*. Local theologizing is thus seen in action rather than as a "received composite of affirmations" (193) and draws not only from theological resources but from any areas that help us understand human experience. This model is constantly evolving, as it "represents a constantly-changing reciprocal interaction between church and context" (194). Reflection on the local situation leads to new readings of Scripture which in turn lead to new theological actions to change oppressive and unjust structures in the setting. This results in new reflection on the local situation and the cycle repeats.

Epistemological

The final model Van Engen discusses is *epistemological* (2005a, 196–201). Again, he draws from other maps and proposes a different label. The epistemological model Van Engen describes incorporates an orientation seen in Hiebert's critical contextualization but is intended to parallel Bevans's countercultural model. He chooses the label "epistemological" because contextualization approaches based on this orientation deal "with an epistemological process of hermeneutical examination and critique of the context and its implications for a missional understanding of the Gospel in that specific context" (2005a, 196).

As described by Bevans, the epistemological model has as its goal to "truly *encounter* and *engage* the context." It uses "respectful yet critical analysis and authentic gospel proclamation in word and deed" (Bevans 2002, 119). This process teaches us new things about God because "Christian knowledge about God is seen as cumulative, enhanced, deepened broadened and expanded as the Gospel takes new shape in each new culture" (Van Engen 2005a, 197). Inspired by Lesslie Newbigin's reflections on bringing the gospel to a post-Christendom environment (1986; 1989), countercultural approaches tend to be seen more in mainline denominations. Evangelicals engaged in the countercultural approach are often critical of selected branches of evangelicalism, perhaps most notably the megachurch movement in the United St., because it is captive to culture rather than engaging it (see, e.g., the essays in Guder 1998). Evangelicals embrace some of the approaches that are within the counter-cultural model, seen in groups such as the Gospel and Our Culture Network (www.gocn.net) and the missional thinking expressed by numerous emerging church advocates (Driscoll and Breshears 2008; Gibbs and Bolger 2005). However, we also dismiss approaches that move too far in the instrumentalist direction (e.g., Emergent, which is described as "an organization promoting a more theologically liberal and non-evangelical version of the missional church," Driscoll and Breshears 2008, 219; see also Hesselgrave 2007).

Van Engen's Map

Van Engen draws on all five perspectives to develop a method of twelve steps needed to construct contextually appropriate mission theology (2005b). In Table C.2, I list the five models and indicate for each model the resulting characteristic of this theology. Van Engen presents a figure incorporating the twelve steps and illustrating the flow of his method (2005b, 221). Because his purpose is different from mine, it does not indicate conceptually where the contextualization models fit. Thus, in Figure C I adapted his diagram by omitting some of the more complex details and using shaded areas indicating where his five models fit in the overall flow. As you examine Figure C, bear in mind that the demarcation of where one model ends and the next begins is fuzzy rather than bounded.

TABLE C.2: CONTEXTUAL MODELS AND IMPACT FOR CHARACTERISTICS OF CONTEXTUAL THEOLOGY	
Model	**Resulting Characteristic**
Communication	Integrational: Understanding the gospel of Jesus Christ
Indigenization	Local: Approaching a new context anew
Translatability	Incarnational: Preparing for new action
Local Theologizing	Praxeological: Living out the gospel in appropriate action
Epistemological	Dialogical: Reshaping our understanding of the gospel

Evaluation

There are significant obstacles to adopting Van Engen's map for evangelical contextualization. He did not intend to map out evangelical models but to show how evangelicals can draw from historical models to construct an appropriate contextual theology. Thus I am evaluating his map on the basis of a different purpose than he had in constructing it, so my critique only relates to my intentions, not to his original purposes.

Van Engen's map offers strengths as a potential taxonomy of evangelical contextualization. His major delineation of one-way and two-way approaches is a good rubric for identifying different models, and I will draw on it in constructing my rubric for mapping evangelical models. Further, tracing the history of contextual models is helpful and enables us to see them in their historical settings. This makes it possible to see what the originators were attempting to do and what they responded to from the models of their historical periods.

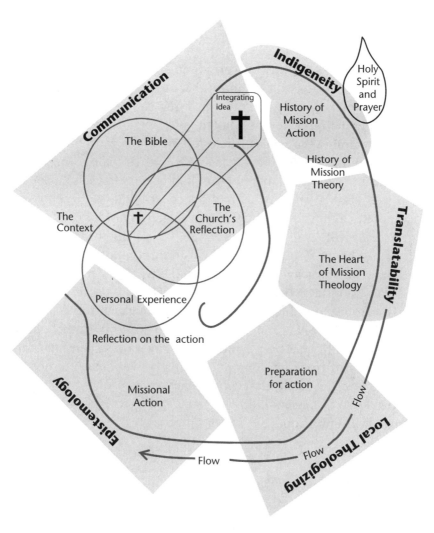

Figure C: Van Engen's Visual Map of Contextual Models

However, the taxonomy also has weaknesses if we want to use it as a map of evangelical models. First, too many of the name changes he proposes are confusing to anyone who is not a historical scholar. The bulk of evangelical missionaries are not acquainted with the original ideas. Van Engen's nomenclature is too confusing to replace Bevans's nomenclature. As we saw in the discussion of other maps in chapters 1, 2, and here, Bevans's terms are widely used as the standards in missiological discourse by those ranging from evangelicals to Roman Catholics.

We can illustrate this by considering Van Engen's proposal to refer to the historical and technical meaning of contextualization as "local theologizing." He is right to identify the need of a new label for the original term, for, as I noted in chapter 1, evangelicals and those in mainline ecumenical circles use the same word but with different meanings. Unfortunately, as with "contextualization," "local theologizing" is also a standard term. Robert Schreiter's use made the term well known, and his method for constructing local theologies incorporates almost everything in Van Engen's map for constructing contextual theology (e.g., Schreiter 1985, 25). Again, for my purposes, this name change results in conceptual confusion rather than clarity.

A final difficulty in using this as a map is whether "translatability" is in reality a model. Sanneh notes, "Translatability became the characteristic mode of Christian expansion through history" (Sanneh 1989, 214, which Shaw and Van Engen cite; 2003, 3). Sanneh is correct; translatability has been a primary *mode* for the expansion of the Christian faith. However, a *mode* of Christian expansion is not the same as a *model* of evangelical contextualization.

Together, these issues indicate that Van Engen's map—while providing key insights—does not fit our purposes.

A Composite Map of Gilliland, Cortez, and Van Engen

In this appendix, I consolidate the maps of Cortez, Gilliland, and Van Engen into a composite map and explore insights that come from this consolidation.

If I can combine and consolidate the categories listed by Gilliland, Cortez, and Van Engen—all intended to portray plausible evangelical models of contextualization—into a single meta-map I may get a useful picture of the evangelical contextualization "universe" they offer (Figure D). Unfortunately, there are major hurdles to overcome in even attempting the task. For example, the authors do not use a common rubric in forming (or naming) their categories. Further, the nomenclature differences make blending them into a single map difficult at best. However, the insights we gain in the process of blending them is worth the effort.

These three authors identify twelve distinct labels in their maps. They are, in alphabetical order: adaptation, anthropological, communication, critical, epistemological, incarnation, indigenization, local theologizing, praxis, synthetic, translatability, and translation.

First, we should drop redundant or overlapping labels from the list. *Translation* and *communication* refer to the same model. Since everyone but Van Engen uses *translation* to name this model, I follow Gilliland's lead and drop *communication*. Gilliland also gives sufficient reasons to drop *incarnation* as a separate model but keep it as the matrix for the composite map. Similarly, I drop *translatability* as a separate model but will use it in the map. I show how I handle these two below.

For the next step, I need to consolidate labels where possible. *Adaptation* and *indigenization* are variations on *translation*, so I group them together under it. Gilliland notes that *critical* may not technically be a model (2005, 508–509), and Van Engen discusses the orientation of *critical* contextualization as fitting in the *epistemological* category (2005a, 201). Bevans indicates in personal correspondence that he sees it as an example of *translation* (2009). Based on that, I decide to list *critical* as a third *translation* example.

Praxis and *local* theologizing also present some difficulty. Van

Engen does not have a *praxis* category, but it is clear from his description that *local theologizing* has essentially a *praxis* orientation. Close examination of how Schreiter uses *local theologizing* shows that he means more than *praxis*. Indeed, he means more than the original understanding of "contextualization" and closer to *synthetic* (see below). Van Engen's restricted use mitigates against using it for the label. However, we need to change the label to avoid confusion with Bevans's *praxis*, in which Scripture is seen as incomplete. To show the difference, we can choose an adjective to moderate *praxis*, such as conditional, constrained, confined, evangelical, guarded, limited, moderated, and so on. I use *constrained praxis* in the composite map to indicate this model and add *local theologizing* in parenthesis simply to indicate the rough equivalence (Figure D). *Praxis* indicates the means by which we engage context and Scripture; *constrained* indicates the grounding on biblical norms rather than economic or sociological ones.

How should I list the three remaining models (*anthropological, epistemological,* and *synthetic*)? As I noted in Appendix A, Gilliland's *anthropological* model involves learning the culture well enough to discover various redemptive analogies and use them as bridges. If I am correct, this is a one-way model. However, as with *praxis,* I will change the label to avoid conflation with Bevans's *anthropological,* which views Scripture as incomplete. *Cultural analysis* is a possible label, but *translation* also uses cultural analysis. As I did with *praxis,* I will add a modifying adjective to *anthropological.* The modifying adjective indicates the difference with Bevans's *anthropological.* Again, *constrained* serves well to modify *anthropological;* indicating the limitations of anthropology as well as the grounding in biblical norms.

Van Engen's *epistemological* is the same as Bevans's *counter-cultural.* Both have strengths and weaknesses. A third option is using a label the practitioners themselves use, such as *emergent* or *missional.* However, these terms carry their own baggage. Ultimately, I chose to use Bevans's label, primarily because it is more descriptive and less confusing to lay readers than Van Engen's.

Gilliland's *synthetic* draws insights from culture (*anthropological*), the local situations (*praxis*) and the history and traditions of the Christian faith. Catholics give this last element more weight than

Protestants (evidenced in Schreiter's and Sedmak's *local theologizing*). However, without saying tradition is on par with biblical revelation, Protestants recognize that we dare not ignore the connection of every local body to every other local body in location and history. This is the essence of Wall's "pilgrim" orientation (see chapter five). As I have shown, Gilliland draws on Bevans's *synthetic* model, but intends that Scripture be normative rather than one source among many other equal sources. Thus, to avoid confusion, I should modify the term in some way. *Pilgrim* is a candidate for the label, but Walls *contrasts* pilgrim with indigenization and this model *combines* them. For consistency with *praxis* and *anthropological*, I use *constrained synthetic* as the label. This maintains Gilliland's primary identifier and indicates differentiation from Bevans's *synthetic*. *Constrained synthetic* indicates the blending of local culture, the need for praxis, and the connection of local bodies to the larger body of Christ and its tradition—but constrained in their roles because we ground the model in biblical authority.

To complete the composite map, I need to incorporate organizational insights from the three source maps, namely: a) Gilliland's incarnation as matrix for the whole map, b) Van Engen's recognition of translatability, c) Van Engen's recognition of the flow of the models, and d) Cortez's layers of discourse for each model. I incorporate them all into Figure D.

Gilliland uses the incarnation as the matrix frame for all contextualization, so I use it to frame the entire map. The translatability of the gospel is a characteristic of all models that *enables* contextualization rather than a model itself.

Van Engen's rubric of *one-way* versus *two*-way models gives an organization for the five models. The one-way category has two models: 1) translation (with three sub-types: adaptation, indigenization, and critical) and 2) constrained anthropological. The two-way category has three models: 3) counter-cultural, 4) praxis, and 5) constrained synthetic. Every model has three layers of discourse (assertion, inference, and speculation).

Cortez's layers of discourse apply to every model, which I indicate by placing to the left of the model name. I use his discourse labels (assertion, inference, and speculation) to avoid confusion.

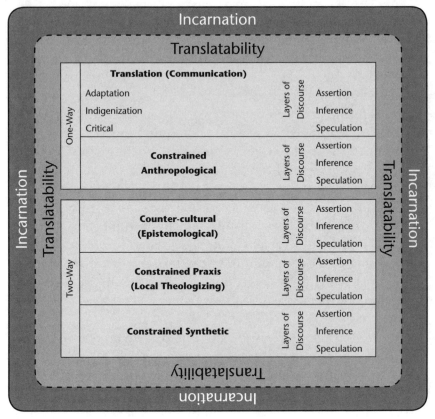

Figure D: Composite Map of Evangelical Models

Evaluation

An important strength of this composite map is that it draws from the combined thinking of evangelicals who have wrestled with contextualization for several decades. However, the fact that each author developed his taxonomy independently from the others presents a fundamental problem that is ultimately impossible to overcome in trying to combine them into a unified map. I doubt that the authors would agree with the way I blended their individual taxonomies in Figure D.

A crucial consideration is whether this map corresponds to the actual models and practices evangelicals have advocated over the past several decades. For example, Gilliland developed his categories from

Bevans's map, which was much broader than evangelicals have practiced. A similar critique applies to Van Engen's "local theologizing" model. Neither author cites evangelical examples for these two models, so we may question whether such even exist. Perhaps the composite map represents more of a type of mandate than a reality.

A Visual Evangelical Semantic

Domain of Contextualization

To offer a cohesive and comprehensive map of practices and models implemented by evangelicals, I need to consider additional insights from evangelical terminology and evangelical practices to see if I need to extend or modify the composite map in Appendix D. In this appendix, I explore evangelical terminology for further help.

Over the past several decades, evangelicals have coined new words or word combinations to capture their orientation toward contextualization. Some created neologisms as a negative reaction to the original intention of the term. Others applied alternate labels to orient us in a particular methodological or theological direction, and still others added adjectives to temper the meaning.

I list in Table D the terms evangelicals proposed in roughly the order they appeared in print. There probably are terms I did not find that would extend the list, but the length of the inventory in Table D demonstrates our mixed reactions of loving the *idea* and being concerned with the *label*.

	TABLE D: EVANGELICAL ALTERNATIVES AND MODIFIERS FOR "CONTEXTUALIZATION"
Year	**Term and Source(s)**
1973	Dynamic equivalence, transculturation (Kraft 1973a); ethnotheology (Kraft 1973d); inculturate (Barney 1973)
1975	Comprehensive *possessio* or possession?(Beyerhaus 1975)
1978	Incarnational theology (Padilla 1979a; Gilliland 2000)
1979	Transformation and Christian transformational change (Kraft 1979d)
1980	Context-indigenization (Fleming 1980)
1984	Actualized theology, theology in context, and transposing (Asia Theological Association 1984); biblically-oriented Asian theology (Ro 1984); pilgrim theology (Tano 1984); actualize (Athyal 1984); wholistic contextualization, relevance (Sumithra 1984); critical contextualization (Hiebert 1984)
1985	Self-theologizing (Hiebert 1985a)
1986	Localization (Tuza 1986)
1988	Metatheology (Hiebert 1988)
1992	Vernacular theology (Dyrness 1992)
1995	Re-clothe (Winter 1995)
1999	Local theology (Stephens 1999—from Schreiter 1985)
2000	Appropriate Christianity (Kraft 1999 and 2005e); deep-level contextualization (Caldwell 2000, 138)
2001	Transcultural theology (Howell 2001)
2003	Enacted theology or theology in practice (Anderson 2003); radical contextualization (Winter 2003a; 2005; Thomas 2005)
2004	Transformational Christopraxis (Gener 2004); comprehensive contextualization (Tallman 2004); comprehensive critical contextualization (Moreau 2005)
2005	Re-incarnation ecclesial translation (Campbell 2005); Beyond Christianity (Winter 2005)

We can organize this catalog of terms using the concept of semantic domains, a "map" of terms that can clarify scope and meaning by showing how they fit—or don't fit—together. Following that lead, I visually arrange the terms from Table D into clusters in Figure E, which serves as a visual map of the evangelical semantic domain for contextualization.

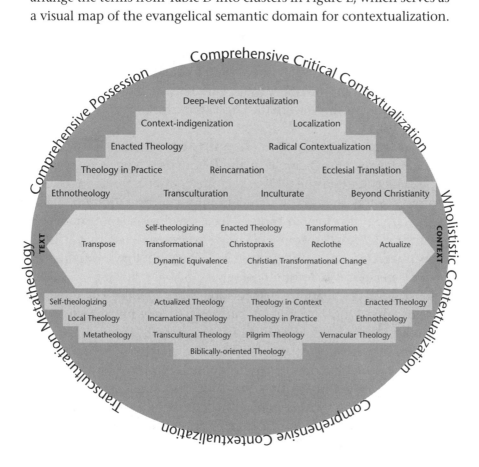

Figure E: Visual Semantic Domain of Evangelical Alternatives for "Contextualization"

This particular arrangement—one among many possibilities—helps us understand the interests and agendas that drive evangelicals as they reflect on contextualization from my vantage point.

Those who are detail-oriented will see that some terms—especially those with two foci, such as "enacted theology"—appear in more than one cluster. The clusters in the visual map indicate which focus I have in mind.

Text and Context (not in a cluster) are the metaphorical walls indicating the two constraining areas of contextualization. Four clusters comprise the rest of the diagram. I arrange three of them together to form a metaphorical house. I frame one cluster in an arrow between the walls indicating movement. I frame the second cluster in a group of bricks underneath the walls, indicating a foundation. I frame the third cluster in a roof on top of the walls. I arrange the fourth cluster in an encompassing oval, showing the larger frame for contextualization.

The Foundation Cluster: The Importance of Theology

The cluster of terms I frame in the foundation have a theological focus, reflecting that the biblical text is a central concern for us and that we see theology as the foundation for contextualization. Terms in the cluster (theology in context, local theology) demonstrate that we acknowledge all theology as being contextual and that it is always integral to the entire process. We value theology firmly rooted in local perspectives (ethnotheology, vernacular theology) and developed local populations (self-theologizing). Theology is not limited to propositional statements but must include praxis (actualized theology, enacted theology, theology in practice, pilgrim theology). Finally, we anchor theology in biblical revelation—biblical truths cross all cultural boundaries (incarnational, metatheology, transcultural). Like a good foundation, good theology will stand the test of time; bad theology will crumble. This cluster corresponds with the evangelical characteristics of the centrality of the gospel, biblicism, and crucicentrism.

The Arrow Cluster: Movement and Action

Terms in the arrow cluster pointing between Text and Context indicate the active methodology of contextualization. The two-way direction of the arrow indicates the movement of contextualization between the two walls. Some terms focus on the action itself (enacted theology, actualize, reclothe) while others indicate the process involved (transposing). "*Self*-theologizing" indicates the actors, and those including *transformation* indicate anticipated change (Christian transformational change, transformational Christopraxis). Dynamic equivalence is an overarching term for this cluster.

Together the terms in this cluster demonstrate that we see contextualization as an active process rather than a passive one. One reason is that people and societies are ever changing. Another is that contextualization itself must be proactive and engaged. This cluster corresponds directly with evangelicals as activists, and implicitly with our emphasis on conversion (an active process).

The Roof Cluster: Text *and* Context Engaged

Terms clustered in the roof overlay Text and Context and indicate the interplay between them. Though the text remains normative, it is also deeply enfleshed in local settings (context-indigenization). We cannot escape the contexts in which contextualization is done, whether in our own homes or in places remote from us (inculturate, localization, ethnotheology), and we must engage them fully (deep-level contextualization, enacted theology) in ways that make a difference (theology in practice, radical contextualization). Contextualization is both "in" and "trans"—both *in* and *beyond* culture (transculturation, beyond Christianity). This reflects the notion of Andrew Walls concerning the nature of Christian faith as simultaneously indigenous *and* pilgrim. Terms in this cluster correspond to the characteristic evangelical beliefs that the gospel is biblical, historical, theological, apostolic, and personal.

The Oval Group: Comprehensive Nature

Terms clustered in the surrounding oval indicate that we see contextualization as comprehensive. As important as theology is, it is only one component of the Christian faith that requires contextualizing. Some terms encapsulate the fact that all of life is fair game for the contextualizing process (comprehensive and wholistic), others that how we frame our approaches matters (metatheology). This cluster may well indicate that the characteristics listed by Bevington and Stott need expansion. Though outsiders have not considered holism a characteristic of evangelicalism through the twentieth century, there is evidence that this needs to be reconsidered (e.g., Corbett and Fikkert 2009).

Evaluation

Visually mapping the semantic domain gives us a more complete picture of how evangelicals conceptualize contextualization and perhaps may help us move past some of the stereotypes. However, this visual semantic domain has at best limited use for an overall map of evangelical contextualization. First, the originators intended the terms we used as *replacements* for contextualization. They were thinking of the entire domain, not individual models. Additionally, almost every term came from academics rather than field missionaries, agency leaders, or church-based evangelicals. The resulting domain necessarily reflects theoretical perspectives rather than contextual practices. Figure E illustrates four *emphases*: a) the importance of theology, b) movement/action, c) text *and* context engaged, and d) comprehensiveness—that they are not necessarily the best categories for mapping evangelical models.

List of Initiator Examples

Following are the 249 examples used in the database to map evangelical contextual models. I list the examples alphabetically in their respective groups. The main groupings are by initiator role in alphabetical order of the role. Within each initiator role, I group the examples by flow (from linear to unclear). A **bold title** indicates that I describe the example in the corresponding chapter of section 2.

Initiator as Facilitator

Linear Facilitator
Community Health Evangelism (Rowland 1985; 2001)

Contextualization as a Developmental Method (Musasiwa 1996; Abebe 1996; McCarty 1996; Tyler 1996)

Contextualizing Development (Bradshaw 1993)

Tentmaking (Blair 1983; Anonymous 1992; Parshall 1998b)

Touching the Mystical Heart Evangelism (Peters 1989)

Urban Leadership Contextual Development (Garriot 1996)

Dialogue Facilitator
Contextual Doctoral Programs (Starcher 2006)

Contextualized Mission Training Model (Lewis 1993)

Indigenization as Incarnation (Gaqurae 1996)

Middle East Theology (Meral 2005)

Missiological Principles as Necessary Foundations for the Contextualization of Theology (Harling 2005)

Patron-Client Indigenous Leadership (Chinchen 1995)

Traditional Arts to Implement Theology (Kafton 1987)

Vernacular Treasure (Hill 2006)

Wider-Sense Biblical Theology (Padilla 1982)

Cyclical Facilitator
Church as Hermeneutical Community (Arrastia 1982)

Organic Facilitator
Church Planting Movements (Garrison 2004a; 2004b; 2004c)
Contextual "Church" Development (Richard 2003; 2004; 2007)
Contextualizing Christian Leadership Development (Elliston, Hoke, and
　Voorhies 1989)
Cross-Cultural Servanthood (Elmer 2006)
Social Development Transformation (Bradshaw 1993; 2002)
Transformational Development (Myers 1999)
Urban Church in Its Community (Algera 1994)

Unclear Facilitator
Case Studies in Holistic Ministry (Myers 1995; 1996)
Cases in Holistic Mission (McAlpine 1995)
Contextual Evangelism (Tooke 1993)

Initiator as Guide

Linear Guide
Betrothal Model (Schlorff 2000; 2006)
Contextual Bookroom Outreach (Parshall 1998b)
Contextual Ethical Guidelines for Church Planters (Payne 2010)
Contextual Pastoral Care (Jongh van Arkel 1995)
Contextualized Teaching Methods (Bowen and Bowen 1989)
Contextualized Youth Ministry (Livermore 2001)
Contextualizing Theological Curriculum (Imasogie 1983)
Conversion in the Cultural Context (Gration 1983)
Critical Contextual Church Planting (Eenigenburg 1997)
Critical Contextualization (Hiebert 1984; 1987)
Culturally Appropriate, Biblically Based Rituals and Institutions (Conkey
　1987)
Culture and Biblical Hermeneutics (Larkin 1988)
Developing Indigenous Theology (Fuller 1997)
Eco-hermeneutical Pastoral Care (Müller 1991)
Eight Phase Church Planting (Scoggins; http://www.dickscoggins.com)

Encouraging Vernacular Use through Bible Storying (Franklin 2005a; 2005b)

Indigenous Art (Jordan and Tucker 2002

Jifu (Chinese acronym: "Theological Training of Christian Workers among the Working Class"; Conn 1992)

Meditation Center (Bali Dhyana Pura) (Mastra 1978)

Nehemiah Model of Cultural Revitalization (Tollefson 1987)

Nomadic Missionary Church (Phillips 2000)

Parables for Understanding Doctrine (M. Shaw 1993)

Pioneer Church Planting Decathalon (Rowland and Bennett 2001)

POUCH Churches (Garrison 2004a)

Rite of Passage Discipling (Courson 1998)

Seven-phase Church Plant (D. Brown 1997; Scoggins 1997)

Storying or Story Telling (Cole 2005; Moreau and O'Rear 2004a)

Storytelling (Steffen 1996; 1999; 2000; 2005)

Theocentric Christology (Obaje 1990)

Theological Workshops (Gration 1984)

Walk Thru the Bible (Dinkins 2000)

Dialogue Guide

Asian Ethnotheologies (Seto 1987)

Aspects of Iman Theology for Islamic Settings (Marantika 1995)

Blended Western and Indigenous Leadership Development (Grant 2004)

Coaching as Contextualized Development (Webb 2008)

Community Life Evangelism (Vincent 1992)

Contextual Christology (Padilla 1986)

Contextual Discipling through Symbols and Ceremonies (Rituals) (Zahniser 1991; 1997)

Contextualized Hymnody (Molyneux 1990; Krabill 1990)

Contextualized Spirituality (Parshall 1983b)

Contextualizing Agency Structures and Leadership (Elder 1991; Walker 1994)

Dream Interpretation Evangelism (Musk 1988; Scott 2008)

Dynamic Christianity (Corwin 1981)

Gospel Communication From Within (Cate 1994)

Holistic Discipleship (Meral 2006)

Indigenous Worship (Collins 1991)

Limits and Bridges in Islamic Theology (Cragg 1979)

Local Village Theology (Hoefer 1981)

May Puritix: Praying into Smoke (Brooks 2000)

Measuring Contextualization (Hayward 1995)

Metaphoric: River (Nicholls 1995)

Metaphoric: Theology as Wisdom (Talman 2004)

Metaphoric: Wisdom (Adeney 1995)

Muslim Friendly Christian Worship (Hoefer 2009)

Muslim Theology of Jesus' Virgin Birth and Death (Borges 2005)

Open Field Contextual Theology (Athyal 1980; 1995)

Oral Skills and Media (Klem 1978; K. Nicholls 1983; Wilson 1991; 1997)

Parabolic Preaching (Goldsmith 1980)

Redeeming a Culture's Music for God (Neeley 1999)

Relational Centers (Nicholls 1979a; 1984, 256–61)

ROPES (Karianjahi—Tanari Trust)

Sesothoization of Liturgy (LaPointe 1995)

Spiritual Journey Evangelism (W. T. Kim 2005; Richardson 2006)

Transforming Barriers into Bridges (Dale 1977)

Trauma Healing Workshops (Carr 2006; Hill et al. 2007)

Video Streaming to Contextualize Theology (Sommer 2006)

Worship as Celebration of God's Existence or Presence (Obaje 1991)

Cyclical Guide

Contextualized Preaching using Redaction Criticism (Osborne 1984)

Contextualizing to an Urban Cultural System (Hall 1983)

Empowering Laity for Urban Ministry (Smith 1995)

Ethno-worship (King 2001)

Four-way Dialogue in Spiral (Shaw and Van Engen 2003, 79–83)

Hermeneutical Circle (Padilla 1979b; 1989; Bautista, Garcia, and Wan 1984, 177)

Hermeneutical Spiral (Osborne 1991)

Metaphoric: Theodrama (Vanhoozer 2006)

New Song Fellowships (King 2006)

Theological Advisory Groups (Gehman 1983; 1987; 1996)

Organic Guide

Comprehensive Critical (Moreau 2005; 2006a; 2007; 2008a)

Contextual African Pastoral Care (Louw 1997)
Contextualized Leadership Training (Harris 2000)
Culture-Sensitive Counseling (Hesselgrave 1986)
Finding Jesus in Dharma (Bharati 2001)
Javanese Church Model (Dixon 2002)
Jesus Hall (Reitz 2006)
Metaphoric (Tano 1984, 106–9)
Metaphoric: Tree (Stephens 1999)
Scripture-Infused Arts (Schrag 2007)

Unclear Guide

Contextualization Conformed to Biblical Worldview while Honoring and
 Maintaining Cultural Customs (Brown 2006d)
Contextualization of Urban Theological Education (Jackson 1993)
House Church as Missiological Model (Birkey 1991)

Initiator as Herald

Linear Herald

Apostolic Accommodation (Hesselgrave 1979; Hesselgrave and Rommen
 1989)
Back to Jerusalem (Hattaway 2003)
Become Like Muslims to Present the Gospel (Terry 1996)
Case Studies as a Means of Contextualizing the Message (Fritz 1995)
Caudillo-Type Pastors (Thornton 1984)
Christian Folk Songs (Baskaran 1989)
Chronological Bible Storying (McIlwain 1987; Steffen 1995; Terry 1997;
 Lovejoy et al. 2001)
Communicating the Gospel in Terms of Shame (Boyle 1984; Francis 1992;
 Blincoe 2001; DeVries 2007)
Contextual Christian Worship (Tarus 1996)
Contextual Ethics (Eitel 1987)
Contextual Preaching (Flemming 2002; Fukuda 2001)
Contextualized Apologetics (Netland 1988)
Evangicube (E3 Resources, www.e3resources.org)
Evangelism Explosion (Kennedy 1997; Ellenberger 1997)
Four Laws for Chinese (Francis 1992)

Jesus Film (Eshleman 1985; Steffen 1993)
P.E.A.C.E. Plan (www.thepeaceplan.com)
Picture Four Spiritual Laws (Africa; Campus Crusade for Christ)
Possessio (Beyerhaus 1975)
Public Debate Evangelism (Smith 1998)

Dialogue Herald
Biblically-oriented Theology Relevant to Asian Needs (Ro 1978)
Bruchko (Olson 1978)
Dialogue with Bible as Normal Pole (Feinberg 1982)
New Christian Apologetic (Larson 1996)
Soularium Cards (Young 2008)
Spirit-First Approach to Muslim Evangelism (Steinhaus 2000)

Cyclical Herald
Disciple a Whole Nation (Montgomery and McGavran 1980; Montgomery 1984; DAWN Ministries)
Pauline Church Planting Model (Hesselgrave 2000b)

Organic Herald
Cultural Chameleon (Poston 2000; Hale 2007)

Unclear Herald
Blended Muslim Evangelism Model (Terry 1996; 1998)
Christian Bhajans (Minz 1996; Hale 2001)
Contextualization in the Local Church (Ramirez 1978)

Initiator as Pathfinder

Linear Pathfinder
Adapting Metaphoric Terms and Expressions (Brown 2000a; 2005a; 2005b; 2007c)
CAMEL Evangelism Method (Greeson 2004)
Central Asian Russian Scriptures (CARS) Project (contextualized Bible; Pierce 2007)
Christological Monotheism and Muslim Evangelism (Teague 2008)
Comprehensive (Talman 2004)

Contextualized Baptism (Parshall 1979)

Contextualizing Needs Assessment for Third World Missionary Training (Lewis 1991)

Contextualizing Research Methods (Engel 1991)

Evangelistic Sacrifices (Nussbaum 1984)

House Masjid for New Creation Muslims (Goble and Munayer 1989)

Issaan Development Foundation (DeNeui 1993; Gustafson 1998)

Jesus Marabou (Vanderaa 2000)

Messianic Synagogues (Goble 1974; 1975; Spielberg and Dauermann 1997)

Radical Contextualization (Winter 2003b)

Theology of Power (Dye 1984a; 1984b)

Underground Jamaats (Churches in Muslim Settings) (Massey 1996)

Using Local and Non-Local Terms in Bible Translation (Hill 2007)

Yoido Full Gospel Church Cell Groups (Cho 1984; Adams 1991; Hong 2000; Hwa 2004b)

Dialogue Pathfinder
Alternative Participation in a Parallel Cultural Event (Ritual) (Perry 1990)

Best Practices Training for Contextual Church Planting (Downey 2008)

Contextual Theology of Mission for the City (Conn 1993)

Contextualized Christian Social Transformation (Elliston 1989)

Contextualized Comics (Chen 1992)

Contextualized Participation in a Cultural Event (Perry 1990)

Creating a Context for the Gospel (Sigg 1995)

Hindu Satsang ("Gathering of Truth," Stevens 2007)

Hindu-Christ Followers (Peterson 2007a)

Integrated Holistic Development (Gustafson 1991; 1998)

Messianic Jews (Goble 1975)

Missionaries Acting Like Insiders (Racey 1996; Fearon 1997; Anonymous 1998; Schlorff 2000)

Muslim-Culture Church Model (Brislin 1996)

New Buddhists (Decker 2005)

Proclaiming a "Theologyless" Christ (Hoefer 2005)

Re-Contextualization Church Renewal (Marchak 1989)

Redeeming the Arts (Harbinson et al. 2005)

Redemptive Analogy Contextualization (Richardson 1974; 2000; Anderson 1998)

Sharia as a Contextual Bridge (Greer 2008)

Three Dimensional Approach to Apostolic Ministry (Love 2008)

Transfer-up Theology (Caldwell 1987a; 1987b)

Using Case Studies to Understand/Evaluate Contextual Ministries (Travis 2000)

Cyclical Pathfinder
Dynamic-equivalence "Churchness" (Kraft 1979c; 1980; 2005)
Expanded Hermeneutical Circle (Adeney 1995)

Narrative Hermeneutics (Redford 2005)

Organic Pathfinder
Accommodating, Reinterpreting, and Innovating Ancestral Practices (Smith 1989)

Chinese Contextual Ecclesiology (Sawatsky 1982; 1983; 1984)

Christian Ashrams (Taylor 1979; Ralston 1987)

Churchless Christianity (Hoefer 2001a; Richard 2002)

Circle Church: Contextualization in a Metropolitan Experience (Ortiz 1991)

Contextualizing Mission Information Management (Conradie 2008)

Dynamic Indigenous Church (Wisley 1979)

Gatherings: Francis Chan's House-type Churches (Brandon 2009)

Grounded Contextualization (Vanden Berg 2009)

Independent Church Movements (Kim 2006; McPhee 2002)

Indigenous Organizational Frameworks (Nelson 1989)

Insider Movements (Garrison 2004b; Travis & Travis 2005b; Higgins 2006; Brown 2007a)

Jesu Bhakta Theology (Hoefer 2002)

Jesus Mosques (Bridges 1997)

Krista Bhakta (Krishna 2007)

Locally Initiated Churches (Aikman 2003; Anderson 2000b; Pew Forum 2006; Zdero 2004)

Messianic Muslim Followers of Isa (Travis 2000)

Movements to Christ within Natural Communities (Lewis 2007a)

New Friars (Bessenecker 2006)

New Ways of Believing, Belonging, and Becoming (McLaren 2001)
Theology in Song (Balisky 1997)
Yeshu-Bhakta Movement (Stevens 2007; Hoefer 2007; Peterson 2007a)

Unclear Pathfinder
Contextualizing as Urban Sensitive Flexibility (Ellison 1988)
Dynamic Equivalent Conversion (Teeter 1990; similar to Tippett 1977)
Indian Instituted Churches (Hedlund 1999)
Out-of-Step Evangelists (Conn 1990)
Radical Decontextualization or Reverse Contextualization (Winter 2003b)
Rethinking Forum (Richard 2002)
Rooted in Traditional Culture (Hoefer 2007)

Initiator as Prophet

Linear Prophet
Contextualizing Universal Values (Adeney 2007)
Delighting in God's Law for Incarnational Witness (Massey 2004b; 2004c)
Seeking the Peace of the City (Seeking 1989)
Theology of Vindication (Harootian 1987)

Dialogue Prophet
Contextual Urban Theology (Monsma 1979; 1981)
Word of Action Liberation (Costas 1991)

Cyclical Prophet
Critical and Constructive Theology (Escobar 1994; Padilla 1985b; Costas 1982; 1989)
Second Generation Contextualization (Ortiz 1993)

Organic Prophet
Environmentalism (AICs; Daneel 1996)
Messianic Movements (Fuchs 1976)
Non-Church (Japan) (Nabetani 1983; Howes 2007)

Unclear Prophet
Contextualization of Theological Education (Kim 1974)

Initiator as Restorer

Linear Restorer
Conflict Management (Palmer 1990)
Contextualized Deliverance Ministry (Cordillera Rehabilitation Center; Cole 2003)
Contextualizing Missionary Medicine (M. C. Kim 2005)
Deep-level Healing (Kraft 1993; 2002; Travis and Travis 2008)
Power Encounter (Tippett 1971)
Social Services Centers (Hwang and Ng 1990)
Spiritual Mapping (Caballeros 1993; Otis 1993; Wagner 1993a; 1993b)
Strategic Level Spiritual Warfare (Wagner 1991a; 1991c; 1992; 1996; 1998)
Truth Encounter (Anderson 1990)

Dialogue Restorer
Allegiance, Truth, and Power Encounters (Kraft 1991c; 2002a; 2005g)
Authentic Vernacular Understanding of Christ (or Bridging Contextual Theology) (Bediako 1993; 2004)
Contextualized Medical Clinics (Parshall 1985b)
Ritual Analysis as an Aid to Contextualization (Conkey 1992)
Theophostic Ministry (Smith 2004)

Cyclical Restorer
No examples.

Organic Restorer
Power Evangelism (Wimber and Springer 1986; Wagner and Pennoyer 1990; Wimber 1990; Wagner 1991a)

Unclear Restorer
Kingdom of God as Organizing and Integrating Theological Paradigm for Contextualization (Love 1994)
Power of the Extended Family (Peters 1987)

References

Abebe, Mulugeta. 1996. "From Relief to Development in Ethiopia." In *Serving with the Poor in Africa*, ed. Tetsunao Yamamori et al., 15–28. Pasadena, CA: MARC.

Adams, Daniel J. 1991. "Reflections on an Indigenous Movement: The Yoido Full Gospel Church." *The Japan Christian Quarterly* 57:1 (Winter): 36–45.

Addison, Steve. 2009. *Movements That Change the World*. Smyrna, DE: Missional Press.

Adeney, Bernard T. 1995. *Strange Virtues: Ethics in a Multicultural World*. Downers Grove, IL: InterVarsity.

Adeney, Frances S. 2007. "Contextualizing Universal Values: A Method for Christian Mission." *International Bulletin of Missionary Research* 31.1 (January): 33–37.

Adeney, Miriam. 2009. *Kingdom without Borders: The Untold Story of Christianity*. Downers Grove, IL: InterVarsity.

"A Different Kind of Mosque: A New Idea Buys Time to Grow." 1997. *Mission Frontiers* (July–October): 20.

Aikman, David. 2003. *Jesus in Beijing: How Christianity Is Transforming China and Changing the Global Balance of Power*. Washington, DC: Regnery Publishing.

Algera, John. 1994. "Urban Pilgrims and Pioneers." *Urban Mission* 11.3 (July): 25–37.

Al kalima Editorial Committee. 2009. "A Response to Jay Smith's Criticisms of Common Ground and of 'The True Meaning of the Gospel'." *St. Francis Magazine* 5.5 (October): 15–20.

"An Extended Conversation about Insider Movements: Responses to the September–October 2005 Mission Frontiers." 2006. *Mission Frontiers* (January–February): 16–23.

Anane-Asane, Andrew, Timothy L. Eckert, Jason Richard Tan, and Robert J. Priest. 2009. "Paul G. Hiebert's 'The Flaw of the Excluded Middle.'" *Trinity Journal* 30NS (Fall): 189–97.

Anderson, Allan H. 2000a. "The Gospel and African Religion." *International Review of Mission* 89.354 (07): 373–83.

———. 2000b. *Zion and Pentecost: The Spirituality and Experience of Pentecostal and Zionist/Apostolic Churches in South Africa*. Pretoria: University of South Africa Press.

———. 2003. "The Contribution of David Yonggi Cho to a Contextual Theology in Korea." *Journal of Pentecostal Theology* 12.1: 85–105.

Anderson, Joy. 1998. "Behold the Ox of God." *Evangelical Missions Quarterly* 34.3 (July): 316–20.

Anderson, Neil T. 1990. *The Bondage Breaker*. Eugene, OR: Harvest House.

Anonymous. 1992."Tentmaking: The Road to People's Hearts." *Evangelical Missions Quarterly* 28.1 (January): 25–28.

Anonymous. 1998. "Jesus in the Muslim City." *Urban Mission* (March): 22–30.

Anonymous. 2004. "H Scale for Hindu Contextualization." *Evangelical Missions Quarterly* 40.3 (July): 316–20.

Archer, Gleason L. 1978. "Contextualization: Some Implications from Life and Witness in the Old Testament." In *New Horizons in World Mission: Evangelicals and the Christian Mission in the 1980s. Papers and Responses Prepared for the Consultation of Theology and Mission, Trinity Evangelical Divinity School, School of World Mission and Evangelism, March 19–22*, ed. David J. Hesselgrave, 199–216. Grand Rapids: Baker.

Arrastia, Cecilio. 1982. "The Church: A Hermeneutical Community." *Occasional Essays* 9.2 (December): 18–25.

Asad, Abdul. 2009a. "Discipling Nations: Imitating Jesus' Goal and Methods." *St. Francis Magazine* 5.2 (April): 1–16.

———. 2009b. "Rethinking the Insider Movement Debate: Global Historical Insights Toward an Appropriate Transitional Model of C5." *St. Francis Magazine* 5.4 (August): 133–59.

Asia Theological Association. 1984. "The Bible and Theology in Asia Today: Declaration of the Sixth Asia Theological Association Theological Consultation." In *The Bible and Theology in Asian Contexts: An Evangelical Perspective on Asian Theology*, ed. Bong Rin Ro and Ruth Eshenaur, 3–20. Taiching, Taiwan: Asia Theological Association.

Athyal, Saphir P. 1980. "Theology and Culture: Certain Preliminary Considerations." In *For the Sake of the Gospel*, ed. Gnana Robinson, 165–80. Madurai, India: T. T. S. Publications.

———. 1984. "Towards an Asian Christian Theology." In *The Bible and Theology in Asian Contexts: An Evangelical Perspective on Asian Theology*, ed.. Bong Rin Ro and Ruth Eshenaur, 49–61. Taiching, Taiwan: Asia Theological Association.

———. 1995. "Towards an Asian Christian Theology." In *Biblical Theology in Asia*, ed. Ken Gnanakan, 77–90. Bangalore, India: Asia Theological Association.

Back, Peter. 1999. *All Things to All Men: A Study of 1 Corinthians Chapter 9:19–23*. 2nd ed. London: Red Sea Team International.

Balisky, Lila W. 1997. "Theology in Song: Ethiopia's Tesfaye Gabbiso." *Missiology* 25.4 (October): 447–56.

Barbour, Ian. 1974. *Myths, Models, and Paradigms*. New York: Harper and Row.

Barney, G. Linwood. 1973. "The Supracultural and the Cultural: Implications for Frontier Missions." In *The Gospel and Frontier Peoples*, ed. R. Pierce Beaver, 48–57. Pasadena, CA: William Carey Library.

Barney, G. Linwood, Kwame Bediako, Ralph R. Covell, Richard B. Gaffin Jr., John Gration, Marie-Louise Martin, Vinay Samuel, Chris Sugden, William A. Smalley, Fred P. Thompson, Harold W. Turner, and Charles C. West. 1979. "Dialogue: Solicited Comments on 'The Contextualization Continuum'." *Gospel in Context* 2.3 (July): 12–22.

Barrett, David. 1968. *Schism and Renewal in Africa: An Analysis of Six Thousand Contemporary Religious Movements*. Nairobi: Oxford.

Barrett, David, and John T. Padwick. 1989. *Rise Up and Walk! Conciliarism and African Indigenous Churches, 1815–1987*. Nairobi: Oxford.

Baskaran, S. Theodore. 1989. "Christian Folk Songs of Tamil Nadu." *Religion and Society (Bangalore)* 33.2 (June): 83–92.

Bautista, Lorenzo. 2005. "The Bible: Servant in the Formation of Communities of Faith." In *Doing Theology in the Philippines*, ed. John Suk, 51–64. Quezon City, Philippines: Asian Theological Seminary.

Bautista, Lorenzo, Hidalbo B. Garcia, and Sze-kar Wan. 1984. "The Asian Way of Thinking in Theology." In *The Bible and Theology in Asian Contexts: An Evangelical Perspective on Asian Theology,* ed. Bong Rin Ro and Ruth Eshenaur, 167–83. Taiching, Taiwan: Asia Theological Association.

Beale, Gregory K. 2008. *The Erosion of Inerrancy in Evangelicalism: Responding to New Challenges to Biblical Authority*. Wheaton, IL: Crossway.

Bebbington, David W. 1989. *Evangelicalism in Modern Britain: A History from the 1730s to the 1980s*. London: Unwin Hyman.

Bediako, Kwame. 1993. "Jesus in African Culture." *Evangelical Review of Theology* 17.1 (January): 54–64.

———. 1995. *Christianity in Africa: The Renewal of the Non-Western Religion*. Maryknoll, NY: Orbis.

———. 1998a. "The Doctrine of Christ and the Significance of Vernacular Terminology." *International Bulletin of Missionary Research* 22.3 (July): 110–11.

———. 1998b. "Understanding African Theology in the 20th Century." In *Issues in African Christian Theology*, eds. Samuel Ngewa, Mark Shaw, and Tite Tiénou, 56–72. Nairobi: East African Educational Publishers.

———. 2004. *Jesus and the Gospel in Africa: History and Experience*. Maryknoll, NY: Orbis.

Bell, William D. 1974. "Muslim World Still Looks Like Impregnable Fortress." *Evangelical Missions Quarterly* 10.1 (January): 75–79.

Bertsche, James. 1966. "Kimbanguism: A Challenge to Missionary Statesmanship." *Practical Anthropology* 13: 13–33.

Bessenecker, Scott. 2006. *The New Friars: The Emerging Movement Serving the World's Poor*. Downers Grove, IL: InterVarsity.

Bevans, Stephen B. 1985. "Models of Contextual Theology." *Missiology* 13.2 (April): 185–202.

_____. 1992. *Models of Contextual Theology.* Maryknoll, NY: Orbis.

_____. 2002. *Models of Contextual Theology: Revised and Expanded Edition.* Maryknoll, NY: Orbis.

_____. 2007. Personal communication from Stephen Bevans; 24 October 2007.

_____. 2009. Personal communication from Stephen Bevans; 7 September 2009.

Beyerhaus, Peter. 1975. "Possessio and Syncretism in Biblical Perspective." In *Christopaganism or Indigenous Christianity?* ed. Tetsunao Yamamori and Charles Russell Taber, 119–42. Pasadena, CA: William Carey Library.

Bharati, Dayanand. 2001. "Lessons from India: Dharma and Christianity According to Chaturvedi Badrinath." *International Journal of Frontier Missions* 18.4 (October): 174–79.

Bill and Jane (pseudonyms). 1990. "Pointing the Way: The Translator's Role in Contextualization." *International Journal of Frontier Missions* 7.3 (July): 85–94.

Billings, Todd J. 2004. "Incarnational Ministry and Christology: A Reappropriation of the Way of Lowliness." *Missiology* 32.2 (April): 187–201.

Birkey, Del. 1991. "The House Church: A Missiological Model." *Missiology* 19.1 (January): 69–80.

Blair, C. F. 1983. "Tentmaking: A Contextualized Approach to Islam." *Missiology* 11.2 (April): 219–27.

Blanton, P. G. 2008. "Integrating Postmodern and Christian Contemplative Thought: Building a Theoretical Framework." *Journal of Psychology and Christianity* 27.1: 73–84.

Blincoe, Robert. 2001. "Faces of Islam: Honor and Shame." *Mission Frontiers* 23.4: 18–20.

Blomberg, Craig. 1993. "Implications of Globalization for Biblical Understanding." In *Globalization of Theological Education,* ed. Alice Frazer Evans, Robert A. Evans, and David A. Roozen, 213–46. Maryknoll, NY: Orbis.

Borges, Jason. 2005. "A Muslim Theology of Jesus' Virgin Birth and His Death." *Evangelical Missions Quarterly* 41.4 (October): 458–63.

Bosch, David J. 1980. *Witness to the World: The Christian Mission in Theological Perspective.* Atlanta: John Knox Press.

_____. 1991. *Transforming Mission: Paradigm Shifts in Theology of Mission.* Maryknoll, NY: Orbis.

_____. 1995. *Believing in the Future: Toward a Missiology of Western Culture.* Valley Forge, PA: Trinity Press International.

Bourne, Phil. 2009. "Summary of the Contextualization Debate." *St. Francis Magazine* 5.w (October): 58–80.

Bowen, Earle, and Dorothy Bowen. 1989. "Contextualizing Teaching Methods in Africa." *Evangelical Missions Quarterly* 25.3 (July): 270–75.

Boyle, Timothy D. 1984. "Communicating the Gospel in Terms of Shame." *The Japan Christian Quarterly* 50.1 (Winter): 41–46.

Bradshaw, Bruce. 1993. *Bridging the Gap: Evangelism, Development, and Shalom.* Pasadena, CA: MARC.

———. 2002. *Change across Cultures: A Narrative Approach to Social Transformation.* Grand Rapids: Baker.

Brandon, John. 2009. "Crazy Passion." *Christianity Today* 53.10 (October): 42–45.

Breslin, Scott, and Mike Jones. 2004. *Understanding Dreams from God.* Pasadena, CA: William Carey Library.

Bridges, Erich. 1997. "Of 'Jesus' Mosques and Muslim Christians." *Mission Frontiers* (July–October): 19.

Brislen, Mike. 1996. "A Model for a Muslim-Culture Church." *Missiology* 24.3: 355–67.

Brooks, Elizabeth. 2000. "*May Puritix*: Praying into Smoke." *International Journal of Frontier Missions* 17.4 (October): 31–41.

Brown, Dan. 1997. "Is Planting Churches in the Muslim World 'Mission Impossible'?" *Evangelical Missions Quarterly* 33.2 (April): 156–61.

———. 2004. "Church-Planting Movements in the Muslim World." *Mission Frontiers* 26.1: 12–13.

Brown, Rick. 2000. "The "Son of God"—Understanding the Messianic Titles of Jesus." *International Journal of Frontier Missions* 17.1 (Spring): 41–52.

———. 2002. "Presenting the Deity of Christ from the Bible." *International Journal of Frontier Missions* 19.1 (Spring): 20–27.

———. 2005a. "Part 1: Explaining the Biblical Term 'Son(s) of God' in Muslim Contexts." *International Journal of Frontier Missions* 22.3 (Fall): 91–96.

———. 2005b. "Part II: Translating the Biblical Term 'Son(s) of God' in Muslim Contexts." *International Journal of Frontier Missions* 22.4 (Winter): 135–45.

———. 2006a. "Muslim Worldviews and the Bible: Bridges and Barriers (Part I: God and Mankind)." *International Journal of Frontier Missions* 23.1 (Spring): 5–12.

———. 2006b. "Muslim Worldviews and the Bible: Bridges and Barriers (Part II: Jesus, the Holy Spirit, and the Age to Come." *International Journal of Frontier Missions* 23.2 (Summer): 48–56.

———. 2006c. "Muslim Worldviews and the Bible: Bridges and Barriers (Part III: Women, Purity, Worship, and Ethics." *International Journal of Frontier Missions* 23.3 (Fall): 93–100.

_____. 2006d. "Contextualization without Syncretism." *International Journal of Frontier Missions* 23.3 (Fall): 127–33.

_____. 2007a. "Brother Jacob and Master Isaac: How One Insider Movement Began." *International Journal of Frontier Missions* 24.1 (Spring): 41–42.

_____. 2007b. "Biblical Muslims." *International Journal of Frontier Missions* 24.2 (Summer): 65–74.

_____. 2007c. "Why Muslims Are Repelled by the Term 'Son of God.'" *Evangelical Missions Quarterly* 43.4 (October): 422–29.

_____. 2008. "A Movement to Jesus Within Islam." *Mission Frontiers* 30.4 (July–August): 16–17.

Brown, Rick, Bob Fish, John Travis, Eric Adams, and Don Allen. 2009. "Movements and Contextualization: Is There Really a Correlation?" *International Journal of Frontier Missions* 26.1 (Spring): 21–23.

Bush, Luis K. 2004. *Transformation: A Unifying Vision of the Church's Mission.* Foreword by Paul Cedar. Thailand: 2004 Forum for World Evangelization.

Buswell, James O., III. 1978. "Contextualization: Is It Only a New Word for Indigenization?" *Evangelical Missions Quarterly* 14.1 (January): 13–19.

Caballeros, Harold. 1993. "Defeating the Enemy with the Help of Spiritual Mapping." In *Breaking Strongholds in Your City: How to Use Spiritual Mapping to Make Your Prayers More Strategic, Effective, and Targeted,* ed. C. Peter Wagner, 123–46. Ventura, CA: Regal.

Caldwell, Larry N. 1987a. "Doing Theology across Cultures: A New Methodology for an Old Task." *International Journal of Frontier Missions* 4: 3–7.

_____. 1987b. "Third Horizon Ethnohermeneutics: Re-Evaluating New Testament Hermeneutical Models for Intercultural Bible Interpreters Today." *Asia Journal of Theology* 1.2: 314–33.

_____. 1999. "Towards the New Discipline of Ethnohermeneutics: Questioning the Relevancy of Western Hermeneutical Methods in the Asian Context." *Journal of Asian Mission* 1.1: 21–43.

_____. 2000. "A Response to the Responses of Tappeiner and Whelchel to Ethnohermeneutics." *Journal of Asian Mission* 2.1: 135–45.

Caldwell, Stuart. 2000. "Jesus in Samaria: A Paradigm for Church Planting among Muslims." *International Journal of Frontier Missions* 17.1 (Spring): 25–31.

Campbell, Jonathan. 2005. "Appropriate Witness to Postmoderns: Re-Incarnating the Way of Jesus in 21st Century Western Culture." In *Appropriate Christianity,* ed. Charles Kraft, 453–73. Pasadena, CA: William Carey Library.

Cantrell, Tim. 2006. "Launching Church Strengthening Movements in Africa." *Evangelical Missions Quarterly* 42.4 (October): 442–48.

Carr, Karen. 2006. "Healing the Wounds of Trauma: How the Church Can Help." *Evangelical Missions Quarterly* 42.3 (July): 318–23.

Carson, D. A. 1983b. "Unity and Diversity in the New Testament: The Possibility of Systematic Theology." In *Scripture and Truth*, ed. D. A. Carson and John D. Woodbridge, 61–95. Leicester: InterVarsity.

_____. 1984. "A Sketch of the Factors Determining Current Hermeneutical Debate in Cross-Cultural Contexts." In *Biblical Interpretation and the Church: Text and Context*, ed. D. A. Carson, 11–29. Exeter: Paternoster.

_____. 1985. "The Limits of Dynamic Equivalence in Bible Translation." *Evangelical Review of Theology* 9: 200–213.

_____. 1986. "Recent Developments in the Doctrine of Scripture." In *Hermeneutics, Authority, and Canon*, ed. D. A. Carson and John D. Woodbridge, 1–48. Leicester: InterVarsity.

_____. 1987. "Church and Mission: Reflections on Contextualization and the Third Horizon." In *The Church in the Bible and the World: An International Study*, ed. D. A. Carson, 213–57. Exeter: Paternoster.

_____. 2008. *Christ and Culture Revisited*. Grand Rapids: Eerdmans.

Cate, Patrick O. 1994. "Gospel Communication from Within." *International Journal of Frontier Missions* 11.2 (April): 93–97.

Chandler, Paul-Gordon. 2007. *Pilgrims of Christ on the Muslim Road— Exploring a New Path between Two Faiths*. Lanham, MD: Cowley Publications.

Chang, Eunhye, J. Rupert Morgan, Timothy Nyasulu, and Robert J. Priest. 2009. "Paul G. Hiebert and Critical Contextualization." *Trinity Journal* 30NS (Fall): 199–207.

Chang, Peter S. C. 1984. "Steak, Potatoes, Peas, and Chopsuey: Linear and Non-linear Thinking." In *Missions and Theological Education in World Perspective*, ed. Harvie M. Conn and Samuel F. Rowen, 113–23. Farmington, MI: Associates of Urbanus.

Chastain, Warren. 1995. "Should Christians Pray the Muslim *Salat?*" *International Journal of Frontier Missions*, 12.3 (July–Sept.): 161–64.

Chen, Elena. 1992. "The Use of Comics for Evangelism among Female Factory Workers." *Evangelical Review of Theology* 16.1 (January): 97–109.

"Chicago Declaration of Evangelical Social Concern." 1973. Online: http://esa-online.org/Display.asp?Page=HistDocs, accessed 27 May 2010.

"Chicago Statement on Biblical Inerrancy." 1978. Online: http://www.bible-researcher.com/chicago1.html, accessed 27 November 2007.

Chinchen, Delbert. 1995. "The Patron-Client System: A Model of Indigenous Leadership." *Evangelical Missions Quarterly* 31.4 (October): 446–51.

Cho, Paul Yonggi. 1984. "A Korean Success Story with Worldwide Implications: Reaching Cities with Home Cells." *Urban Mission* 1.3 (October): 4–14.

Clark, Mathew S. 2001. "The Challenge of Contextualization and Syncretism to Pentecostal Theology and Missions in Africa." *Journal of Asian Mission* 3.1: 79–99.

Coe, Shoki. 1976. "Contextualizing Theology." In *Mission Trends No. 3: Asian, African, and Latin American Contributions to a Radical, Theological Realignment in the Church*, ed. Gerald H. Anderson and Thomas F. Stransky, C.S.P., 19–24. Grand Rapids: Eerdmans.

Cole, Graham A. 1981. "Christianity in Culture." *Reformed Theological Review* 40.3: 87–88.

Cole, Harold L. 2003. "A Model of Contextualized Deliverance Ministry: A Case Study: The Cordillera Rehabilitation Center." *Journal of Asian Mission* 5.2: 259–73.

———. 2005. "Stories Aren't Just for Kids Anymore: A Case for Narrative Teaching in Missions." *Journal of Asian Mission* 7.1: 23–38.

Colgate, Jack. 2008a. "Part 1: Relational Bible Storying and Scripture Use in Oral Muslim Contexts." *International Journal of Frontier Missions* 25.3 (Fall): 135–42.

———. 2008b. "Part 2: Relational Bible Storying and Scripture Use in Oral Muslim Contexts." *International Journal of Frontier Missions* 25.4 (Winter): 199–207.

Collins, Travis M. 1991. "Understanding Worship from a Missiological Perspective." *Ogbomoso Journal of Theology* 6 (December): 32–39.

Conkey, Calvin W. 1987. "Doing Theology among the Zuni." *International Journal of Frontier Missions* 4.1–4: 39–51.

———. 1992. "The Malay Funeral Rite." *International Journal of Frontier Missions* 9.2 (April): 45–55.

Conn, Harvie M. 1978. "Contextualization: A New Dimension for Cross-Cultural Hermeneutic." *Evangelical Missions Quarterly* 14.1 (January): 39–48.

———. 1979a. "Conversion and Culture: A Theological Perspective with Reference to Korea." In *Gospel and Culture. The Papers of a Consultation on the Gospel and Culture, Convened by the Lausanne Committee's Theology and Education Group*, ed. John R. W. Stott and Robert T. Coote, 195–239. Pasadena, CA: William Carey Library.

———. 1979b. "The Muslim Convert and His Culture." In *The Gospel and Islam: A 1978 Compendium*, ed. Don M. McCurry, 97–111. Monrovia, CA: MARC.

———. 1982. *Evangelism: Doing Justice and Preaching Grace*. Grand Rapids: Zondervan.

———. 1984. *Eternal Word and Changing Worlds: Theology, Anthropology, and Mission in Trialogue*. Grand Rapids: Zondervan.

———. 1988. "Normativity, Relevance, and Relativism." In *Inerrancy and*

Hermeneutic: A Tradition, A Challenge, A Debate, ed. Harvie M. Conn, 185–209. Grand Rapids: Baker.

———. 1990. "Editor's Viewpoint: Odds and Ends for the City." *Urban Mission* 8.1 (January): 3–5.

———. 1992. "A Neglected People Group." *Missionary Monthly* 99A.2 (February): 14–15.

———. 1993. "A Contextual Theology of Mission for the City." In *The Good News of the Kingdom: Mission Theology for the Third Millennium*, ed. Charles van Engen, Dean S. Gilliland, and Paul Pierson, 96–104. Maryknoll, NY: Orbis.

———. 2000. *Evangelical Dictionary of World Mission*, gen. ed. A. Scott Moreau, s.v. "Indigenization." Grand Rapids: Baker.

Connor, John H. 1991. "When Culture Leaves Contextualized Christianity Behind." *Missiology* 19.1 (January): 21–29.

Conradie, Sal. 2008. "Contextualizing Mission Information Management in the 21st Century." *Connections* (Fall): xx. Online: http://www.weaconnections.com/Back-issues/Contextualization-Revisited---A-global-and-mission/Contextualizing-Mission-Information-Management-in-.aspx, accessed 26 June 2012.

Corbett, Steve, and Brian Fikkert. 2009. *When Helping Hurts: How to Alleviate Poverty without Hurting the Poor . . . and Yourself*. Chicago: Moody Press.

Cortez, Marc. 2005a. "Context and Concept: Contextual Theology and the Nature of Theological Discourse." *Westminster Theological Journal* 67: 85–102.

———. 2005b. "Creation and Context: A Theological Framework for Contextual Theology." *Westminster Theological Journal* 67: 347–62.

Corwin, Charles. 1981. "Cultural Diversity as a Dynamic for Growth." *Evangelical Missions Quarterly* 17.1 (January): 15–22.

Corwin, Gary. 1998. "A Second Look: Reaching the Resident." *Evangelical Missions Quarterly* 34.2 (April): 144–45.

———. 2004. "A Second Look: Telling the Difference." *Evangelical Missions Quarterly* 40.3 (July): 282–83.

———. 2006. "A Second Look: Insider Movements and Outsider Missiology." *Evangelical Missions Quarterly* 42.1 (January): 10–11.

———. 2007. "A Humble Appeal to C5/Insider Movement Muslim Ministry Advocates to Consider Ten Questions." *International Journal of Frontier Missions* 24.1 (Spring): 5–20.

———. 2008. "A Second Look: The Believer's Identity in the Muslim Context: Common Ground?" *Evangelical Missions Quarterly* 44.1 (January): 8–9.

Costas, Orlando. 1979. "Conversion as a Complex Experience: A Personal Case Study." In *Gospel and Culture. The Papers of a Consultation on the Gospel and Culture, Convened by the Lausanne Committee's Theology and*

Education Group, ed. John R. W. Stott and Robert T. Coote, 240–62. Pasadena, CA: William Carey Library.

_____. 1982. *Christ outside the Gate*. Maryknoll, NY: Orbis.

_____. 1989. *Liberating News*. Grand Rapids: Eerdmans.

_____. 1991. "The Subversiveness of Faith: A Paradigm for Doing Liberation Theology." In *Doing Theology in Today's World: Essays in Honor of Kenneth S. Kantzer*, ed. John D. Woodbridge and Thomas E. McComiskey, 377–96. Grand Rapids: Zondervan.

Courson, Jim. 1998. "Deepening the Bonds of Christian Community: Applying Rite of Passage Structure to the Discipling Process in Taiwan." *Missiology* 26.3 (July): 301–13.

Cragg, Kenneth A. 1979. "Islamic Theology: Limits and Bridges." In *The Gospel and Islam: A 1978 Compendium*, ed. Don M. McCurry, 196–204. Monrovia, CA: MARC.

Culver, Jonathan. 2000. "The Ishmael Promise and Contextualization among Muslims." *International Journal of Frontier Missions* 17.1 (Spring): 61–70.

Dale, Kenneth J. 1977. "Transforming Barriers into Bridges." *The Japan Christian Quarterly* 43.3 (Summer): 153–60.

Daneel, M. L. 1996. "Earthkeeping in Missiological Perspective: An African Challenge." *Mission Studies* 13.1–2: 130–88.

Davids, Peter H. 1978. "Comments." *Gospel in Context* 1.1 (January): 18.

Davies, John R. 1997. "Biblical Precedence for Contextualization." *Evangelical Review of Theology* 21.3 (July): 197–214.

Davis, John Jefferson. 1981. *Theology Primer: Resources for the Theological Student*. Grand Rapids: Baker.

De Carvalho, Levi T. 1999. "Charles H. Kraft: Ethnotheology in Mission." In *Footprints of God: A Narrative Theology of Mission*, ed. Charles Van Engen, Nancy Thomas, and Robert Gallagher, 62–73. Monrovia, CA: World Vision.

Decker, Frank. 2005. "When 'Christian' Does Not Translate." *Mission Frontiers* (September–October): 8.

Demarest, Bruce. 1983. "A Flawed Attempt to Merge Hindu and Christian Theology." *Evangelical Missions Quarterly* 18.1 (January): 21–24.

DeNeui, Gretchen. 1993. "The Making of a Sodality in Northeastern Thailand." Thailand Covenant Church. Online: http://www.strategicnetwork.org/index.php?loc=kb&view=v&id=6655&fto=974&, accessed 26 June 2012.

DeNeui, Paul. 2002. "Contextualizing with Thai Folk Buddhists." Online: http://www.agts.edu/syllabi/ce/summer2002/mthm639oleson_sum02_np_r2.pdf, accessed 27 May 2010.

DeVries, Grant. 2007. "Explaining the Atonement to the Arabic Muslim in terms of Honor and Shame." *St. Francis Magazine* 2.4 (March): 1–68.

Dinkins, Larry. 2000. "Walk-Thru the Bible: A Cross-cultural Tool?" *Evangelical Missions Quarterly* 36.4 (October): 484–88.

Dixon, Roger. 2002. "The Major Model of Muslim Ministry." *Missiology* 30.4 (October): 443–54.

———. 2007. "Identity Theft: Retheologizing the Son of God." *Evangelical Missions Quarterly* 43.2 (April): 220–26.

———. 2009. "Moving on from the C1–C6 Spectrum." *St. Francis Magazine* 5.4 (August): 3–19.

Donovan, Vincent. 1968. *Christianity Rediscovered*. Chicago: Fides/Claretian.

Downey, Steven. 2008. "What Are 'Best Practices' of Church Planting among Muslims?" *Evangelical Missions Quarterly* 44.3 (July): 368–73.

Driscoll, Mark, and Gerry Breshears. 2008. *Vintage Church: Timeless Truths and Timely Methods*. Wheaton, IL: Crossway.

Droogers, André. 2005. "Syncretism and Fundamentalism: A Comparison." *Social Compass* 52.4 (December): 463–71.

Dulles, Avery Robert. 1983. *Models of Revelation*. Garden City, NY: Doubleday.

Dutch, Bernard. 2000. "Should Muslims Become Christians?" *International Journal of Frontier Missions* 17.1 (Spring): 15–24.

Dye, T. Wayne. 1984a. "Toward a Theology of Power for Melanesia: Part 1." *Catalyst* 14.1: 57–75.

———. 1984b. "Toward a Theology of Power for Melanesia: Part 2." *Catalyst* 14.2: 158–80.

Dyrness, William A. 1990. *Learning about Theology from the Third World*. Grand Rapids: Zondervan.

———. 1992. *Invitation to Cross-Cultural Theology: Case Studies in Vernacular Theologies*. Grand Rapids: Zondervan.

Eenigenburg, Don. 1997. "The Pros and Cons of Islamicized Contextualization." *Evangelical Missions Quarterly* 33.3 (July): 310–15.

Effa, Allan L. 2007. "Prophet, Kings, Servants, and Lepers: A Missiological Reading of an Ancient Drama." *Missiology* 35.3 (July): 305–13.

Eitel, Keith E. 1987. "The Transcultural Gospel—Crossing Cultural Barriers." *Evangelical Missions Quarterly* 23.2 (April): 130–37.

Ekka, Jhakmak Neeraj. 2007. "Indigenous Christian Theology: Questions and Directions in Making." *Bangalore Theological Forum* 39.1: 102–25.

Elder, Annette. 1991. "Boomers, Busters, and the Challenge of the Unreached People." *International Journal of Frontier Missions* 8.2 (March): 51–55.

Ellenberger, John D. 1997. "Evangelism Explosion and Communication: A Response." *Evangelical Missions Quarterly* 33 (July): 304–6.

Ellison, Craig W. 1988. "Growing Urban Churches Biblically." *Urban Mission* 6.2 (April): 7–18.

Elliston, Edgar J. 1989. "Contextualized Christian Social Transformation."

In *The Word Among Us: Contextualizing Theology for Mission Today*, ed. Dean S. Gilliland, 199–218. Dallas: Word.

Elliston, Edgar, Stephen Hoke, and Samuel Voorhies. 1989. "Issues in Contextualizing Christian Leadership Development." In *Christian Relief and Development: Developing Workers for Effective Ministry*, ed. Edgar Elliston, 179–210. Dallas: Word.

Elmer, Duane. 2006. *Cross-Cultural Servanthood: Serving the World in Christlike Humility*. Downers Grove, IL: InterVarsity.

Engel, James F. 1991. "Using Research Strategically in Urban Ministry." *Urban Mission* 8.4 (October): 6–12.

Engel, James F., and H. Wilbert Norton. 1975. *What's Gone Wrong with the Harvest? A Communication Strategy for the Church and World Evangelization*. Grand Rapids: Zondervan.

Ericson, Norman R. 1978. "Implications from the New Testament for Contextualization." In *New Horizons in World Mission: Evangelicals and the Christian Mission in the 1980s. Papers and Responses Prepared for the Consultation of Theology and Mission, Trinity Evangelical Divinity School, School of World Mission and Evangelism, March 19–22*, ed. David J. Hesselgrave, 71–85. Grand Rapids: Baker.

Escobar, Samuel. 1994. "The Search for a Missiological Christology for Latin America." In *Emerging Voices in Global Christian Theology*, ed. William A Dyrness, 199–228. Grand Rapids: Zondervan.

———. 2002. *Changing Tides: Latin America and World Mission Today*. American Society of Missiology series, no. 31. Maryknoll, NY: Orbis.

———. 2003. *The New Global Mission: The Gospel from Everywhere to Everywhere*. Downers Grove, IL: InterVarsity.

Eshleman, Paul. 1985. *I Just Saw Jesus*. San Bernardino, CA: Here's Life Publishers.

———. 2002. "The 'Jesus' Film: A Contribution to World Evangelism." *International Bulletin of Missionary Research* 26.2 (April): 68–70, 72.

Espiritu, Daniel L. 2001. "Ethnohermeneutics or Oikohermeneutics? Questioning the Necessity of Caldwell's Hermeneutics." *Journal of Asian Mission* 3.2: 267–81.

Fearon, Josiah. 1997. "The Ethics of Contextualization." *World Evangelization Magazine* (September/October): 20–22.

Feinberg, Paul D. 1982. "An Evangelical Approach to Contextualization of Theology." *Trinity World Forum* 7.3 (Spring): 7.

Felde, Marcus Paul Bach. 1989. "Local Theologies—License to Sing." *The Hymn* 40 (July): 15–20.

Fernando, Ajith. 2002. *Jesus Driven Ministry*. Wheaton, IL: Crossway.

Fleming, Bruce C. E. 1980. *Contextualization of Theology: An Evangelical Assessment*. Pasadena, CA: William Carey Library.

Flemming, Dean. 2002. "Contextualizing the Gospel in Athens." *Missiology: An International Review* 30.2 (April): 198–214.

_____. 2005. *Contextualization in the New Testament: Patterns for Theology and Mission.* Downers Grove, IL: InterVarsity.

Francis, Glen R. 1992. "The Gospel for a Sin/Shame-Based Society." *Taiwan Mission Quarterly* 2.2 (October): 5–16.

Franklin, Karl. 2005a. "Re-Thinking Stories." *International Journal of Frontier Missions* 22.1 (Spring): 6–12.

_____. 2005b. "Part II: Proposing an Alternative Initial Strategy for Small Language Groups in the Pacific." *International Journal of Frontier Missions* 22.2 (Summer): 45–52.

Fritz, Paul. 1995. "Contextualizing the Message through Use of Case Studies." *International Journal of Frontier Missions* 12.3 (July–September): 147–52.

Frost, Michael. 2006. *Exiles: Living Missionally in a Post-Christian Culture.* Peabody, MA: Hendrickson.

Frost, Michael, and Alan Hirsch. 2003. *The Shaping of Things to Come: Innovation and Mission for the 21st Century Church.* Peabody, MA: Hendrickson.

Fuchs, Stephen. 1976. "Messianic Movements: A New Mission Method for India?" *Catalyst* 6.1: 3–17.

Fudge, Eric. 1987. "Can Doctrinal Statements Be Objective?" In *Objective Knowledge: A Christian Perspective,* ed. Paul Helm, 109–28. Leicester: InterVarsity.

Fukuda, Mitsuo. 2001. "Sermon Topics Contextualized for Japan." *Journal of Asian Mission* 3.1: 141–48.

Fuller, Lois. 1997. "The Missionary's Role in Developing Indigenous Christian Theology." *Evangelical Missions Quarterly* 33.4 (October): 404–9.

Gaqurae, Joe. 1996. "Indigenization as Incarnation: The Concept of a Melanesian Christ." *Evangelical Review of Theology* 20.3 (July): 240–47.

Garriott, Craig W. 1996. "Leadership Development in the Multiethnic Church." *Urban Mission* 13.4 (October): 24–37.

Garrison, David. 1999. *Church Planting Movements.* Richmond, VA: International Mission Board of the Southern Baptist Convention.

_____. 2004a. *Church Planting Movements: How God Is Redeeming a Lost World.* Bangalore, India: WIGTake.

_____. 2004b. "Church Planting Movements vs. Insider Movements: Missiological Realities vs. Mythological Speculations." *International Journal of Frontier Missions* 21.4 (October–December): 151–54.

_____. 2004c. "Church Planting Movements: The Next Wave?" *International Journal of Frontier Missions* 21.3 (July–September): 118–21.

_____. 2004d. "How to Kill a Church-Planting Movement." *Mission Frontiers* 26.6: 14–17.

Gehman, Richard J. 1983. "Guidelines in Contextualization." *East African Journal of Evangelical Theology* 2.1: 24–36.

_____. 1987. *Doing African Christian Theology: An Evangelical Perspective*. Nairobi: Evangel Publishing House.

_____. 1996. "Doing African Christian Theology: A Response and a Revelation." *The Africa Journal of Evangelical Theology* 15.2: 85–113.

Geleta, Amsalu Tadesse. 2002. "Demonization and Exorcism in Ethiopian Churches." In *Deliver Us From Evil: An Uneasy Frontier in Christian Mission*, ed. A. Scott Moreau, Tokunboh Adeyemo, David Burnett, Bryant Myers, and Hwa Yung, 91–103. Monrovia, CA: MARC.

Gener, Timoteo D. 2004. "Re-visioning Local Theology: An Integral Dialogue with Practical Theology: A Filipino Evangelical Perspective." *Journal of Asian Mission* 6.2: 133–66.

_____. 2005. "Every Filipino Christian a Theologian: A Way of Advancing Local Theology for the 21st Century." In *Doing Theology in the Philippines*, ed. John Suk, 3–23. Quezon City, Philippines: Asian Theological Seminary.

Gibbs, Eddie, and Ryan K. Bolger. 2005. *Emerging Churches: Creating Christian Community in Postmodern Cultures*. Grand Rapids: Baker.

Gilliland, Dean S. 1989a. "Contextual Theology as Incarnational Mission." In *The Word among Us: Contextualizing Theology for Mission Today*, ed. Dean S. Gilliland, 9–31. Dallas: Word.

_____. 1989b. "Contextualization Models." In *The Word among Us: Contextualizing Theology for Mission Today*, ed. Dean S. Gilliland, 313–17. Dallas: Word.

_____. 1989c. "New Testament Contextualization: Continuity and Particularity in Paul's Theology." In *The Word among Us: Contextualizing Theology for Mission Today*, ed. Dean S. Gilliland, 52–73. Dallas: Word.

_____. 1998. "Context Is Critical in 'Islampur' Case." *Evangelical Missions Quarterly* 34.4 (October): 415–17.

_____. 2000a. In *Evangelical Dictionary of World Missions*, gen. ed. A. Scott Moreau, s.v. "Contextualization." Grand Rapids: Baker.

_____. 2000b. "Modeling the Incarnation for Muslim People: A Response to Sam Schlorff." *Missiology* 28.3 (July): 305–28.

_____. 2005. "The Incarnation as Matrix for Appropriate Theologies." In *Appropriate Christianity*, ed. Charles Kraft, 493–519. Pasadena, CA: William Carey Library.

Glasser, Arthur F. 1989. "Old Testament Contextualization: Revelation and Its Environment." In *The Word Among Us: Contextualizing Theology for Mission Today*, ed. Dean S. Gilliland, 32–51. Dallas: Word.

_____. 1995. "A Study of Acts 15." *Missionary Monthly* 99D.6 (June): 13–15, 31.

Gnanakan, Ken. 1994. "Creation, New Creation, and Ecological

Relationships." In *Emerging Voices in Global Christian Theology*, ed. William A Dyrness, 127–54. Grand Rapids: Zondervan.

Gnanakan, Ken, and Sunand Sumithra. 1995. "Theology, Theologization, and the Theologian." In *Biblical Theology in Asia*, ed. Ken Gnanakan, 39–46. Bangalore, India; Theological Book Trust.

Goble, Phillip E., and Salim Munayer. 1989. *New Creation Book for Muslims*. Pasadena, CA: Mandate Press.

Goble, Phil. 1974. *Everything You Need to Grow a Messianic Synagogue*. Pasadena, CA: William Carey Library.

———. 1975. "Reaching Jews through Messianic Synagogues." *Evangelical Missions Quarterly* 11.2 (April): 80–87.

Goldsmith, Martin. 1980. "Parabolic Preaching in the Context of Islam." *Evangelical Review of Theology* 4.2 (October): 218–22.

Gort, Gerald D. 1989. "Syncretism and Dialogue: Christian Historical and Earlier Ecumenical Perception." *Mission Studies* 6.1: 9–22.

Grafas, Basil. 2007. "Evaluation of Scriptural Support for Insider Movements." *St. Francis Magazine* 2.4 (March): 1–17.

Grant, Beth. 2004. "Theological Education in the 21st Century." *Evangelical Missions Quarterly* 40.2 (April): 184–89.

Gration, John A. 1983. "Conversion in the Cultural Context." *International Bulletin of Missionary Research* 7.4 (October): 157–62.

———. 1984. "Willowbank to Zaire: The Doing of Theology." *Missiology* 12: 95–112.

Gray, Andrea, and Leith Gray. 2008. "A Muslim Encounters the Gospel of Mark: Theological Implications of Contextual Mismatch." *International Journal of Frontier Missions* 25.3 (Fall): 127–34.

———. 2009a. "Paradigms and Practice Part I: Social Networks and Fruitfulness in Church Planting." *International Journal of Frontier Missions* 26.1 (Spring): 19–28.

———. 2009b. "Paradigms and Praxis Part II: Why Are Some Workers Changing Paradigms?" *International Journal of Frontier Missions* 26.2 (Summer): 63–73.

Greenspahn, Frederick E. 2004. "Syncretism and Idolatry in the Bible." *Vetus Testamentum* 54.4: 480–94.

Greer, Bradford. 2008. "The Sharia of God: A Contextual Bridge for Islamic Contexts." *Evangelical Missions Quarterly* 44.3 (July).

———. 2009. "Toward More Meaningful Interaction: Rethinking How We Articulate Our Faith." *International Journal of Frontier Missions* 26.1 (Spring): 16–22.

Greeson, Kevin. 2004. *Camel Training Manual*. Bangalore, India: WIGTake.

Grenz, Stanley. 1993. *Revisioning Evangelical Theology: A Fresh Agenda for the 21st Century*. Downers Grove, IL: InterVarsity.

_____. 2000. "Culture and Spirit: The Role of Cultural Context in Theo-
logical Reflection." *Asbury Theological Journal* 55.2 (Fall): 37–51.

Grudem, Wayne A. 1988. *The Gift of Prophecy in the New Testament and
Today*. Westchester, IL: Crossway.

Guder, Darrell L., ed. 1998. *Missional Church: A Vision for the Sending of the
Church in North America*. Grand Rapids: Eerdmans.

Gustafson, James W. 1991. "The Integration of Development and Evangelism." *International Journal of Frontier Missions* 8.4 (October): 115–20.

_____. 1998. "The Integration of Development and Evangelism." *Missi-
ology: An International Review* 26.2 (April): 131–42.

Guthrie, Stan. 2004. *Missions in the Third Millennium: 21 Key Trends for the
21st Century*. Waynesboro, GA: Authentic.

Haines, John. 1983. "Worship: The Neglected Way to Reach Muslims."
Evangelical Missions Quarterly 19.1 (January): 42–45.

Hale, Chris. 2001. "Reclaiming the Bhajan." *Mission Frontiers* 23.2 (June):
16–17.

_____. 2007. "Aradhna: From Comfort to Discomfort, from Church to
Temple." *International Journal of Frontier Missions* 24.3 (Fall): 147–50.

Haleblian, Krikor. 1983. "The Problem of Contextualization." *Missiology*
11.1: 95–111.

Hall, Douglas. 1983. "Case Study: Emmanuel Gospel Center Boston: Contextualized Urban Ministry." *Urban Mission* 1.2 (April): 31–36.

Harbinson, Colin; John Franklin, James Tughan, and Phyllis Novak. 2005.
"Redeeming the Arts: The Restoration of the Arts to God's Creational
Intention." Lausanne Occasional Paper (LOP) No. 46. Online: http://
www.lausanne.org/documents/2004forum/LOP46_IG17.pdf, accessed 7
November 2009.

Hardin, Daniel C. 1981. "Review of Christianity in Culture." *Journal of the
Evangelical Theological Society* 24.4 (December): 351–53.

Harling, Mack. 2005. "De-Westernizing Doctrine and Developing Appropriate Theology in Mission." *International Journal of Frontier Missions*
22.4 (Winter): 159–66.

Harootian, Abigail F. Ramientos. 1987. "Doing Theology among Filipino
Peasant-Farmers." *International Journal of Frontier Missions* 4: 81–90.

Harris, Mark. 2000. "Contextualized Education for Russian Leaders."
Online: http://www.cvi2.org/pages/harris/spiritualtrainingprogrampro-
posal.rtf Accessed 12 October 2009.

Harris, R. Laird. 1971. *Inspiration and Canonicity of the Bible: An Historical
and Exegetical Study*. Grand Rapids: Zondervan.

Hattaway, Paul. 2003. *Back to Jerusalem: Three Chinese House Church Leaders
Share Their Vision to Complete the Great Commission*. Waynesboro, GA:
Gabriel Resources.

Hayward, Douglas. 1995. "Measuring Contextualization in Church and

Missions." *International Journal of Frontier Missions* 12.3 (July–September): 135–38.

Hedlund, Roger E. 1999. "Indian Instituted Churches: Indigenous Christianity Indian Style." *Mission Studies* 46.1: 26–42.

Heideman, Eugene P. 1997. "Syncretism, Contextualization, Orthodoxy, and Heresy." *Missiology* 25.1 (January): 37–49.

Heldenbrand, Richard. 1982. "Missions to Muslims: Cutting the Nerve." *Evangelical Missions Quarterly* 18.3 (July): 134–38.

Henry, Carl H. 1980. "The Cultural Relativizing of Christianity." *Trinity Journal* 1: 153–64.

Henson, Les. 2008. "Cultural Bridges and Momina Traditional Religion: Seeking a Key Redemptive Analogy and Mission Many." *Evangelical Missions Quarterly* 44.2 (April): 224–32.

Hesselgrave, David J. 1978. *Communicating Christ Cross-Culturally: An Introduction to Missionary Communication*. Grand Rapids: Zondervan.

———. 1979. "The Contextualization Continuum." *Gospel in Context* 2.3 (July): 4–11.

———. 1984. "Contextualization and Revelational Epistemology." In *Hermeneutics, Inerrancy, and the Bible*, ed. Earl D. Radmacher and Robert D. Preus, 693–738. Grand Rapids: Zondervan.

———. 1986. "Culture-Sensitive Counseling and the Christian Mission." *International Bulletin of Missionary Research* 10.3 (July): 109–13.

———. 1995a. "Contextualization that Is Authentic and Relevant." *International Journal of Frontier Missions* 12.3 (July–September): 115–19.

———. 1995b. "Great Commission Contextualization." *International Journal of Frontier Missions* 12.3 (July–September): 139–44.

———. 2000a. "Third Millennium Missiology: 'Use of Egyptian Gold.'" *International Journal of Frontier Missions* 16.4 (Winter): 191–97.

———. 2000b. *Planting Churches Cross-Culturally: North America and Beyond*. 2nd ed. Grand Rapids: Baker.

———. 2005. *Paradigms in Conflict: 10 Key Questions in Christian Missions Today*. Grand Rapids: Kregel.

———. 2006. "Syncretism: Mission and Missionary Induced?" In *Contextualization and Syncretism: Navigating Cultural Currents*, ed. Gailyn Van Rheenen, 71–98. Pasadena, CA: William Carey Library.

———. 2007. "Brian McLaren's Contextualization of the Gospel." *Evangelical Missions Quarterly* 43.1 (January): 92–100.

Hesselgrave, David J., and Edward Rommen. 1989. *Contextualization: Meanings, Methods, and Models*. Grand Rapids: Baker.

Hiebert, Paul. 1979. "The Gospel and Culture." In *The Gospel and Islam: A 1978 Compendium*, ed. Don M. McCurry, 58–65. Monrovia, CA: MARC.

———. 1982. "The Flaw of the Excluded Middle." *Missiology* 10 (January): 35–48.

_____. 1984. "Critical Contextualization." *Missiology* 12.3 (July): 287–96.

_____. 1985a. *Anthropological Insight for Missionaries.* Grand Rapids: Baker.

_____. 1985b. "Epistemological Foundations for Science and Theology." *Theological Students Fellowship Bulletin* 8.4 (March–April): 5–10.

_____. 1987. "Critical Contextualization." *International Bulletin of Missionary Research* 11: 104–11.

_____. 1988. "Metatheology: The Step Beyond Contextualization." In *Reflection and Projection: Mission at the Threshold of 2001: Festschrift in Honor of George W. Peters for his Eightieth Birthday,* ed. Hans Kasdorf and Klaus W. Muller, 383–95. Bad Liebenzell: Verlag der Liebenzeller Mission.

_____. 1989. "Form and Meaning in Contextualization of the Gospel." In *The Word Among Us: Contextualizing Theology for Mission Today,* ed. Dean S. Gilliland, 101–20. Dallas: Word.

_____. 1991. "Checks against Syncretism." *Christianity Today* 35.2 (February): 39–40.

_____. 1994. *Anthropological Reflections on Missiological Issues.* Grand Rapids: Baker.

_____. 2006. "Syncretism and Social Paradigms." In *Contextualization and Syncretism: Navigating Cultural Currents,* ed. Gailyn Van Rheenen, 31–46. Pasadena, CA: William Carey Library.

_____. 2008. *Transforming Worldviews: An Anthropological Understanding of How People Change.* Grand Rapids: Baker.

_____. 2009. *The Gospel in Human Contexts: Anthropological Explorations for Contemporary Missions.* Grand Rapids: Baker.

Hiebert, Paul, Daniel Shaw, and Tite Tiénou. 1999. *Understanding Folk Religions: A Christian Response to Popular Beliefs and Practices.* Grand Rapids: Baker.

Higgins, Kevin. 2006. "Identity, Integrity, and Insider Movements: A Brief Paper Inspired by Timothy C. Tennent's Critique of C–5 Thinking." *International Journal of Frontier Missions* 23.3 (Fall): 117–23.

_____. 2007. "Acts 15 and Insider Movements among Muslims: Questions, Process, and Conclusions." *International Journal of Frontier Missions* 24.1 (Spring): 29–40.

_____. 2009. "Inside What? Church, Culture, Religion, and Insider Movements in Biblical Perspective." *St. Francis Magazine* 5.4 (August): 74–91.

Hill, Harriet. 1990. "Incarnational Ministry." *Evangelical Missions Quarterly* 26.2 (April): 196–201.

_____. 1993. "Lifting the Fog on Incarnational Ministry." *Evangelical Missions Quarterly* 29.3 (July): 262–68.

_____. 2006. "The Vernacular Treasure: A Century of Mother-Tongue Bible Translation." *International Bulletin of Missionary Research* 30.2 (April): 82–86, 88.

_____. 2007. "The Effect of Using Local and Non-Local Terms in Mother-Tongue Scripture." *Missiology* 35.4 (October): 384–96.

Hill, Margaret V., Harriet Hill, Richard Baggé, and Pat Miersma. 2007. *Healing the Wounds of Trauma: How the Church Can Help.* Nairobi: Paulines Publications Africa, 2007.

"History Reveals Questions about This Approach." 1998. *Evangelical Missions Quarterly* 34.1 (January): 36–38.

Hoefer, Herbert E. 1981. "Local Village Theology in India." *Catalyst* 11.2: 121–30.

_____. 2001a. *Churchless Christianity.* Pasadena, CA: William Carey Library.

_____. 2001b. "The Conversion Confusion." *International Journal of Frontier Missions* 18.1 (Spring): 47–49.

_____. 2002. "Gospel Ferment in India among Both Hindus and Christians: Jesus, My Master: 'Jesu Bhakta' Hindu Christian Theology." *International Journal of Frontier Missions* 19.3 (Fall): 39–42.

_____. 2005. "Proclaiming a 'Theologyless' Christ." *International Journal of Frontier Missions* 22.3 (Fall): 97–100.

_____. 2007a. "Church in Context." *Evangelical Missions Quarterly* 43.2 (April): 200–208.

_____. 2007b. "Rooted or Uprooted: The Necessity of Contextualization in Missions." *International Journal of Frontier Missions* 24.3 (Fall): 131–38.

_____. 2008. "How Do We Deal with the Baggage of the Past? What's in a Name? The Baggage of Terminology in Contemporary Mission." *International Journal of Frontier Missions* 25.1 (January): 25–29.

_____. 2009. "Muslim-Friendly Christian Worship." *Evangelical Missions Quarterly* 45.1 (January): 48–53.

Hong, Yong-gi. 2000. "The Backgrounds and Characteristics of the Charismatic Mega-Churches in Korea." *Asian Journal of Pentecostal Studies* 3.1: 99–118.

Horden, William E. 1966. *New Directions in Theology Today.* Philadelphia: Westminster.

Horner, Norman A. 1987. "The Association of Professors of Mission." *International Bulletin of Missionary Research* 11.3 (July): 120–24.

Horrell, J. Scott. 2005. "Doing Theology: An International Task." *Evangelical Missions Quarterly* 41.4 (October): 474–78.

Howell, Brian. 2009. "Contextualizing Context—Exploring Christian Identity in the Global Church through Six Contemporary Cases." In *Power and Identity in the Global Church: Six Contemporary Cases,* ed. Brian M. Howell and Edwin Zehner, 1–25. Pasadena, CA: William Carey Library.

Howell, Brian M., and Edwin Zehner, eds. 2009. *Power and Identity in the*

Global Church: Six Contemporary Cases. Pasadena, CA: William Carey Library.

Howell, Richard. 2001. "Transcultural Theology and Contextualization." *Evangelical Review of Theology* 25.1: 31–37.

Howes, John F. 2007. "Christian Prophecy in Japan: Uchimura Kanzō." *Japanese Journal of Religious Studies* 34.1: 127–50.

Hwa, Yung. 1997. *Mangoes or Bananas? The Quest for an Authentic Asian Christian Theology.* Regnum Studies in Mission. Oxford: Regnum International.

————. 2002. "Case Studies in Spiritual Warfare from East Asia." In *Deliver Us from Evil: An Uneasy Frontier in Christian Mission*, ed. A. Scott Moreau, Tokunboh Adeyemo, David Burnett, Bryant Myers, and Hwa Yung, 146–51. Monrovia, CA: MARC.

————. 2004a. "Strategic Issues in Missions." *Evangelical Missions Quarterly* 40.1 (January): 26–34.

————. 2004b. "Missiological Implications of Dr. David Yonggi Cho's Theology." *Cyberjournal for Pentecostal-Charismatic Research* 13 (April). Online: http://www.pctii.org/cyberj/cyberj13/yung.html, accessed 2 November 2009.

Hwang, Andrew, and Richard Ng. 1990. "Case Study: Singapore: Uniting Social Concern and Evangelism." *Urban Mission* 7.4 (October): 36–44.

Imasogie, Osalador. 1983. "Contextualization: Constructive Interaction between Culture, People, Church, and Theological Programme." *East Africa Journal of Evangelical Theology* 2.1: 19–23.

————. 1984. *Guidelines for Christian Theology in Africa.* Achimota, Ghana: Africa Christian Press.

Inch, Morris A. 1982. *Doing Theology across Cultures.* Grand Rapids: Baker.

————. 1984. "A Response to 'Contextualization and Revelational Epistemology.'" In *Hermeneutics, Inerrancy, and the Bible*, ed. Earl D. Radmacher and Robert D. Preus, 741–50. Grand Rapids: Zondervan.

International Orality Network. 2007. *Making Disciples of Oral Learners.* Richmond, VA: International Mission Board SBC.

Jackson, Bruce W. 1993. "Urban Theological Education for Church Leadership." *Urban Mission* 11.2 (April): 32–43.

Jacobs, Adrian. 2000. "Drumming, Dancing, Chanting, and Other Christian Things." *Mission Frontiers* (September). Online: http://www.mission-frontiers.org/issue/article/drumming-dancing-chanting-and-other-christian-things; accessed 26 June, 2012.

Jacobs, Donald R. 1979. "Conversion and Culture: An Anthropological Perspective with Reference to East Africa." In *Gospel and Culture. The Papers of a Consultation on the Gospel and Culture, Convened by the Lausanne Committee's Theology and Education Group*, ed. John R. W. Stott and Robert T. Coote, 175–94. Pasadena, CA: William Carey Library.

Jameson, Richard, and Nick Scalevich. 2000. "First-Century Jews and Twentieth-Century Muslims." *International Journal of Frontier Missions* 17.1 (Spring): 33–39.

Jamison, Todd. 2007. "House Churches in Central Asia: An Evaluation." *Evangelical Missions Quarterly* 43.2 (April): 188–96.

Jenkins, Orville Boyd. 2007. "Orality in Christian Mission." Online: http://orvillejenkins.com/orality/oralityinchristianmission.html; accessed 22 May 2010.

Jenkins, Philip. 2002. *The Next Christendom: The Coming of Global Christianity*. New York: Oxford University Press.

————. 2006. *The New Faces of Christianity: Believing the Bible in the Global South*. New York: Oxford University Press.

Johnson, Mark. 2006. "Grace and Greed in a People Movement to Christ in Nepal." *Evangelical Missions Quarterly* 42.1 (January): 26–32.

Jongh van Arkel, Jan T. de. 1995. "Teaching Pastoral Care and Counseling in an African Context: A Problem of Contextual Relevancy." *Journal of Pastoral Care* 49: 189–99.

Jordan, Ivan, and Frank Tucker. 2002. "Using Indigenous Art to Communicate the Christian Message." *Evangelical Missions Quarterly* 38.3 (July): 302–9.

Kafton, Sheri. 1987. "Doing Theology among Cambodian Refugees." *International Journal of Frontier Missions* 4: 23–37.

Kato, Byang. 1975. "The Gospel, Cultural Context, and Religious Syncretism." In *Let the Earth Hear His Voice*, ed. J. D. Douglas, 1216–28. Minneapolis: World Wide Publications.

Kennedy, D. James. 1997. "Evangelism Explosion: 'Reaching All the Nations' and Its Impact on World Missions." *Evangelical Missions Quarterly* 33 (July): 298–301.

Kim, Chong H. 2006. "Another Reformation on the Horizon." *International Journal of Frontier Missions* 23.1 (January): 17–29.

Kim, Chung-choon. 1974. "The Contextualization of Theological Education." *Northeast Asia Journal of Theology* 12 (March): 1–9.

Kim, Kirsteen. 2004. "Missiology as Global Conversation of (Contextual) Theologies." *Mission Studies* 21.1: 39–53.

Kim, Min Chul. 2005. "Missionary Medicine in a Changing World." *Evangelical Missions Quarterly* 41.4 (October): 430–37.

Kim, Wong Tok. 2005. "Discovering God's Prior Work in Bringing People to Himself." *Evangelical Missions Quarterly* 41.1 (January): 78–85.

King, Roberta. 2001. "Worship That Moves the Soul: A Conversation with Professor Roberta King on the Impact of Ethno-worship." *Mission Frontiers* 23.2 (June): 10–15.

————. 2006. "Singing the Lord's Song in a Global World: The Dynamics of Doing Critical Contextualization through Music." *Evangelical Missions Quarterly* 42.1 (January): 68–74.

Kinsler, F. Ross. 1978. "Mission and Context: The Current Debate about Contextualization." *Evangelical Missions Quarterly* 14.1 (January): 23–29.

Kirk, J. Andrew. 1979. *Liberation Theology: An Evangelical View from the Third World*. Atlanta: John Knox.

Kivengere, Festo, with Dorothy Smoker. 1977. *I Love Idi Amin: The Story of Triumph under Fire in the Midst of Suffering and Persecution in Uganda*. Old Tappan, NJ: Revell.

Klem, Herbert V. 1978. "The Bible as Oral Literature in Oral Societies." *International Review of Mission* 67.268 (October): 479–86.

Koehler, Paul. 2009. *Telling God's Stories with Power*. Pasadena, CA: William Carey Library.

Kraft, Charles. 1973a. "Church Planters and Ethnolinguistics." In *God, Man, and Church Growth: A Festschrift in Honor of Donald Anderson McGavran*, ed. Alan R. Tippett, 226–49. Grand Rapids: Eerdmans.

_____. 1973b. "Dynamic Equivalence Churches." *Missiology* 1.1: 39–57.

_____. 1973c. "The Incarnation, Cross-Cultural Communication, and Communication Theory." *Evangelical Missions Quarterly* 9.3 (Fall): 277–84.

_____. 1973d. "Toward a Christian Ethnotheology." In *God, Man, and Church Growth: A Festschrift in Honor of Donald Anderson McGavran*, ed. Alan R. Tippett, 109–26. Grand Rapids: Eerdmans.

_____. 1974. "Psychological Stress Factors among Muslims." In *Report [of] Conference on Media in Islamic Culture*, ed. C. R. Shumaker, 137–44. Wheaton, IL: Evangelical Literature Overseas.

_____. 1978. "The Contextualization of Theology." *Evangelical Missions Quarterly* 14.1 (January): 31–38.

_____. 1979a. "Dynamic Equivalence Churches in Muslim Society." In *The Gospel and Islam: A 1978 Compendium*, ed. Don McCurry, 114–28. Monrovia, CA: MARC.

_____. 1979b. "Communicating the Gospel God's Way." *Ashland Theological Bulletin* 12.1 (Spring): 3–60.

_____. 1979c. The Church in Culture: A Dynamic Equivalence Model." In *Gospel and Culture. The Papers of a Consultation on the Gospel and Culture, Convened by the Lausanne Committee's Theology and Education Group*, ed. John R. W. Stott and Robert T. Coote, 285–312. Pasadena, CA: William Carey Library.

_____. 1979d. "Measuring Indigeneity." In *Gospel and Culture. The Papers of a Consultation on the Gospel and Culture, Convened by the Lausanne Committee's Theology and Education Group*, ed. John R. W. Stott and Robert T. Coote, 118–52. Pasadena, CA: William Carey Library.

References

_____. 1979e. *Christianity in Culture: A Study in Dynamic Biblical Theologizing in Cross-Cultural Perspective.* Maryknoll, NY: Orbis.

_____. 1979f. "Dynamic Equivalence Theologizing." In *Readings in Dynamic Indigeneity,* ed. Charles H. Kraft and Tom N. Wisley, 258–85. Pasadena, CA: William Carey Library.

_____. 1980. "The Church in Culture: A Dynamic Equivalence Model." In *Down to Earth: Studies in Christianity and Culture,* ed. John R. Stott and Robert Coote, 211–30. Grand Rapids: Eerdmans.

_____. 1982. "My Distaste for the Combative Approach." *Evangelical Missions Quarterly* 18.3 (July): 138–41.

_____. 1991a. *Communication Theory for Christian Witness,* Rev. ed. Maryknoll, NY: Orbis.

_____. 1991b. "Receptor-oriented Ethics in Cross-cultural Intervention." *Transformation* 8: 20–25.

_____. 1991c. "What Kind of Encounters Do We Need in Our Christian Witness?" *Evangelical Missions Quarterly* 27.3 (July): 258–65.

_____, with Ellen Kearney and Mark H. White. 1993. *Deep Wounds, Deep Healing: Discovering the Vital Link between Spiritual Warfare and Inner Healing.* Ann Arbor, MI: Vine Books/Servant Publications.

_____. 1995. "'Christian Animism' or God-Given Authority?" In *Spiritual Power and Missions: Raising the Issues,* ed. Edward Rommen, 88–136. Pasadena, CA: William Carey Library.

_____. 1996. *Anthropology for Christian Witness.* Maryknoll, NY: Orbis.

_____. 1999. "Culture, Worldview, and Contextualization." In *Perspectives on the World Christian Movement,* 2nd ed., eds. Ralph D. Winter and Steven C. Hawthorne, 384–91. Pasadena, CA: William Carey Library.

_____. 2002a. "Contextualization and Spiritual Power." In *Deliver Us from Evil: An Uneasy Frontier in Christian Mission,* ed. A. Scott Moreau, Tokunboh Adeyemo, David G. Burnett, Bryant L. Myers, and Hwa Yung, 290–308. Monrovia, CA: MARC/World Vision.

_____. 2002b. *Culture, Communication, and Christianity: A Selection of Writings by Charles H. Kraft.* Pasadena, CA: William Carey Library.

_____, ed. 2005a. *Appropriate Christianity.* Pasadena, CA: William Carey Library.

_____. 2005b. "Appropriate Contextualization of Spiritual Power." In *Appropriate Christianity,* ed. Charles Kraft, 375–95. Pasadena, CA: William Carey Library.

_____. 2005c. *Christianity in Culture: A Study in Dynamic Biblical Theologizing in Cross-Cultural Perspective.* 25th Anniversary Edition. Maryknoll, NY: Orbis.

_____. 2005d. "The Development of Contextualization Theory in Euroamerican Missiology." In *Appropriate Christianity,* ed. Charles Kraft, 15–34. Pasadena, CA: William Carey Library.

_____. 2005d. "Spiritual Power: A Missiological Issue." In *Appropriate Christianity*, ed. Charles Kraft, 361–74. Pasadena, CA: William Carey Library.

_____. 2005e. "Why Appropriate?" In *Appropriate Christianity*, ed. Charles Kraft, 3–14. Pasadena, CA: William Carey Library.

_____. 2005f. "Why Isn't Contextualization Implemented?" In *Appropriate Christianity*, ed. Charles Kraft, 67–79. Pasadena, CA: William Carey Library.

_____. 2005g. "Contextualization in Three Crucial Dimensions." In *Appropriate Christianity*, ed. Charles Kraft, 99–115. Pasadena, CA: William Carey Library.

_____. 2005h. "Meaning Equivalence Contextualization." In *Appropriate Christianity*, ed. Charles Kraft, 155–68. Pasadena, CA: William Carey Library.

_____. 2007. Personal communication from Charles Kraft; 30 November 2007.

_____. 2008. *Worldview for Christian Witness*. Pasadena, CA: William Carey Library.

Kraft, Marguerite G. 1995. *Understanding Spiritual Power: A Forgotten Dimension of Cross-Cultural Mission and Ministry*. Maryknoll, NY: Orbis.

Krabill, James R. 1990. "Dida Harrist Hymnody (1913–1990)." *Journal of Religion in Africa* 20.2: 118–52.

Krass, Alfred C. 1979. "Contextualization for Today." *Gospel in Context* 2.3 (July): 27–30.

Krishna, Raghav. 2007. "India: Debating Global Missiological Flashpoints: From 'Krishna Bhakta' to 'Christianity' to 'Krista Bhakta'." *International Journal of Frontier Missions* 24.4 (October): 173–77.

Kwan, Simon S. M. 2005. "From Indigenization to Contextualization: A Change in Discursive Practice Rather Than a Shift in Paradigm." *Studies in World Christianity* 11.2: 236–50.

Lam, Wing-hung. 1984. "Patterns of Chinese Theology." In *The Bible and Theology in Asian Contexts: An Evangelical Perspective on Asian Theology*, ed. Bong Rin Ro and Ruth Eshenaur, 327–42. Taiching, Taiwan: Asia Theological Association.

LaPointe, Eugene. 1995. "Africans' Ancestors Veneration and Christian Worship." *Mission* 2: 207–18.

Larkin, William J. 1988. *Culture and Biblical Hermeneutics: Interpreting and Applying the Authoritative Word in a Relativistic Age*. Grand Rapids: Baker.

Larson, Warren F. 1996. "Critical Contextualization and Muslim Conversion." *International Journal of Frontier Missions* 13.4 (October–December): 189–91.

Lausanne Committee for World Evangelization. 1974. *The Lausanne*

Covenant. Online: http://www.lausanne.org/covenant. Accessed 7 September 2009.

———. 1978. *The Willowbank Report: Report of a Consultation on Gospel and Culture held at Willowbank, Somerset Bridge, Bermuda, from 6th to 13th January 1978.* Lausanne Occasional Papers, no. 2. Online: http://www.lausanne.org/en/documents/lops/73-lop-2.html; Accessed 26 June, 2012.

———. 2002. "Deliver Us from Evil Consultation Statement." In *Deliver Us from Evil: An Uneasy Frontier in Christian Mission,* ed. A. Scott Moreau, Tokunboh Adeyemo, David G. Burnett, Bryant L. Myers, and Hwa Yung, xvii–xxviii. Monrovia: MARC/World Vision.

———. 2004. Holistic Mission. Lausanne Occasional Paper No. 33. Online: http://www.lausanne.org/documents/2004forum/LOP33_IG4.pdf, accessed 21 May 2010.

Lewis, Jonathan P. 1991. "Contextualizing Needs Assessment for Third World Missionary Training." *International Journal of Frontier Missions* 8.4 (October): 121–26.

———. 1993. "Profiling the Latin Missionary: A Report of Contextualized Curriculum Research." *International Journal of Frontier Missions* 10.2 (March): 83–86.

Lewis, Rebecca. 2004. "Strategizing for Church Planting Movements in the Muslim World: Informal Reviews of Rodney Stark's *The Rise of Christianity* and David Garrison's *Church Planting Movements.*" *International Journal of Frontier Missions* 21.2 (April–June): 73–77.

———. 2007a. "Promoting Movements to Christ within Natural Communities." *International Journal of Frontier Missions* 24.2 (Summer): 75–76.

———. 2007b. "A Note about the C-scale." *International Journal of Frontier Missions* 24.2 (Summer): 76.

———. 2009. "Insider Movements: Honoring God-Given Identity and Community." *International Journal of Frontier Missions* 26.1 (Spring): 16–19.

Lim, David, Steve Spaulding, and Paul De Neui, eds. 2005. *Sharing Jesus Effectively in the Buddhist World.* Pasadena, CA: William Carey Library.

Lind, Millard C. 1982. "Refocusing Theological Education to Mission: The Old Testament and Contextualization." *Missiology* 10.2 (April): 141–60.

Livermore, David. 2001. "Billions to Be Won: Going after the Largest Mission Field in the World—Youth!" *Evangelical Missions Quarterly* 37.3 (July): 330–35.

Loewen, Jacob A. 1965. "Missionaries and Anthropologist Cooperate in Research." *Practical Anthropology* 12.4 (1965): 158–90.

Lonergan, Bernard J. F. 1972. *Method in Theology.* New York: Herder and Herder.

Lord, Andrew M. 2001. "The Holy Spirit and Contextualization." *Asian Journal of Pentecostal Studies* 4.2: 201–23.

Louw, Daniel J. 1997. "Pastoral Care in an African Context." *Missionalia* 25.3 (November): 392–407.

Love, Richard D. 1994. "Church Planting among Folk Muslims." *International Journal of Frontier Missions* 11.2 (April): 86–91.

_____. 2000. *Muslims, Magic, and the Kingdom of God: Church Planting Among Folk Muslims*. Pasadena, CA: William Carey Library.

Love, Rick. 2008. "How Do We Deal with the Baggage of the Past? Blessing the Nations in the 21st Century: A 3D Approach to Apostolic Ministry." *International Journal of Frontier Missions* 25.1 (January): 31–37.

Lovejoy, Grant, James B. Slack, J. O. Terry, and Bob A. Licio, eds. 2001. *Chronological Bible Storying Manual: A Methodology for Presenting the Gospel to Oral Communicators*. Online: http://www.oralitystrategies.org/resources.cfm?id=459&t=14; accessed 26 June, 2012.

Lowe, Chuck. 1998. *Territorial Spirits and World Evangelization?* Mentor/OMF.

Luzbetak, Louis J. 1963. "Toward an Applied Missionary Anthropology." *Practical Anthropology* 10.05 (1963): 199–208.

_____. 1988. *The Church and Cultures: New Perspectives in Missiological Anthropology*. Maryknoll, NY: Orbis.

Ma, Julie C. 2000. "*Santuala*: A Case of Pentecostal Syncretism." *Asian Journal of Pentecostal Studies* 3.1 (January): 61–82.

Madany, Bassam M. 2009. "The New Christians of North Africa and the Insider Movement." *St. Francis Magazine* 5.5 (October): 49–57.

Mallouhi, Mazhar. 2009. "Comments on the Insider Movement." *St. Francis Magazine* 5.5 (October): 3

Marantika, Chris. 1995. "Towards an Evangelical Theology in an Islamic Culture." In *Biblical Theology in Asia*, ed. Ken Gnanakan, 181–200. Bangalore, India: Asia Theological Association.

Marchak, Mark. 1989. "Nibbling the Big Apple." *Urban Mission* 7.1 (January): 35–41.

Martin, Marie-Louise. 1976. *Kimbangu: An African Prophet and His Church*. Translated by D. M. Moore. Grand Rapids: Eerdmans.

_____. 1978. "Kimbanguism: A Prophet and His Church." In *Dynamic Religious Movements*, ed. David J. Hesselgrave, 37–69. Grand Rapids: Baker.

Massey, Joshua. 1996. "Planting the Church Underground in Muslim Contexts." *International Journal of Frontier Missions* 13.3 (July September): 139–53.

_____. 2000. "God's Amazing Diversity in Drawing Muslims to Christ." *International Journal of Frontier Missions* 17.1 (Spring): 5–14.

_____. 2004a. "Misunderstanding C–5: His Ways Are Not Our Orthodoxy." *Evangelical Missions Quarterly* 40.3 (July): 296–304.

_____. 2004b. "Part I: Living Like Jesus, a Torah-Observant Jew: Delighting in God's Law for Incarnational Witness to Muslims." *International Journal of Frontier Missions* 21.1 (January): 12–23.

_____. 2004c. "Part II: Living Like Jesus, a Torah-Observant Jew: Delighting in God's Law for Incarnational Witness to Muslims." *International Journal of Frontier Missions* 21.2 (April): 54–71.

Mastra, I. Wayan. 1978. "A Contextualized Church." *Gospel in Context* 1.2 (April): 4–15; 20–21.

_____. 1984. "Christology in the Context of Life and Religion of the Balinese." In *Sharing Jesus in the Two Thirds World: Evangelical Christologies from the Contexts of Poverty, Powerlessness, and Religious Pluralism*, ed. Vinay Samuel and Chris Sugden, 157–74. Grand Rapids: Eerdmans.

Maxey, James A. 2009. *From Orality to Orality: A New Paradigm for Contextual Translation of the Bible*. Eugene, OR: Wipf & Stock.

May, Stan. 2005. "Ugly Americans or Ambassadors of Christ?" *Evangelical Missions Quarterly* 41.3 (July): 346–52.

McAlpine, Thomas H. 1995. *By Word, Work, and Wonder: Cases in Holistic Mission*. Monrovia, CA: MARC.

McCarty, Kathy A. 1996. "Home Care for AIDS Patients in Zimbabwe." In *Serving with the Poor in Africa*, ed. Tetsunao Yamamori et al,, 51–66. Pasadena, CA: MARC.

McCurry, Don. 1976. "Cross-Cultural Models for Muslim Evangelism." *Missiology* 4.3 (July): 267–84.

McElhanon, Kenneth. 1991. "Don't Give Up on the Incarnational Model." *Evangelical Missions Quarterly* 27.4 (October): 390–93.

McGavran, Donald A. 1963. *Church Growth in Mexico*. Grand Rapids: Eerdmans.

_____. 1980. *Understanding Church Growth*. Rev. ed. Grand Rapids: Eerdmans.

McIlwain, Trevor. 1987. *Building on Firm Foundations: Guidelines for Evangelism and Teaching Believers*. Sanford, FL: New Tribes Mission.

McPhee, Art. 2002. "Gospel Ferment in India among Both Hindus and Christians." *International Journal of Frontier Missions* 19.3 (July): 30–37.

McLaren, Brian 2001. *A New Kind of Christian: A Tale of Two Friends on a Spiritual Journey*. San Francisco: Jossey-Bass.

McQuilkin, J. Robertson. 1980. "Limits of Cultural Interpretation." *Journal of the Evangelical Theological Society* 23: 113–24.

_____. 1984. "Problems of Normativeness in Scripture: Cultural versus Permanent." In *Hermeneutics, Inerrancy, and the Bible*, ed. Earl D. Radmacher and Robert D. Preus, 217–40. Grand Rapids: Zondervan.

Meral, Ziya. 2005. "Toward a Relevant Theology for the Middle East." *Evangelical Missions Quarterly* 41.2 (April): 210–15.

_____. 2006. "Conversion and Apostasy: A Sociological Perspective." *Evangelical Missions Quarterly* 42.4 (October): 508–13.

"Micah Declaration on Integral Mission." 2001. Online: http://www.micahnetwork.org/sites/default/files/doc/page/mn_integral_mission_declaration_en.pdf; accessed 26 June, 2012.

Minz, Nirmal. 1996. "A Theological Interpretation of Modern Kuruky Christian Bhajans." In *Culture, Religion, and Society: Essays in Honor of Richard W. Taylor*, ed. Richard W. Taylor, Saral Kumar Chatterji, and Hunter P. Mabry, 154–76. Bangalore, India: The Christian Institute for the Study of Religion & Society Bangalore.

Miura, Hiroshi. 1996. *The Life and Thought of Kanzo Uchimura, 1861–1930*. Grand Rapids: Eerdmans.

Molyneux, K. Gordon, 1990. "The Place and Function of Hymns in the EJCSK (*Eglise de Jésus-Christ sur terre par le Prophète Simon Kimbangu*). *Journal of Religion in Africa* 20.2 (June): 153–87.

_____. 1993. *African Christian Theology: The Quest for Selfhood*. San Francisco: Mellen Research University Press.

Monsma, Timothy M. 1979. *An Urban Strategy for Africa*. Pasadena, CA: William Carey Library.

_____. 1981. "Urban Explosion and Missions Strategy." *Evangelical Missions Quarterly* 17.1 (January): 5–12.

Montgomery, Jim. 1984. "Can We Disciple Whole Countries?" *Evangelical Missions Quarterly* 20.1 (January): 48–57.

Montgomery, James H., and Donald A. McGavran. 1980. *The Discipling of a Nation*. Milpitas, CA: Global Church Growth Bulletin.

Moo, Douglas J. 1986. "The Problem of *Sensus Plenior*." In *Hermeneutics, Authority, and Canon*, ed. D. A. Carson and John D. Woodbridge, 177–211. Leicester: InterVarsity.

Moon, Jay. 2004. "Sweet Talk in Africa, Using Proverbs in Ministry." *Evangelical Missions Quarterly* 40.2 (April): 162–69.

_____. 2009. *African Proverbs Reveal Christianity in Culture: A Narrative Portrayal of Builsa Proverbs Contextualizing Christianity in Ghana*. ASM Monograph Series. Eugene, OR: Wipf & Stock.

Moreau, A. Scott. 1995a. "The Human Universals of Culture: Implications for Contextualization." *International Journal of Frontier Missions* 12.3 (July–September): 121–25.

_____. 1995b. "Religious Borrowing as a Two-Way Street: An Introduction to Animistic Tendencies in the Euro-North American Context." In *Christianity and the Religions: A Biblical Theology of World Religions*, ed. Ed Rommen and Harold Netland, 166–83. EMS 2. Pasadena, CA: William Carey Library.

_____. 1995c. *Twentieth-Century Dictionary of Christian Biography*, ed. J.

D. Douglas, s.v. "Sundar Singh, Sadhu (1889-c.1929)." Grand Rapids: Baker.

_____. 1995d. *Twentieth-Century Dictionary of Christian Biography*, ed. J. D. Douglas, s.v. "Sung, John (1901–1944)." Grand Rapids: Baker.

_____. 1995e. *Twentieth-Century Dictionary of Christian Biography*, ed. J. D. Douglas, s.v. "Uchimura, Kanzo (1861–1930)." Grand Rapids: Baker.

_____. 1997. "Broadening the Issues: Historiography, Advocacy, and Hermeneutics: Response to C. Peter Wagner." In *The Holy Spirit and Mission Dynamics*, ed. C. Douglas McConnell, 123–35. EMS 5. Pasadena, CA: William Carey Library.

_____, gen. ed. 2000a. *Evangelical Dictionary of World Mission*. Grand Rapids: Baker.

_____. 2000b. *Evangelical Dictionary of World Mission,* gen. ed. A. Scott Moreau, s.v. "Syncretism." Grand Rapids: Baker.

_____. 2005. "Contextualization: From an Adapted Message to an Adapted Life." In *The Changing Face of World Missions*, ed. Michael Pocock, Gailyn Van Rheenen, and Douglas McConnell, 321–48. Grand Rapids: Baker.

_____. 2006a. "Contextualization That Is Comprehensive." *Missiology* 34.3 (July): 325–35.

_____. 2006b. "Contextualization, Syncretism and Spiritual Warfare: Identifying the Issues." In *Contextualization and Syncretism: Navigating Cultural Currents,* ed. Gailyn Van Rheenen, 47–69. Pasadena, CA: William Carey Library.

_____. 2007. "Contextualization That Is Comprehensive." *Lausanne World Pulse* (April). Online: http://www.lausanneworldpulse.com/perspectives/673, accessed 31 October 2009.

_____. 2008a. "Holistic Contextualization: Ensuring That Every Facet of Christian Faith Is Localized." In *Mission to the World: Communicating the Gospel in the 21st Century. Essays in Honor of Knud Jørgensen*, ed. Tormod Engelsviken and Thor Strandenæs, 193–204. Oxford: Regnum.

_____. 2008b. "Mapping Evangelical Models of Contextualization." In *Med Kristus til Jordens Enger: Festskrift til Tormod Engelsviken*, ed. Kjell Olav Sannes et al., 55–64. Trondheim, Norway: Tapir Akademisk Forlag.

_____. 2009. "Paul Hiebert's Legacy of Worldview." *Trinity Journal* 30NS (Fall): 223–33.

_____. 2010. "Evangelical Models of Contextualization." In *Local Theology for the Global Church: Principles for an Evangelical Approach to Contextualization*, ed. Matthew Cook, Rob Haskell, Natee Tanchanpongs, and Ruth Julian. World Evangelical Alliance Theological Commission. Pasadena, CA: William Carey Library (in press).

Moreau, A. Scott, Gary Corwin, and Gary McGee. *Introducing World Missions*. Grand Rapids: Baker.

Moreau, A. Scott, and Mike O'Rear. 2004a. "Missions on the Web: And So the Story Goes . . . Web Resources on Storytelling, Myths and Proverbs." *Evangelical Missions Quarterly* 40.2 (April): 236–42.

_____ . 2004b. "Missions on the Web: A World Tour of Contextual Theologies." *Evangelical Missions Quarterly* 40.3 (July): 374–79.

_____. 2005. "Missions on the Web: Internet Resources on Contextualizing Ministry among Muslims." *Evangelical Missions Quarterly* 41.4 (October): 516–20.

Moreau, A. Scott, Tokunboh Adeyemo, David G. Burnett, Bryant L. Myers, and Hwa Yung, eds. 2002. *Deliver Us from Evil: An Uneasy Frontier in Christian Mission*. Monrovia: MARC/World Vision.

Müller, Julian. 1991. "African Contextual Pastoral Theology." *Scriptura* 39: 77–88.

Musasiwa, Roy. 1996. "Missiological Reflections." In *Serving with the Poor in Africa*, ed. Tetsunao Yamamori et al., 193–210. Pasadena, CA: MARC.

Musk, Bill. 1988. "Dreams and the Ordinary Muslim." *Missiology* 16.2 (April): 163–72.

Myers, Bryant. 1995. "At the End of the Day." In *Serving with the Poor in Asia*, ed. Tetsunao Yamamori et al., 195–201. Pasadena, CA: MARC.

_____. 1996. "At the End of the Day." In *Serving with the Poor in Africa*, ed. Tetsunao Yamamori et al., 213–24. Pasadena, CA: MARC.

_____. 1999. *Walking with the Poor: Principles and Practices of Transformational Development*. Maryknoll, NY: Orbis.

Nabetani, Gyoji. 1983. "An Asian Critique of Church Movements in Japan." *Evangelical Review of Theology* 7.1 (April): 73–78.

Nagasawa, Mkito. 2002. "Religious Truth: From a Cultural Perspective in the Japanese Context." *Journal of Asian Mission* 4.1: 43–62.

Naja, Ben. 2007. *Releasing the Workers of the Eleventh Hour: The Global South and the Task Remaining*. Pasadena, CA: William Carey Library.

Naugle, David K. 2002. *Worldview: The History of a Concept*. Grand Rapids: Eerdmans.

Ndofunso, Diakanua. 1978. "The Role of Prayer in the Kimbanguist Church." In *Christianity in Independent Africa*, ed. Edward Fashole-Luke, Richard Gray, Adrian Hastings, and Godwin Tasie, 577–96. Bloomington: Indiana University Press.

Neeley, Paul. 1999. "Noted Ministry." *Evangelical Missions Quarterly* 35.2 (April): 156–60.

Nelson, Reed E. 1989. "Five Principles of Indigenous Church Organization." *Missiology* 17.1 (January): 39–51.

Netland, Harold. 1988. "Toward Contextualized Apologetics." *Missiology* 16.3 (July): 289–303.

Newbigin, Lesslie. 1986. *Foolishness to Greeks: The Gospel and Western Culture*. London: SPCK.

_____. 1989. *The Gospel in a Pluralist Society*. Grand Rapids: Eerdmans.

Nguapitshi, Léon. 2005. "Kimbanguism: Its Present Christian Doctrine and the Problems Raised by It." *Exchange* 34.3: 135–55.

Nicholls, Bruce J. 1979a. *Contextualization: A Theology of Gospel and Culture*. Downers Grove, IL: InterVarsity.

_____. 1979b. "Towards a Theology of Gospel and Culture." In *Gospel and Culture. The Papers of a Consultation on the Gospel and Culture, Convened by the Lausanne Committee's Theology and Education Group*, ed. John R. W. Stott and Robert T. Coote, 69–82. Pasadena, CA: William Carey Library.

_____. 1984. "Hermeneutics, Theology, and Culture with Special Reference to Hindu Culture." In *The Bible and Theology in Asian Contexts: An Evangelical Perspective on Asian Theology*, ed. Bong Rin Ro and Ruth Eshenaur, 243–64. Taiching, Taiwan: Asia Theological Association.

_____. 1987. "Doing Theology in Context." *Evangelical Review of Theology* 11.1: 101–6.

_____. 1995. "Contextualisation in Chinese Culture." *Evangelical Review of Theology* 19.4: 368–80.

Nicholls, Kathleen D. 1983. "Tell the Story Powerfully in Local Cultural Forms." *Evangelical Missions Quarterly* 19.4 (October): 298–306.

Nicole, Roger. 1983. "The Biblical Concept of Truth." In *Scripture and Truth*, ed. D. A. Carson and John D. Woodbridge, 287–302. Leicester: InterVarsity.

Nida, Eugene A., and William D. Reyburn. 1981. *Meaning across Cultures*. ASM 4. Maryknoll, NY: Orbis.

Niebuhr, H. Richard. 1951. *Christ and Culture*. New York: Harper.

Nikides, Bill. 2006a. "Evaluating Insider Movements: C5 (Messianic Muslims)." *St. Francis Magazine* 2.3 (March): 1–14.

_____. 2006b. "Special Translations of the Bible for Muslims? Contemporary Trends in Evangelical Missions." *St. Francis Magazine* 2.3 (March): 1–9.

_____. 2009. "A Response to Kevin Higgins' 'Inside What? Church, Culture, Religion, and Insider Movements in Biblical Perspective.'" *St. Francis Magazine* 5.4 (August): 92–113.

Niles, D. Preman. 1980. "Example of Contextualization in the Old Testament." *The South East Asia Journal of Theology* 21.2: 19–33.

Nishioka, Yoshiyuki Billy. 1998. "Worldview Methodology in Mission Theology: A Comparison between Kraft's and Hiebert's Approaches." *Missiology* 26.4 (October): 457–76.

North, Eric M. 1974. "Eugene A. Nida: An Appreciation." In *On Language, Culture, and Religion: In Honor of Eugene A. Nida*, ed. Matthew Black and William A. Smalley, vii–xx. The Hague: Mouton.

Nuñez, Emilio A. 1985. *Liberation Theology.* Translated by Paul E. Sywulka. Chicago: Moody Press.

Nussbaum, Stan. 1984. "Re-Thinking Animal Sacrifice: A Response to Some Sotho Independent Churches." *Missionalia* 12.2 (August): 49–63.

Obaje, Yusufu Ameh. 1990. "Theocentric Christology as a Basis for a More Relevant Doctrine of Christ for the African Christian." *Ogbomoso Journal of Theology* 5 (December): 1–7.

———. 1991. "The Theology of Worship from an African Perspective." *Ogbomoso Journal of Theology* 6 (December): 40–47.

Oksnevad, Roy. 2007. "Contextualization in the Islamic Context." *Lausanne World Pulse* (April): Online: http://www.lausanneworldpulse.com/themedarticles.php/686/?pg=all, accessed 7 November 2009.

Olsen, Rolv. 2002. "True Or False? Contextualization Efforts of Karl Ludwig Reichelt and the Tao Fong Shan Christian Institute, 1930–55." *Svensk Missionstidskrift* 90.1: 103–28.

Olson, Bruce. 1978. *Bruchko.* Carol Stream, IL: Creation House.

Ong, Walter J. 1982. *Orality and Literacy: the Technologizing of the Word.* New York: Methuen.

Ortiz, Manny. 1991. "Circle Church: A Case Study in Contextualization." *Urban Mission* (January): 6–18.

———. 1993. "Insights into the Second Generation Hispanic." *Urban Mission* 10.4 (October): 21–33.

Osborne, Grant. 1984. "Preaching the Gospels: Methodology and Contextualization." *Journal of the Evangelical Theological Society* 27.1 (March): 27–42.

———. 1991. *The Hermeneutical Spiral: A Comprehensive Introduction to Biblical Interpretation.* Downers Grove, IL: InterVarsity.

Otis, Gerald E. 1980. "Power Encounter: The Way to Muslim Breakthrough." *Evangelical Missions Quarterly* 16.4 (October): 217–20.

Otis, George. 1993. "An Overview of Spiritual Mapping." In *Breaking Strongholds in Your City: How to Use Spiritual Mapping to Make Your Prayers More Strategic, Effective, and Targeted,* ed. C. Peter Wagner, 29–47. Ventura, CA: Regal.

Ott, Craig, and Stephen Strauss, with Timothy C. Tennent. 2010. *Encountering Theology of Mission: Biblical Foundations, Historical Developments, and Contemporary Issues.* Encountering Missions Series, ed. A. Scott Moreau. Grand Rapids: Baker.

Owens, Larry. 2007. "Syncretism and the Scriptures." *Evangelical Missions Quarterly* 43.1 (January): 74–80.

Padilla, C. René. 1979a. "The Contextualization of the Gospel." In *Readings in Dynamic Indigeneity,* ed. Charles H. Kraft and Tom N. Wisely, 286–312. Pasadena, CA: William Carey Library.

———. 1979b. "Hermeneutics and Culture: A Theological Perspective." In

Gospel and Culture. The Papers of a Consultation on the Gospel and Culture, Convened by the Lausanne Committee's Theology and Education Group, ed. John R. W. Stott and Robert T. Coote, 83–108. Pasadena, CA: William Carey Library.

_____. 1979c. "The Fullness of Mission." *Occasional Bulletin of Missionary Research* 3.1: 6–11.

_____. 1981. "The Interpreted Word: Reflections on Contextual Hermeneutics." *Themelios* 7.1 (September): 18–23.

_____. 1982. "Toward a Biblical Foundation for a Two-Thirds World Evangelical Theology." *Theological Fraternity Bulletin* 6.4: 29–36.

_____. 1985a. "How Evangelicals Endorsed Social Responsibility 1966–1983." *Transformation* 2.3: 27–32.

_____. 1985b. *Mission between the Times: Essays on the Kingdom*. Grand Rapids: Eerdmans.

_____. 1986. "Toward a Contextual Christology from Latin America." In *Conflict and Context: Hermeneutics in the Americas*, ed. Mark Lau Branson and C. René Padilla, 81–91. Grand Rapids: Eerdmans.

_____. 2009. *Global Poverty and Integral Mission*. Oxford: Church Mission Society.

Palau, Luis, with David Sanford. 1994. *Calling America and the Nations to Christ*. Nashville: Thomas Nelson.

Palmer, Donald C. 1990. *Managing Conflict Creatively: A Guide for Missionaries and Christian Workers*. Pasadena, CA: William Carey Library, 1990.

Parshall, Phil. 1979. "Contextualized Baptism for Muslim Converts." *Missiology* 7.4 (October): 501–15.

_____. 1980. *New Paths in Muslim Evangelism: Evangelical Approaches to Contextualization*. Grand Rapids: Baker.

_____. 1982a. "I Am Really Only Asking Questions." *Evangelical Missions Quarterly* 18.3 (July): 141–43.

_____. 1982b. "Muslim Misconceptions about 'Missionary'." *Evangelical Missions Quarterly* 18.1 (January): 31–34.

_____. 1983a. *Bridges to Islam: A Christian Perspective on Folk Islam*. Grand Rapids: Baker.

_____. 1983b. "Applied Spirituality in Ministry among Muslims." *Missiology: An International Review* 11.4 (October): 435–47.

_____. 1985a. *Beyond the Mosque: Christians within Muslim Community*. Grand Rapids: Baker.

_____. 1985b. "How to Change Medicine to Muslims." *Evangelical Missions Quarterly* 21.3 (July): 253–55.

_____. 1994. *Inside the Community: Understanding Muslims through Their Traditions*. Grand Rapids: Baker.

_____. 1998a. "Danger! New Directions in Contextualization. Do Some

Approaches to Muslims Cross the Line into Syncretism?" *Evangelical Missions Quarterly* 34.4 (October): 404–6, 409–10.

_____. 1998b. "Other Options for Muslim Evangelism." *Evangelical Missions Quarterly* 34.1 (January): 38–42.

_____. 2001. "Muslim Evangelism: Mobilizing the National Church." *Evangelical Missions Quarterly* 37.1 (January): 44–47.

_____. 2003. *Muslim Evangelism: Contemporary Approaches to Contextualization*. Waynesboro, GA: Gabriel Publications.

Payne, J. D. 2003. "Problems Hindering North American Church Planting Movements." *Evangelical Missions Quarterly* 39.2 (April): 220–28.

_____. 2010. "Ethical Guidelines for Church Planters." *Evangelical Missions Quarterly* 46.1 (January): 90–94.

P.E.A.C.E. Plan. n.d. Online: http://www.thepeaceplan.com/, accessed 1 November 1, 2009.

Perry, Cindy. 1990. "Bhai-Tika and Tij Braka: A Case Study in the Contextualization of Two Nepali Festivals." *Missiology* 18.2 (April): 177–83.

Pesebre, John Ricafrente. 2005. "Balik-Loob: Towards a Filipino Evangelical Theology of Repentance." In *Doing Theology in the Philippines*, ed. John Suk, 117–30. Quezon City, Philippines: Asian Theological Seminary.

Peters, Clifford. 1987. "Doing Theology among the Ibanags." *International Journal of Frontier Missions* 4: 69–78.

Peters, Ken. 1989. "Touching the Mystical Heart of Islam." *Evangelical Missions Quarterly* 25.4 (October): 364–69.

Peterson, Brian K. 2007a. "The Possibility of a 'Hindu Christ-Follower': Hans Staffner's Proposal for the Dual Identity of Disciples of Christ within High Caste Hindu Communities." *International Journal of Frontier Missions* 24.2 (Summer): 87–97.

_____. 2007b. "A Brief Investigation of Old Testament Precursors to the Pauline Missiological Model of Cultural Adaptation." *International Journal of Frontier Missions* 24.3 (Fall): 117–29.

Pew Forum on Religion and Public Life. 2006. *Spirit and Power: A 10 Country Survey of Pentecostals*. Online: http://pewforum.org/newassets/surveys/pentecostal/pentecostals-08.pdf, accessed 9 December 2009.

Phil. 2009. "A Response to Kevin Higgins' 'Inside What? Church, Culture, Religion, and Insider Movements in Biblical Perspective.'" *St. Francis Magazine* 5.4 (August): 114–26.

Phillips, David J. 2000. "Factors in Training Workers for Nomadic Peoples." *International Journal of Frontier Missions* 17.3 (July): 41–43.

Pierce, Alexander. 2007. "Contextualizing Scriptures for Ethno-linguistic Minorities: Case Study of Central Asian Muslims." *Evangelical Missions Quarterly* 43.1 (January): 52–56.

Pierson, Paul. 2003. "Lessons in Mission from the Twentieth Century: Conciliar Missions." In *Between Past and Future: Evangelical Mission Entering the Twenty-first Century*, ed. Jonathan J. Bonk, 67–84. EMS 10. Pasadena, CA: William Carey Library.

———. 2009. *The Dynamics of Christian Mission: History through a Missiological Perspective*. Pasadena, CA: William Carey Library.

Pinnock, Clark H. 1984. *The Scripture Principle*. San Francisco: Harper & Row.

Plueddemann, James E. 2010. *Leading Across Cultures: Effective Ministry and Mission in the Global Church*. Downers Grove, IL: InterVarsity.

Pocock, Michael, Gailyn VanRheenen, and Douglas McConnell. 2005. *The Changing Face of World Missions: Engaging Contemporary Issues and Trends*. Encountering Mission series, gen. ed. A. Scott Moreau. Grand Rapids: Baker.

Ponraj, S. Devasahayam, and Chandon K. Sah. 2003. "Communication Bridges to Oral Cultures: A Method That Caused a Breakthrough in Starting Several Church Planting Movements in North India." *International Journal of Frontier Missions* 20.1 (January–March): 28–31.

Poston, Larry. 2000. "Cultural Chameleon: Contextualization from a Pauline Perspective." *Evangelical Missions Quarterly* 36.4 (October): 460–69.

———. 2006. "'You Must Not Worship in Their Way . . .' When Contextualization becomes Syncretism (Syncretism among Messianic Jews)." In *Contextualization and Syncretism: Navigating Cultural Currents*, ed. Gailyn Van Rheenen, 243–63. Pasadena, CA: William Carey Library.

Priest, Doug, Jr. 1990. *Doing Theology with the Maasai*. Pasadena, CA: William Carey Library.

Priest, Robert J. 1994. "Missionary Elenctics: Conscience and Culture." *Missiology* 22.3 (July): 291–315.

———. 2009a. Christians, World View, and Contemporary Anthropology–3–A Personal Essay. http://igca.blogspot.com/2009/01/christians-world-view-and-contemporary_15.html.

———. 2009b. Christians, World View, and Contemporary Anthropology–1. http://igca.blogspot.com/2009/01/christians-world-view-and-contemporary.html.

Priest, Robert J., Thomas Campbell, and Bradford A. Mullen. 1995. "Missiological Syncretism: The New Animistic Paradigm." In *Spiritual Power and Missions: Raising the Issues*, ed. Edward Rommen, 9–87. Pasadena, CA: William Carey Library.

Racey, David. 1996. "Contextualization: How Far Is Too Far?" *Evangelical Missions Quarterly* 32.3 (July): 304–9.

Ralston, Helen. 1987. *Christian Ashrams: A New Religious Movement in Contemporary India*. Lewiston, NY: Edwin Mellen.

Ramirez, Eduardo Miguel. 1978. "Contextualization in the Local Church." *Evangelical Missions Quarterly* 14.1 (January): 49–58.

Redford, Shawn B. 2005. "Appropriate Hermeneutics." In *Appropriate Christianity*, ed. Charles Kraft, 227–53. Pasadena, CA: William Carey Library.

Register, Ray G., Jr. 2000. *Back to Jerusalem: Church Planting Movements in the Holy Land.* Enumclaw, WA: WinePress.

Reid, Michael S. B. 2002. *Strategic Level Spiritual Warfare: A Modern Mythology?* Fairfax, VA: Xulon Press.

Reitz, George. 2006. "Jesus Hall: A Case Study of a Bengali Muslim Ministry in New York City." *Evangelical Missions Quarterly* 42.3 (July): 364–69.

Richard, H. L. 1994. "Is Extraction Evangelism Still the Way to Go?" *Evangelical Missions Quarterly* 30.2 (April): 170–74.

———. 1998. *Following Jesus in the Hindu Context: The Intriguing Implications of N. V. Tilak's Life and Thought.* Pasadena, CA: William Carey Library.

———. 2001. "Evangelical Approaches to Hindus." *Missiology* 29.3: 307–16.

———. 2002. "Rethinking 'Rethinking'." *International Journal of Frontier Missions* 19.3 (Fall): 7–17.

———. 2003. "New Paradigms for Understanding Hinduism and Contextualization." *Voice of Bhakti* 2.2 (May). Online: http://bhaktivani.com/volume2/number2/paradigms.html, accessed 23 October 2009.

———. 2004. "New Paradigms for Understanding Hinduism and Contextualization." *Evangelical Missions Quarterly* 40.3 (July): 308–15.

———. 2007a. "Religious Movements in Hindu Social Contexts: A Study of Paradigms for Contextual "Church" Development." *International Journal of Frontier Missions* 24.3 (July): 139–45.

Richardson, Don. 1974. *Peace Child.* Glendale, CA: Regal.

———. 1977. *Lords of the Earth.* Glendale, CA: Regal.

———. 1981. *Eternity in Their Hearts.* Ventura, CA: Regal.

———. 2000. In *Evangelical Dictionary of World Missions,* gen. ed. A. Scott Moreau, s.v. "Redemptive Analogies." Grand Rapids: Baker.

Richardson, Rick. 2006. *Reimagining Evangelism: Inviting Friends on a Spiritual Journey.* Downers Grove, IL: InterVarsity.

Ro, Bong Rin. 1978. "Contextualization: Asian Theology." *Evangelical Review of Theology* 2.1 (April): 15–23.

———. 1984. "Contextualization: Asian Theology." In *The Bible and Theology in Asian Contexts: An Evangelical Perspective on Asian Theology,* ed. Bong Rin Ro and Ruth Eshenaur, 63–77. Taiching, Taiwan: Asia Theological Association.

Robert, Dana L. 2002. "The First Globalization: The Internationalization of the Protestant Missionary Movement between the World Wars." *International Bulletin of Missionary Research* 26.2 (April): 50.

Rowland, Stan. 1985. "Training Local Villagers to Provide Health Care." *Evangelical Missions Quarterly* 21.1 (January): 44–50.

———. 2001. "What Is Community Health Evangelism?" *Medical*

Ambassadors International Online: http://www.strategicnetwork.org/index.php?loc=kb&view=v&id=4179, accessed 3 November, 2009.

Rowland, Trent, and Shane Bennett. 2001. "Qualifying for the Pioneer Church Planting Decathalon." *Evangelical Missions Quarterly* 37.3 (July): 348–54.

Sasaki, Kei. 2009. "Kanzo Uchimura's Christian Faith as "パウロ道 (Paul-Dou)." *Journal of the Graduate School of Letters, Hokkaido University* 4 (March): 37–46.

Samuel, Vinay. 1982. "Current Trends in Theology." *Missionalia* 10.3: 113–22.

Samuel, Vinay, and Chris Sugden, eds. 1984. *Sharing Jesus in the Two Thirds World: Evangelical Christologies from the Contexts of Poverty, Powerlessness, and Religious Pluralism.* Grand Rapids: Eerdmans.

Samuel, Vinay, and Chris Sugden. 1984a. "Current Trends in Theology: A Third World Guide." In *The Bible and Theology in Asian Contexts: An Evangelical Perspective on Asian Theology,* eds. Bong Rin Ro and Ruth Eshenaur, 139–66. Taiching, Taiwan: Asia Theological Association.

_____. 1987. *The Church in Response to Human Need.* Grand Rapids: Eerdmans.

Sanchez, Daniel R. 1998."Contextualization and the Missionary Endeavor." In *Missiology: An Introduction to the Foundations, History, and Strategy of World Missions,* ed. John Mark Terry, Ebbie Smith, and Justice Anderson, 318–33. Nashville: Broadman and Holman.

Sanneh, Lamin. 1989. *Translating the Message: The Missionary Impact on Culture.* Maryknoll, NY: Orbis.

_____. 2003. *Whose Religion Is Christianity? The Gospel beyond the West.* Grand Rapids: Eerdmans.

Sawatsky, Sheldon. 1982. "Chinese Ecclesiology in Context." *Mission Focus* 10.4 (December): 53–58.

_____. 1983. "Chinese Ecclesiology in Context." *Taiwan Journal of Theology* 5: 149–64.

_____. 1984. "Church Images and Metaphorical Theology." *Taiwan Journal of Theology* 6: 109–30.

Schafer, Joseph L., Mark Yoon, and A. Scott Moreau. 2009. "University Bible Fellowship: What Happens When Missionaries from Korea Descend on North American College Campuses?" In *Missions from the Majority World: Progress, Challenges, and Case Studies.* EMS 17, ed. Michael Pocock and Enoch Wan, 121–49. Pasadena, CA: William Carey Library.

Schineller, Peter. 1992. "Inculturation and Syncretism: What Is the Real Issue?" *International Bulletin of Missionary Research* 16.2 (April): 50–53.

Schlorff, Sam. 2000. "The Translational Model for Mission in a Resistant Muslim Society: A Critique and an Alternative." *Missiology* 28.3 (July): 305–28.

_____. 2006. *Missiological Models in Ministry to Muslims*. Upper Darby, PA: Middle East Resources.

Schrag, Brian. 2007. "India: Debating Global Missiological Flashpoints: Why Local Arts Are Central to Mission." *International Journal of Frontier Missions* 24.4 (December): 199–202.

Schreiter, Robert J. 1985. *Constructing Local Theologies*. London: SCM Press.

_____. 1993. "Defining Syncretism: An Interim Report." *International Bulletin of Missionary Research* 17.2 (April): 50–53.

_____. 2002. Foreword in *Doing Local Theology: A Guide for Artisans of a New Humanity*, Clemens Sedmak. Maryknoll, NY: Orbis.

Scoggins, Dick. 1997. "Seven Phases of Church Planting and Activity List." *Evangelical Missions Quarterly* 33.2 (April): 161–65.

Scott, Randal. 2008. "Evangelism and Dreams: Foundational Presuppositions to Interpret God-given Dreams of the Unreached." *Evangelical Missions Quarterly* 44.2 (April): 176–84.

Sedmak, Clemens. 2002. *Doing Local Theology: A Guide for Artisans of a New Humanity*. Maryknoll, NY: Orbis.

"Seeking the Peace of the City: The Valle de Bravo Affirmation." 1989. *Urban Mission* 7.1 (January): 18–24.

Segundo, Juan Luis. 1976. *Liberation of Theology*. Maryknoll, NY: Orbis.

Seto, Wing-luk. 1987. "An Asian Looks at Contextualization and Developing Ethnotheologies." *Evangelical Missions Quarterly* 23.2 (April): 138–41.

Shaw, Mark. 1993. *Doing Theology with Huck and Jim: Parables for Understanding Doctrine*. Downers Grove, IL: InterVarsity.

Shaw, R. Daniel. 1995. "Contextualizing the Power and the Glory." *International Journal of Frontier Missions* 12.3 (July–September): 155–60.

Shaw, R. Daniel, and Charles E. Van Engen. 2003. *Communicating God's Word in a Complex World: God's Truth or Hocus Pocus?* Lanham, MD: Rowman and Littlefield.

Sider, Ronald J. 1977. *Rich Christians in an Age of Hunger: A Biblical Study*. Downers Grove, IL: InterVarsity.

_____. 2005. *The Scandal of the Evangelical Conscience, Why Are Christians Living Just Like the Rest of the World?* Grand Rapids: Baker.

Sigg, Samuel. 1995. "The French University Students." *Urban Mission* 12.4 (October): 37–50.

Simson, Wolfgang. 1999. *Houses That Change the World: The Return of the House Churches*. Waynesboro, GA: Authentic.

Smalley, William A. 1955. "Culture and Superculture." *Practical Anthropology* 2.3: 58–71.

_____. 1958. "Cultural Implications of an Indigenous Church." *Practical Anthropology* 5.2: 51–65.

Smart, Ninian. 1996. *Dimensions of the Sacred: An Anatomy of the World's Beliefs*. Berkeley: University of California Press.

Smith, Edward M. 2004. *Healing Life's Deepest Hurts: Let the Light of Christ Dispel the Darkness in Your Soul*. Ventura, CA: Regal.

Smith, Glenn. 1995. "Urban Mission in the French North Atlantic." *Urban Mission* 12.4 (October): 5–21.

Smith, Henry N. 1989. "Christianity and Ancestor Practices in Hong Kong: Toward a Contextualized Strategy." *Missiology* 17.1 (January): 27–38.

Smith, Jay. 1998. "Courage in Our Convictions: The Case for Debate in Islamic Outreach." *Evangelical Missions Quarterly* 34.1 (January): 28–35.

_____. 2009. "An Assessment of the Insider's Principle Paradigms." *St. Francis Magazine* 5.4 (August): 20–51.

Sommer, Donald. 2006. "Integrating Technology in Leadership Training." *Evangelical Missions Quarterly* 42.2 (April): 166–73.

Span, John. 2009. "Jesus the Ultimate Insider? A Response to Proponents of the Insider Movement That Jesus Is the 'Ultimate Insider' and the Ultimate Justification for the Methodology." *St. Francis Magazine* 5.5 (October): 41–48.

Speers, John. 1991. "Ramadan: Should Missionaries Keep the Muslim Fast?" *Evangelical Missions Quarterly* 27.4 (October): 356–59.

Spielberg, Faña, and Stuart Dauermann. 1997. "Contextualization: Witness and Reflection Messianic Jews as a Case." *Missiology* 25.1 (January): 15–35.

Starcher, Rich. 2006. "A Really Useful Theological Doctorate for Africa." *Evangelical Missions Quarterly* 42.2 (April): 206–13.

Steele, William. 2009. "The Insider Movement as a Strategy for Evangelizing Muslims." *St. Francis Magazine* 5.4 (August): 127–32.

Steffen, Tom A. 1993. "Don't Show the 'Jesus' Film'. . . ." *Evangelical Missions Quarterly* 29.3 (July): 272–76.

_____. 1995. "Storying the Storybook to Tribals." *International Journal of Frontier Missions* 12.2 (April–June): 99–104.

_____. 1996. *Reconnecting God's Story to Ministry: Cross-cultural Storytelling at Home and Abroad*. La Habra, CA: Center for Organizational & Ministry Development.

_____. 1999. "Why Communicate the Gospel through Stories?" In *Perspectives on the World Christian Movement*, 2nd ed., ed. Ralph D. Winter and Steven C. Hawthorne, 404–7. Pasadena, CA: William Carey Library.

_____. 2000. "Reaching 'Resistant' People through Intentional Narrative." *Missiology* 28.4 (October): 471–86.

_____. 2005. "My Journey from Propositional to Narrative Evangelism." *Evangelical Missions Quarterly* 41.2 (April): 200–209.

Steffen, Tom A., and Lois McKinney-Douglas. 2008. *Encountering Missionary Life and Work*. Grand Rapids: Baker.

Steinhaus, S. P. 2000. "The Spirit-First Approach to Muslim Evangelism." *International Journal of Frontier Missions* 17.4 (October): 23–30.

Stephens, Sunil H. 1999. "Doing Theology in a Hindu Context." *Journal of Asian Mission* 1.2: 181–203.

Stevens, Ryan. 2007. "India: Debating Global Missiological Flashpoints: Bridging the Gap between Western Workers and India's Hindus." *International Journal of Frontier Missions* 24.4 (October): 179–84.

Stott, John. 2003. *Evangelical Truth*. Rev. ed. Downers Grove, IL: InterVarsity.

Stott, John R. W., and Robert T. Coote. 1980. *Down to Earth: Studies in Christianity and Culture: The Papers of the Lausanne Consultation on Gospel and Culture*. Grand Rapids: Eerdmans.

Strand, Mark. 2000. "Explaining Sin in a Chinese Context." *Missiology* 28.4 (October): 427–41.

Strauss, Steve. 2006. "The Role of Context in Shaping Theology." In *Contextualization and Syncretism: Navigating Cultural Currents,* ed. Gailyn Van Rheenen, 99–128. Pasadena, CA: William Carey Library.

Strom, Donna. 1987. "Cultural Practices: Barriers or Bridges." *Evangelical Missions Quarterly* 23.3 (July): 248–56.

Stutzman, Linford. 1991. "An Incarnational Approach to Mission in Modern, Affluent Societies." *Urban Mission* (May): 35–43.

Sumithra, Sunand. 1984. "Towards Evangelical Theology in Hindu Cultures." In *The Bible and Theology in Asian Contexts: An Evangelical Perspective on Asian Theology,* ed. Bong Rin Ro and Ruth Eshenaur, 217–41. Taiching, Taiwan: Asia Theological Association.

Taber, Charles R. 1975. "Concluding Thoughts." In *Christopaganism or Indigenous Christianity?* ed. Tetsunao Yamamori and Charles R. Taber, 179–82. Pasadena, CA: William Carey Library.

_____. 1978. "Is There More Than One Way to Do Theology?" *Gospel in Context* 1.1 (January): 4–10, 22–40.

_____. 1979a. "Contextualization: Indigenization and/or Transformation." In *The Gospel and Islam: A 1978 Compendium,* ed. Don M. McCurry, 143–50. Monrovia, CA: MARC.

_____. 1979b. "Hermeneutics and Culture: A Theological Perspective." In *Gospel and Culture. The Papers of a Consultation on the Gospel and Culture, Convened by the Lausanne Committee's Theology and Education Group,* ed. John R. W. Stott and Robert T. Coote, 83–108. Pasadena, CA: William Carey Library.

_____. 1983. "Contextualization." In *Exploring Church Growth,* ed. Wilbert R. Shenk, 117–31. Grand Rapids: Eerdmans.

Taber, Charles R. 1991. *The World Is Too Much with Us—'Culture' in Modern Protestant Missions*. Macon, GA: Mercer University Press.

Talman, Harley. 2004. "Comprehensive Contextualization." *International Journal of Frontier Missions* 21.1 (Spring): 6–12.

Tanari Trust. n.d. "Ropes." Online: http://tanari.org/index. php?option=com_content&task=view&id=16&Itemid=30, accessed 1 November 2009.

Tano, Rodrigo D. 1981. *Theology in the Philippine Setting: A Case Study in the Contextualization of Theology.* Quezon City, Philippines: New Day Publishers.

_____. 1984. "Towards an Evangelical Asian Theology." In *The Bible and Theology in Asian Contexts: An Evangelical Perspective on Asian Theology,* ed. Bong Rin Ro and Ruth Eshenaur, 93–118. Taiching, Taiwan: Asia Theological Association.

Tappeiner, Daniel A. 1999. "A Response to Caldwell's Trumpet Call to Ethnohermeneutics." *Journal of Asian Mission* 1.2: 223–32.

Tarus, Abraham. 1996. "Music in Christian Worship." *Africa Journal of Evangelical Theology* 15.2: 114–27.

Taylor, Howard. 2004. "Contextualized Mission in Church History." In *Encountering New Religious Movements: A Holistic Evangelical Approach,* ed. Irving Hexham, Stephen Rost, John Morehead, and John W. Morehead II, 43–60. Grand Rapids: Kregel.

Taylor, William D. 2000. "Setting the Stage. From Iguassu to the Reflective Practitioners of the Global Family of Christ." In *Global Missiology for the 21st Century: The Iguassu Dialogue,* ed. William D. Taylor, 3–13. Grand Rapids: Baker.

Teague, David. 2008. "Christological Monotheism and Muslim Evangelism." *Evangelical Missions Quarterly* 44.4 (October): 466–70.

Teeter, David. 1990. "Dynamic Equivalent Conversion for Tentative Muslim Believers." *Missiology* 18.3 (July): 305–13.

Tennent, Timothy C. 2005. "The Challenge of Churchless Christianity: An Evangelical Assessment." *International Bulletin of Missionary Research* 29.4 (October): 171–77.

_____. 2006. "Followers of Jesus (Isa) in Islamic Mosques: A Closer Examination of C–5 'High Spectrum' Contextualization." *International Journal of Frontier Missions* 23.23 (Fall): 101–15.

_____. 2007. *Theology in the Context of World Christianity: How the Global Church Is Influencing the Way We Think about and Discuss Theology.* Grand Rapids: Zondervan.

Terry, John Mark. 1996. "Approaches to the Evangelization of Muslims." *Evangelical Missions Quarterly* 32.2 (April): 168–73.

_____. 1998. "Contextual Evangelism Strategies." In *Missiology: An Introduction to the Foundations, History, and Strategies of World Missions,* ed. John Mark Terry, Ebbie Smith, and Justice Anderson, 450–66. Nashville: Broadman and Holman.

Terry, J. O. 1997. "Chronological Bible Storying to Tribal and Nomadic Peoples." *International Journal of Frontier Missions* 14.4 (October-December): 167–72.

Thiessen, Elmer J. 2007. "Refining the Conversation: Some Concerns about Contemporary Trends in Thinking about Worldviews, Christian Scholarship, and Higher Education." *Evangelical Quarterly* 79.2: 133–52.

Thomas, Juliet. 2002. "Issues from the Indian Perspective." In *Deliver Us from Evil: An Uneasy Frontier in Christian Mission,* ed. A. Scott Moreau, Tokunboh Adeyemo, David Burnett, Bryant Myers, and Hwa Yung, 146–51. Monrovia, CA: MARC.

Thomas, Norman E. 2005. "Radical Mission in a Post-9/11 World: Creative Dissonances." *International Bulletin of Missionary Research* 29.1 (January): 2–4, 6–8.

Thornton, W. Philip. 1984. "The Cultural Key to Developing Strong Leaders." *Evangelical Missions Quarterly* 20.3 (July): 234–41.

Tiénou, Tite. 1984. "The Church in African Theology: Description and Analysis of Hermeneutical Presuppositions." In *Biblical Interpretation and the Church: Text and Context,* ed. D. A. Carson, 151–65. Exeter: Paternoster.

_____. 1992. "Which Way for African Christianity: Westernization or Indigenous Authenticity?" *Evangelical Missions Quarterly* 28.3 (July): 256–63.

Tippett, Alan R. 1971. *People Movements in Southern Polynesia: Studies in the Dynamics of Church-Planting and Growth in Tahiti, New Zealand, Tonga, and Samoa.* Chicago: Moody Press.

_____. 1973. *Verdict Theology in Missionary Theory.* Pasadena, CA: William Carey Library.

_____. 1975. "The Meaning of Meaning." In *Christopaganism or Indigenous Christianity?* ed. Tetsunao Yamamori and Charles R. Taber, 129–51. Pasadena, CA: William Carey Library.

_____. 1977. "Conversion as a Dynamic Process in Christian Mission." *Missiology* 5.2 (April): 202–21.

_____. 1987. *Introduction to Missiology.* Pasadena, CA: William Carey Library.

Tollefson, Kenneth. 1987. "The Nehemiah Model for Christian Missions." *Missiology* 15.1 (January): 31–55.

Tooke, J. V. 1993. "Toward Contextual Evangelism: The Case of Africa Enterprise." *Missionalia* 21.2 (August): 124–37.

"Transformation: The Church in Response to Human Need." 1984. Online: http://www.lausanne.org/all-documents/transformation-the-church-in-response-to-human-need.html, accessed 31 May 2010.

Travis, John. 1998a. "The C1 to C6 Spectrum." *Evangelical Missions Quarterly* 34.4 (October): 407–8.

_____. 1998b. "Must All Muslims Leave 'Islam' to Follow Jesus?" *Evangelical Missions Quarterly* 34.4 (October): 4011–15.

_____. 2000. "Messianic Muslim Followers of Isa: A Closer Look at C5 Believers and Congregations." *International Journal of Frontier Missions* 19.1 (Spring): 53–59.

Travis, John, and Anna Travis. 2005a. "Appropriate Approaches in Muslim Contexts." In *Appropriate Christianity*, ed. Charles Kraft, 397–414. Pasadena, CA: William Carey Library.

_____. 2005b. "Contextualization among Hindus, Muslims, and Buddhists, A Focus on 'Insider Movements'." *Mission Frontiers* 27.5 (September–October): 12–15.

_____. 2008. "Deep-Level Healing Prayer in Cross-Cultural Ministry." In *Paradigm Shifts in Christian Witness: Insights from Anthropology, Communication, and Spiritual Power*, ed. Charles E. Van Engen, J. Dudley Woodberry, and Darrell Whiteman, 106–15. Maryknoll, NY: Orbis.

Tsu-kung, Chuang. 1996. "Communicating the Concept of Sin in the Chinese Context." *Taiwan Mission Quarterly* 6.2 (July): 49–55.

Turpie, Bill, and Billy Graham, eds. 2000. *Ten Great Preachers: Messages and Interviews*. Grand Rapids: Baker.

Tuza, Esau. 1986. "Who Decides What in a Local Church: An Attempt to Understand Localization in Relation to the Missionary Era of the United Church." *Point Series* 8: 175–84.

Tyler, Mary. 1996. "AIDS Awareness and Challenge, Uganda." In *Serving with the Poor in Africa*, ed. Tetsunao Yamamori et al., 29–40. Pasadena, CA: MARC.

Vanden Berg, Todd. 2009. "Contextualization from the Ground: Longuda Lutherans in Nigeria." In *Power and Identity in the Global Church: Six Contemporary Cases*, ed. Brian M. Howell and Edwin Zehner, 55–79. Pasadena, CA: William Carey Library.

Vanderaa, Larry. 2000. "Strategy for Mission among the Fulbe (Part Two)." *International Journal of Frontier Missions* 17.3 (July): 49–55.

Van Engen, Charles. 2005a. "Five Perspectives of Contextually Appropriate Missional Theology." In *Appropriate Christianity*, ed. Charles Kraft, 183–202. Pasadena, CA: William Carey Library.

_____. 2005b. "Toward a Contextually Appropriate Methodology in Mission Theology." In *Appropriate Christianity*, ed. Charles Kraft, 203–26. Pasadena, CA: William Carey Library.

_____. 2009. Personal communication from Charles Van Engen; 6 September 2009.

Vanhoozer, Kevin J. 1986. "The Semantics of Biblical Literature: Truth and Scripture's Diverse Literary Forms." In *Hermeneutics, Authority, and Canon*, ed. D. A. Carson and John D. Woodbridge, 49–104. Leicester: InterVarsity.

_____. 2006. "'One Rule to Rule Them All?' Theological Method in an Era of World Christianity." In *Globalizing Theology: Belief and Practice in an Era of World Christianity*, ed. Craig Ott and Harold Netland, 85–126. Grand Rapids: Baker.

Van Rheenen, Gailyn, ed. 2006a. *Contextualization and Syncretism: Navigating Cultural Currents*. EMS 13. Pasadena, CA: William Carey Library.

_____. 2006b. "Syncretism and Contextualization: The Church on a Journey Defining Itself." In *Contextualization and Syncretism: Navigating Cultural Currents*, ed. Gailyn Van Rheenen, 1–29. Pasadena, CA: William Carey Library.

Vincent, David. 1992. "Evangelism for Melanesia: Towards a More Culturally Appropriate Ministry." *Catalyst* 22.2: 71–80.

Von Allmen, Daniel. 1975. "The Birth of Theology: Contextualization as the Dynamic Element in the Formation of New Testament Theology," *International Review of Mission* 64: 37–52.

Wagner, C. Peter, ed. 1991a. *Engaging the Enemy: How to Fight and Defeat Territorial Spirits*. Ventura, CA: Regal.

_____. 1991b. "Spiritual Power in Urban Evangelism." *Evangelical Missions Quarterly* 27.2 (April): 130–37.

_____. 1991c. "Territorial Spirits." In *Engaging the Enemy: How to Fight and Defeat Territorial Spirits*, ed. C. Peter Wagner, 43–50. Ventura, CA: Regal.

_____. 1992. *Warfare Prayer: How to Seek God's Power and Protection in the Battle to Build His Kingdom*. Ventura, CA: Regal.

_____, ed. 1993a. *Breaking Strongholds in Your City: How to Use Spiritual Mapping to Make Your Prayers More Strategic, Effective, and Targeted*. Ventura, CA: Regal.

_____. 1993b. "Summary: Mapping Your Community." In *Breaking Strongholds in Your City*, ed. C. Peter Wagner, 223–32. Ventura, CA: Regal.

_____. 1996. *Confronting the Powers: How the New Testament Church Experienced the Power of Strategic-level Spiritual Warfare*. Ventura, CA: Regal.

_____. 1998. *Confronting the Queen of Heaven*. Colorado Springs, CO: Wagner Institute for Practical Ministry.

Wagner, C. Peter and F. Douglas Pennoyer, eds. 1990. *Wrestling with Dark Angels: Toward a Deeper Understanding of the Supernatural Forces in Spiritual Warfare*. Ventura, CA: Regal.

Walker, Larry. 1994. "Seven Dynamics for Advancing Your Church in Missions." *International Journal of Frontier Missions* 11.3 (July): 147–51.

Walls, Andrew. 1982. "The Gospel as the Prisoner and Liberator of Culture." *Missionalia* 10.3 (November): 93–105.

_____. 1990. "The Translation Principle in Christian History." In *Bible Translation and the Spread of the Church: The Last Two Hundred Years*, ed. Philip C. Stine, 24–39. Leiden: E. J. Brill.

_____. 1996. *The Missionary Movement in Christian History: Studies in the Transmission of Faith.* Maryknoll, NY: Orbis.

_____. 2002. *The Cross-Cultural Process in Christian History.* Maryknoll, NY: Orbis.

Waterman, Laurence. D. 2007. "Do the Roots Affect the Fruits?" *International Journal of Frontier Missions* 24.2 (Summer): 57–63.

_____. 2008. "Contextualization: A Few Basic Questions." *Evangelical Missions Quarterly* 44.2 (April): 166–72.

Webb, Keith E. 2008. "Coaching for On-field Development." *Evangelical Missions Quarterly* 44.3 (July): 284–91.

Weerasingha, Tissa. 1984. "A Critique of Theology from Buddhist Cultures." In *The Bible and Theology in Asian Contexts: An Evangelical Perspective on Asian Theology,* ed. Bong Rin Ro and Ruth Eshenaur, 290–314. Taiching, Taiwan: Asia Theological Association.

Weerstra, Hans M. 2000. "Editorial: Challenges in the Muslim World." *International Journal of Frontier Missions* 17.4 (Winter): 3–4.

Wells, David. 1985. "The Nature and Function of Theology." In *The Use of the Bible in Theology: Evangelical Options,* ed. Robert K. Johnston, 175–99. Atlanta: John Knox.

Whelchel, James R. 2000. "Ethnohermeneutics: A Response." *Journal of Asian Mission* 2.1: 125–33.

Whiteman, Darrell L. 1989. "Archives and Oral Theology Traditional Historiography and Ethnohistory: Strange Bedfellows, or Necessary Companions in Missiology?" *Mission Studies* 6.1: 96–98.

_____. 1997. "Contextualization: The Theory, the Gap, the Challenge." *International Bulletin of Missionary Research* 21 (January): 2–7.

_____. 2004a. "Part I: Anthropology and Mission: The Incarnational Connection." *International Journal of Frontier Missions* 21.1 (Spring): 34–45.

_____. 2004b. "Part II: Anthropology and Mission: The Incarnational Connection." International Journal of Frontier Missions 21.2 (Summer): 78–89.

_____. 2005. "The Function of Appropriate Contextualization in Mission." In *Appropriate Christianity,* ed. Charles Kraft, 49–79. Pasadena, CA: William Carey Library.

_____. 2006. "Anthropological Reflections on Contextualizing Theology in a Globalizing World." In *Globalizing Theology: Belief and Practice in an Era of World Christianity,* edI Craig Ott and Harold Netland, 52–69. Grand Rapids: Baker.

Wilder, John W. 1977. "Some Reflections on Possibilities for People Movements among Muslims." *Missiology* 5.3: 301–20.

Williams, Mark S. 2003. "Aspects of High-Spectrum Contextualization in Ministries to Muslims." *Journal of Asian Mission* 5.1: 75–91.

References

Wilson, John D. 1991. "What It Takes to Reach People in Oral Cultures." *Evangelical Missions Quarterly* 27.2 (April): 154–58.

———. 1997. "Let the Earth Hear His Voice." *International Journal of Frontier Missions* 14.4 (October): 177–80.

Wimber, John. 1990. "Power Evangelism: Definitions and Directions." In *Wrestling with Dark Angels: Toward a Deeper Understanding of the Supernatural Forces in Spiritual Warfare*, ed. C. Peter Wagner and F. Douglas Pennoyer, 13–42. Ventura, CA: Regal.

Wimber, John, and Kevin Springer. 1986. *Power Evangelism*. London: Hodder and Stoughton.

Winter, Ralph. 1995. "Christian History in Cross-Cultural Perspective." *International Journal of Frontier Missions* 12.3 (July): 126–32.

———. 2003a. " "Eleven Frontiers of Perspective." *International Journal of Frontier Missions* 20.3 (July): 76–81.

———. "Eleven Frontiers of Perspective (7–11)." *International Journal of Frontier Missions* 20.4 (October): 134–41.

———. 2005a. "When Business Can Be Mission: Where Both Business and Mission Fall Short." *International Journal of Frontier Missions* 22.3 (July): 110–17.

Wisley, Tom N. 1979. "Towards a Dynamic Indigenous Church." In *Readings in Dynamic Indigeneity*, ed. Charles H. Kraft and Tom N. Wisley, 207–25. Pasadena, CA: William Carey Library.

Woodberry, J. Dudley. 1989. "Contextualization among Muslims: Reusing Common Pillars." In *The Word among Us: Contextualizing Theology for Mission Today*, ed. Dean S. Gilliland, 282–312. Dallas: Word.

———. 1996. "Contextualization among Muslims: Reusing Common Pillars." *International Journal of Frontier Missions* 13.4 (October–December): 171–86.

———. 2006. "To the Muslim I Become a Muslim?" In *Contextualization and Syncretism: Navigating Cultural Currents*, ed. Gailyn Van Rheenen, 143–57. Pasadena, CA: William Carey Library.

———. 2007. "To the Muslim I Became a Muslim?" *International Journal of Frontier Missions* 24.1 (Winter): 23–28.

———, ed. 2008. *From Seed to Fruit: Global Trends, Fruitful Practices, and Emerging Issues among Muslims*. Pasadena, CA: William Carey Library.

Woods, Scott. 2003. "A Biblical Look at C5 Muslim Evangelism." *Evangelical Missions Quarterly* 39.2 (April): 188–95.

Wright, Christopher J. H. 2006. *The Mission of God: Unlocking the Bible's Grand Narrative*. Downers Grove, IL: InterVarsity.

———. 2007. "Following Jesus in the Globalized Marketplace." *Evangelical Review of Theology* 31.4: 320–30.

"The X Spectrum: A Helpful Way to Categorize Evangelistic Approaches."

Online: http://www.internetevangelismday.com/x-spectrum.php; accessed 26 June, 2012.

Yamamori, Tetsunao, and Charles R. Taber, eds. 1975. *Christopaganism or Indigenous Christianity?* Pasadena, CA: William Carey Library.

Yates, Timothy. 1994. *Christian Mission in the Twentieth Century.* Cambridge: Cambridge University Press.

Yego, Josphat K. 1980. "Appreciations for and Warnings about Contextualization." *Evangelical Mission Quarterly* 16.3 (July): 153–56.

Yoder, Michael L., Michael H. Lee, Jonathan Ro, and Robert J. Priest. 2009. "Understanding Christian Identity in Terms of Bounded and Centered Set Theory in the Writings of Paul G. Hiebert." *Trinity Journal* 30NS (Fall) 177–88.

Young, Kevin. 2008. "Re-Imagining the Four Spiritual Laws: A New Kind of Evangelism for a New Generation." Online: http://web.archive.org/web/20090212213331/http://www.thejournalofstudentministries.com/authors/103/Kevin-Young; accessed 26 June 2012.

Zahniser, A. H. Mathias. 1991. "Ritual Process and Christian Discipling: Contextualizing a Buddhist Rite of Passage." *Missiology* 19.1 (January): 3–19.

———. 1997. *Symbol and Ceremony: Making Disciples across Cultures.* Monrovia, CA: MARC.

Zdero, Rad. 2004. *The Global House Church Movement.* Pasadena, CA: William Carey Library.

———. 2005. "Launching House Church Movements." *Mission Frontiers* 27.2: 16–19.

Zoba, Wendy Murray. 2005. *The Beliefnet Guide to Evangelical Christianity.* New York: Three Leaves Press.